Lititz 9.22.94

To Deb —

It's always a personal & professional pleasure to work together!

Best wishes,

[signature]

Training for the Healthcare Manufacturing Industries

Tools and Techniques to Improve Performance

James L. Vesper

Interpharm Press, Inc.
Buffalo Grove, IL

NEW BOOK CONCEPTS

Interpharm Press specializes in publishing books related to applied technology and regulatory affairs impacting the biotechnology, chemical, cosmetic, device, diagnostic or drug manufacturing industries. If you have a manuscript in progress, or are planning to write a book that will be applicable to development, medical, regulatory, manufacturing, quality or engineering professionals, please contact our editorial director.

SOCIAL RESPONSIBILITY PROGRAMS

Interpharm Resources Replenishment Program

Interpharm Press is significantly concerned with the worldwide loss of trees, and the impact of such loss on the environment and the availability of new drug sources. Losses to tropical rain forests are particularly remarkable in that only 3% of all possible endangered plant species have been evaluated for their active drug potential.

Interpharm Press commits to replant trees sufficient to replace those destroyed in meeting the paper needs for Interpharm's publications and advertising. Interpharm is actively supporting reforestation programs in Bangladesh, Israel, Kenya and the United States.

Pharmakos-2000

To foster the teaching of pharmaceutical technology, Interpharm Press has initiated its Pharmakos-2000 program. Under this program, one copy of this book is being sent, at no charge, to every College and School of Pharmacy worldwide. The program covers all 504 establishments listed by the Commonwealth Pharmaceutical Association (CPA) and the Federation Internationale Pharmaceutique (FIP).

It is hoped that this book will be a suitable reference resource to faculty and students advancing the theory and practice of pharmaceutical technology.

10 9 8 7 6 5 4 3 2 1

ISBN: 0-935184-43-0

Interpharm Press, Inc.
1358 Busch Parkway
Buffalo Grove, IL 60089, USA

Phone: + 1 + 708 + 459-8480
Fax: + 1 + 708 + 459-6644

Contents

Preface

It was a phone call that started all of this: my manager called me while I was working in France and asked if I would establish a corporate group to develop training programs on the U.S. FDA's Current Good Manufacturing Practice regulations (cGMPs) and the company's standard operating procedures. Maybe it was because I had taught several "standup," leader-led programs or had taught at Indiana University, or maybe because I had been labeled a "creative" type—I'm still not sure. But, as they say, it was an opportunity I couldn't refuse.

Entering into the task, I encountered professions and jargon I had never known: instructional designers, instructional technologists, front-end analysis, mastery learning—the list could go on and on. But what was exciting was getting a glimpse of how *different* training *could be* **if** approached from the perspective of human performance. It was there and then I discovered that "training" was much more complex than I had been told or had experienced.

Despite the complexity, there was a simplicity in the goal: getting a person or persons to perform tasks safely, correctly, and effectively, time after time.

In trying to understand and deal with this seeming paradox, I began reading about human performance, adult learning theory, and what other industries were and are doing in instructing and training their employees. I discovered a variety of ways to deliver instruction, some of which have been around for generations and others just now becoming practical and useful.

Also, I began talking with and visiting other pharmaceutical and medical device firms to learn and share approaches, tools, frustrations, and ideas.

And yes, I talked with some of the *users* of training programs to learn what they liked, what they did not like, and how they thought learning could be best be integrated into their operational or professional activities.

This book is the result of the learning and experiences I have had regarding training and performance since receiving that phone call in September 1989. It is a book I wish I had had when I started that job.

Several people to whom I have described this project have said, "Oh . . . it's going to be a cookbook for doing training." I think it all depends on what you mean by "cookbook."

There is a cook who comes to mind who meticulously follows a recipe. Her use of timers, thermometers, and measuring cups would make the director of the National Bureau of Standards proud. Her successes, though frequent, are uninspired. A crisis occurs when she discovers there are only two cups of flour and she needs three, or when the sauce breaks down and separates into globules even though she followed the recipe *precisely*. Variations and surprises throw her into turmoil.

Another person comes to mind—my father. Raised in his family's bakery and studying the subject in college, he learned that recipes were guides. Temperature and humidity were factors to be reckoned with just as the time in the oven. He learned there are rules of thumb about what you can substitute if you run out of a particular item. If you discovered you were out of flour, that gave you the opportunity to try something else. Occasionally it did not work, but most of the time, the results were sensational.

The point is this: if you try to use this volume as a step-by-step, do-it-without-thinking cookbook, you will succeed to a limited degree. But, if you *understand the concepts and principles, and apply them to your specific situation* with creativity and courage, using this book as a guide, you will do far better.

Getting the best and most from the people who are doing a particular job is not a validated process. Neither is producing a training course or lesson that will yield optimal results on the first (or second or third) try. There are, however, some guidelines and approaches that will greatly increase the probability of success. If you understand something about how people—*adults*—learn, how to systematically define the problem and how to solve it, the learner's needs and how to meet them, you'll be 80 percent there. The more frequently you do it, the more you will learn, and the better the results.

There is science and technology involved in training, but there is also some art. You are fighting for the attention and concentration of people who usually would rather be elsewhere, doing almost anything. Creatively developed and visually appealing handouts, engaging computer-based training, videos, slides, or the use of a well-told story in any medium can help get people to focus on the knowledge and skills you are helping to provide to them.

Julia Child, one of America's greatest chefs, with her co-authors wrote:

> Cooking is not a particularly difficult art, and the more you cook and learn about cooking, the more sense it makes. But like any art it requires practice and experience. The most important ingredient you can bring to it is love of cooking for its own sake.

Change the verb from "cook" to "teach" or "train," add some rigor and technology, mix well, and there you have it.

There is a basic model of instructional systems design, with as many variations as practitioners, used to systematically produce a "training intervention." The approach you will find here is a mix of (what I have found to be) the best of the variations, plus some new ideas, realism, and experience gained while working for a large pharmaceutical corporation and, more recently, consulting in the U.S. and abroad. Included are examples or situations where people (including me) have learned something from the College of Painful Experience.

This book will not make you an instructional designer or a performance technologist; it does not intend to do that. This book should help you make 80 percent of your training programs 80 percent more effective than what one professional calls the "spray and pray" approach to training. To go much beyond that 80/80 estimate, and for complex or unusual projects, you will need the experience, expertise, and unique perspective of professional instructional designers.

If you have an opportunity to be involved with training and human performance, you are very fortunate. You will learn an incredible amount about people, various topics, and using a systematic process for solving problems that will help you in every other position that you will have. You will make a difference in the lives of people and in the quality of your firm's products and in the company's profitability.

And, if you do it right, you will also have a whole lot of fun.

Jim Vesper
June 1993
Rochester, New York

Acknowledgements

Where do I begin?

First, thanks to my friends and past colleagues at Eli Lilly and Company with whom I have worked and learned. Special thanks to Mike Akers for encouraging me to write this; and Susan Hatgas, Paul Harber, Debbie Meyers, John Yergler, Christine Hood, and Peter Burbidge who were members of the most creative and productive group I have ever had the chance to be part of—it was a great two years. Thanks also to Carmen Rosa Sabater for her collaborations and friendship over the years, especially her valuable comments on this manuscript.

There are other associates in Indianapolis and throughout the world: Ron Meyer, Tom Engelking, Paul Moriconi, Vincent Griffoul, Jacques Leger, Peter Gough, Caridad Purcell, and Roberto Alvarenga.

There were people I worked for and learned from: Bill Chiasson, Ken Martledge, Jim Landes, and a gentleman of wisdom I hold in high regard, Gordon Mallett.

Second, I'd like to thank my family and friends in Grand Rapids, Indianapolis, and Rochester for their encouragement, telephone calls, and taking care of the dogs. Special people here are Dr. Mary Jo Brandt, Skip Sauvain, John Aleshire, Mike Mathis, and Aaron Brace.

Finally, to Sherri Casterline, a mountain of thanks for reading the early versions of this; for her help, coaching, and suggestions.

For Michael Thomas,

who has shown me

that to be an artist,
is to be a communicator

Introduction

Everything should be made as simple as possible, but no simpler.
—Albert Einstein

The goal of this book is to describe a systematic method for producing instructional programs, courses, and materials that will have results. This goal is based on experiences that have shown that training, when done correctly and for the appropriate reasons, can be an investment with measurable benefits.

There are three intended audiences for this book:

- Pharmaceutical industry training professionals looking for a more effective, systematic, performance-based approach for solving problems;
- Management with responsibilities for training or drug manufacturing or control; and
- People who suddenly find themselves involved with producing training programs and want to know more about them

The question used to help determine material to be included and how it is presented was, "*What information is needed or useful for someone 'doing' training of operational, technical, or support personnel?*"

The topics covered and the methods described in this book are appropriate for producing instruction for all types of content, whether it be on topics important to drug manufacturing, dry product operations, parenteral product operations, quality control laboratories, maintenance, regulatory requirements (FDA, OSHA, EPA), etc. **The instructional systems design (ISD) process presented and other information discussed is valid for *all* types of industries;** however, examples and cases used here have largely been taken from the pharmaceutical industry for a clearer, more direct application by the intended audiences.

Chapter 7, "Overview of the Instructional Systems Design Process," is written particularly for management and presents a summary of Sections II–VI.

Section I is the foundation. It contains concepts important to the ISD process and should be read *before* starting to produce a course using the ISD method.

Sections II–VI each focus on a phase of the ISD model (overviewed in Chapter 7). Each phase contains several tasks (e.g., "Define the scope," "Select topics," etc.). Each task is composed of steps and substeps. Tasks vary significantly in the amount of time needed to complete them. Time is a function of the scope of the project, the complexity of the learners' job/task, and the like. The tasks are arranged based on "classical" models of instructional design, as well as on how information from one task or step flows into others downstream. There is an introduction to each of the ISD phases describing what will be done and where information used in that phase comes from.

Sections VII and VIII are more supplemental in nature—"nice-to-know" information that may or may not be applicable to the training intervention you are producing.

Section VIII (Looking into the Future) presents information about how audiences and technologies are changing. On one hand, some of the applications discussed might appear dated five years from now. On the other, and more importantly, people involved in training today need to understand how technological tools and media can be used now to solve today's problems.

The chapters in Sections I, VII, and VIII each have *goals* at the beginning. The chapters that present the ISD process do not have them listed but, instead, share the common goals listed below.

- Define the task;
- Describe why it is done;
- Identify who is involved with the task;
- Identify the output of the completed task;
- Discuss issues related to the task;
- List the steps and substeps used in performing the task; and
- Provide examples related to the task.

The chapters describing the ISD process are best understood if read in sequence as most steps build on the information obtained and activities of previous steps. The tasks and steps are not rigid. They should be considered a well-traveled path that, when followed, will significantly increase the effectiveness and benefits of the resulting training intervention.

I

Before You Begin . . .

1

Why Training Is *NOT* the Answer

An example

Karen, a director of employee training, described an inspection the U.S. Food and Drug Administration (FDA) conducted in the pharmaceutical manufacturing facility where she worked. The investigators systematically reviewed a stack of batch manufacturing records—entry after entry, page after page, batch after batch. After two days, they had reviewed 43 records.

At the close of their inspection, the investigators wrote their observations on the agency's standard form (called a "483") and included one particular point regarding the 43 batch records reviewed.

> *All batch records reviewed contained documentation deficiencies. Most contained multiple corrections or changes.*

When the FDA investigators left, the plant's senior management met to formulate a plan of action to respond to the 483 observations. They told the director of training to immediately develop a training program on documentation to prevent the reoccurrence of the problems.

The director of employee training agreed *some* action needed to be taken, but was reluctant about conducting training on "documentation deficiencies." She said the problem needed more study and, with difficulty, persuaded management to allow her time to investigate.

Karen formed a task group to review the batch records—all those reviewed by the FDA plus seven more. The team first looked at the instances of errors in the documentation and categorized them into three groups: dates, numbers, and words. Table 1.1 shows the results.

Table 1.1. Errors seen in 50 manufacturing documents

Document	Dates	Numbers	Words	Total	Pages
Manufacturing tickets	44 (15%)	178 (61%)	72 (24%)	294 (100%)	1411

In a brief update meeting, the task group presented their results to management. Management suggested that implementing a course teaching arithmetic would solve at least 60 percent of their problems. The training director emphasized the study was not yet complete; she was able to get a little more time to finish it.

Karen and her group then went back to the manufacturing tickets containing errors involving numbers and categorized them, as shown in Table 1.2.

Table 1.2. Results of analysis of errors involving numbers

Category	Instances	Percent
calculation	66	38
transposition	18	10
illegible entry	13	7
rounding	1	0
wrong place	47	27
other	31	18

The team was getting closer. They decided to focus on the two largest error categories—calculations and wrong place (meaning a number was written on one line, then crossed out and written on the proper line). They watched people perform the tasks; they talked to supervisors and quality control representatives. They prepared their report including recommended action steps and presented it at a meeting with management.

The action steps were

- Buy new calculators,
- Modify tickets, and
- Inform personnel of changes before and when they take place.

While the management group knew this action plan was very different from the one they had proposed, they listened for the reasons as to why training did not appear anywhere on the recommendations list.

A supervisor led off by talking about the need for new calculators. He said the ones currently in use were quite old and had displays that were difficult to read. Also, when the batteries got weak, the devices wouldn't blink or give an error message like newer models. Instead, they gave incorrect answers. Operators would write the initial answer on the ticket, as they were required to do, then, checking their work by recalculating the numbers, got a different answer. They crossed out the old and put the new one in, and then checked their work again. This took time. It caused numerous crossouts on the batch record. The solution to this was the purchase of new calculators that used solar cells and had larger number displays.

Another member of the task group described the recommendation to modify manufacturing tickets. As examples, she showed several tickets for different products. The arrangement of fill-in blanks varied from one ticket to another. For example, for one product, the operator needed to record the gross, tare, and net weights (in that order), while another asked for the tare, gross, and net weights (in that order). In other words, the operator had to pay very close attention to each form because there was little consistency.

One member of the management group suggested that people be more careful. Another countered by saying, "But shouldn't we make a job as easy to do as we can?"

The management committee was starting to understand. They decided to immediately purchase new calculators with the condition that operations people—the users—have a major role in selecting them. They also agreed to begin the change process to make the manufacturing documents more consistent, and as part of that, inform all affected personnel about the changes.

Within a week new calculators were in use. Calculations were being recorded more accurately without the need for corrections due to calculator problems. The story ends here only temporarily—the team is still monitoring the manufacturing documents and studying what else can be done to reduce errors. The team and management are seeking continual improvements.

Possible solutions

This real example shows there are situations when using training as a solution would have been a waste of time, money, and people. It might have caused a temporary improvement, but the root cause of the problem would still be there, waiting to appear again.

Training is not necessarily the answer to a problem. It should only be used when there is reason to use it.

Training is not a good solution in situations where

- There is lack of motivation;
- Reward systems (formal and informal) do not support the desired performance;
- Expectations and/or technology are rapidly changing;
- The process/job/task is not well designed or coordinated;
- Tools, information, and other resources are lacking;
- Control systems are not in place or effective;
- Feedback is not provided or is inappropriate;
- Poor management or organizational structure exists; or
- Expectations are not understood or are unreasonable.

Penicillin was considered a wonder drug when it first appeared and continues to be a very effective tool when used to fight specific infections. However, it is not the cure for all diseases. It won't do much to heal a broken arm. It also can cause serious side effects to those allergic to it. The prescribing physician must know both the disease he or she is treating, as well as the patient.

Frequently, a physician recommends more than just a drug product—"drink plenty of fluids, get lots of bed rest, and stay warm." These are part of the total prescription and are needed, together with the medicine, for the patient to become healthy again.

Instruction is a powerful tool. It is also a very costly tool. To make the most of the investment, instruction needs to be selected as an intervention in the appropriate situations. It needs to be geared to the needs of those participating in it. Training also needs to be supported by structures and systems that can give it integrity and strength, and maximize its effectiveness as a solution.

Before you say, or agree, that "training is the answer," consider that it might *not be*. Then prove to yourself that it is.

2

Focusing on Human Performance

Solutions to problems are like keys in locks: they don't work if they don't fit. And if solutions aren't the right ones, the problem doesn't get solved.

—Robert Mager

Goals

- Define performance.
- Describe the goals of performance analysis.
- List the steps and describe the process of conducting a performance analysis.

In the previous chapter, we saw an example of where there was a problem and that a solution other than training was used to effectively correct it. Here we will look at methods for determining what type of actions—training and otherwise—may be needed.

Human performance

Performance is behavior plus accomplishment (Gilbert 1978). Since we are focused on human performance, we are looking at the behavior and resulting accomplishments made by a person or group of people.

Organizations—businesses, clubs, not-for-profit groups, etc.—frequently have problems involving people. The performance that is observed does not meet the requirements, goals, or expectations that may or may not be written or even known by all involved.

Conducting a performance analysis identifies reasons why the people are not performing as well as desired. The analysis looks at trying to maximize the performance.

Example: Identify the need

Your phone rings; you pick it up and it is the manager of the injectable products manufacturing department. She tells you that during the routine bacterial monitoring of the aseptic gowns worn by personnel entering the area, five people (about 15%) had results that were over the action limits, meaning something needs to be done. (You recall that monitoring, using rodac plates, is periodically conducted on the outside of the gowns to be sure personnel are gowning up properly, i.e., in a way that does not cause microbiological contamination of the gown.)

The production manager continues to say she is very concerned about this because it could affect the manufacturing environment and the purity of the injectable products being made. She asks if you could put the five persons through a one-hour training program in order to solve the problem.

You understand what she *really* wants. You also understand that one or five or nineteen hours spent in a training program won't necessarily achieve the goal. You say, "I understand that you want to reduce the microbial levels on the gowns. Let me take a look at the situation, see what we need to do, and then get back with you." The manager agrees.

Three things resulted from your response. First, you realized that what was being asked for, a training program, would not *necessarily* accomplish the goal. Second, you acknowledged to the requestor that you understood what she really wants to accomplish. Third, you gave yourself the assignment to begin solving the problem.

Now what?

Sometimes people involved in training have a very limited vision of their positions. Frequently, they get this from their supervisors or management.

"Trainers" can and should do more than simply train. They can help solve performance problems, sometimes with training, other times by pointing out other, more appropriate solutions.

Problem solving and performance analysis

As a training professional who has a broader understanding of your role, you are now ready to solve the gowning problem in the best possible way.

There are a number of different problem-solving methods published. Frequently, they are found in quality improvement programs. Other authors, such as Robert Mager, have very usable and thorough approaches for Performance Analysis. For our discussions, we will use the model shown in Figure 2.1.

One of the most important things in most problem-solving methods is to clearly define the goal, or, in our case, the desired performance. Then, with the same clarity and precision, you define the current performance. The difference is the performance "gap" or the performance discrepancy.

To obtain the desired performance, that is, eliminate the gap or discrepancy, you need to

- Identify and remove or modify the barriers that are blocking the path to the desired performance; and
- Identify structures that need to be provided or strengthened that will support and encourage the desired performance.

The performance barriers that need to be removed or modified and the structures that need to be added or strengthened generally fall into seven categories (Spitzer 1990):

- The person's aptitude and capability of doing the job;
- The design of the job;
- Clear, known performance requirements and expectations;
- Appropriate feedback;
- Appropriate rewards are provided;
- Adequate and appropriate tools and opportunities for practice are provided; and
- Persons have the knowledge and skills necessary to perform the required task.

Spitzer states his experience in performance technology has shown that at least 80 percent of the performance problems he has encountered could not be solved by instruction, that is, 80 percent of the solutions fall into one of the first six categories.

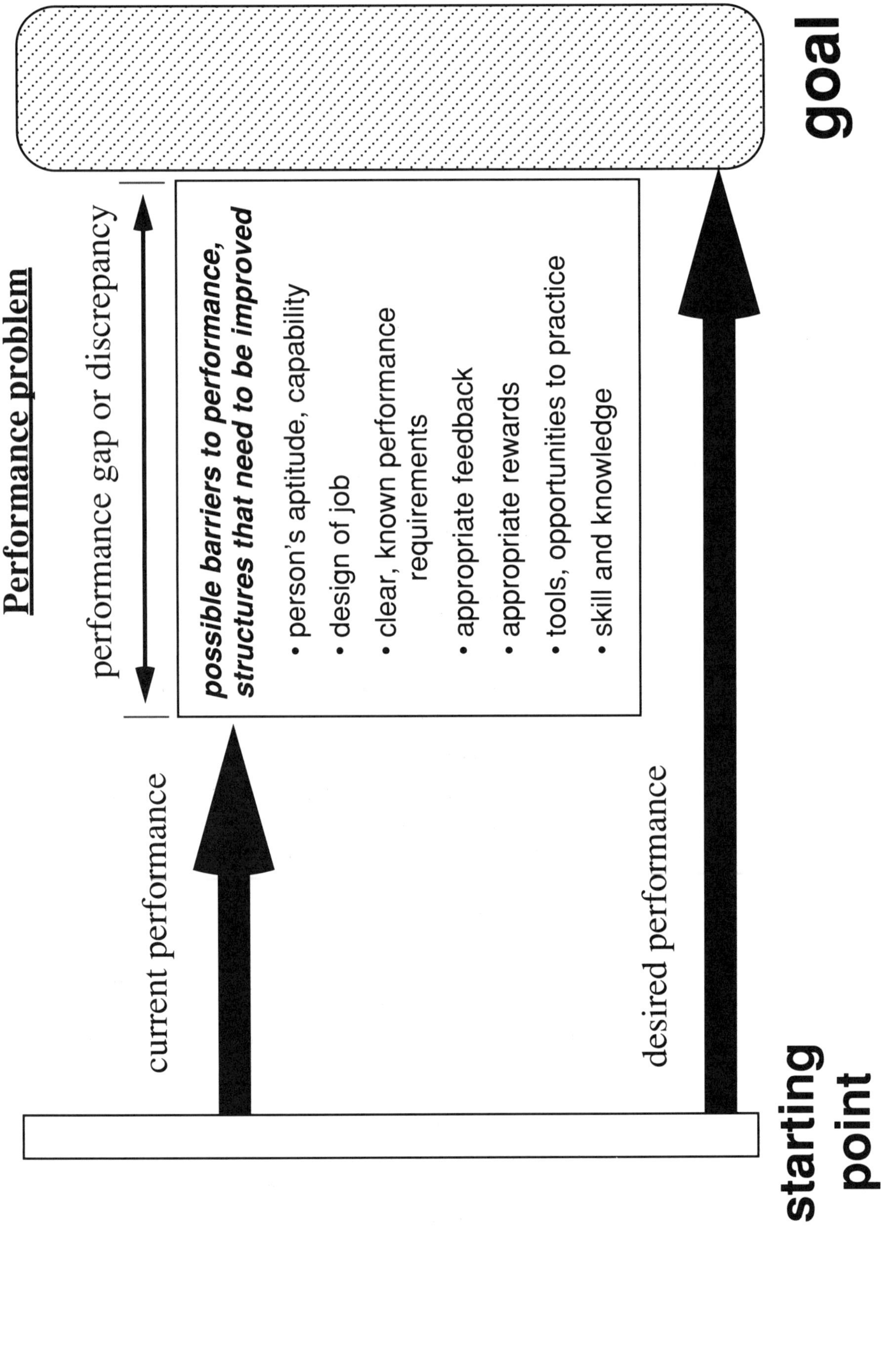

Figure 2.1. Model of a performance problem.

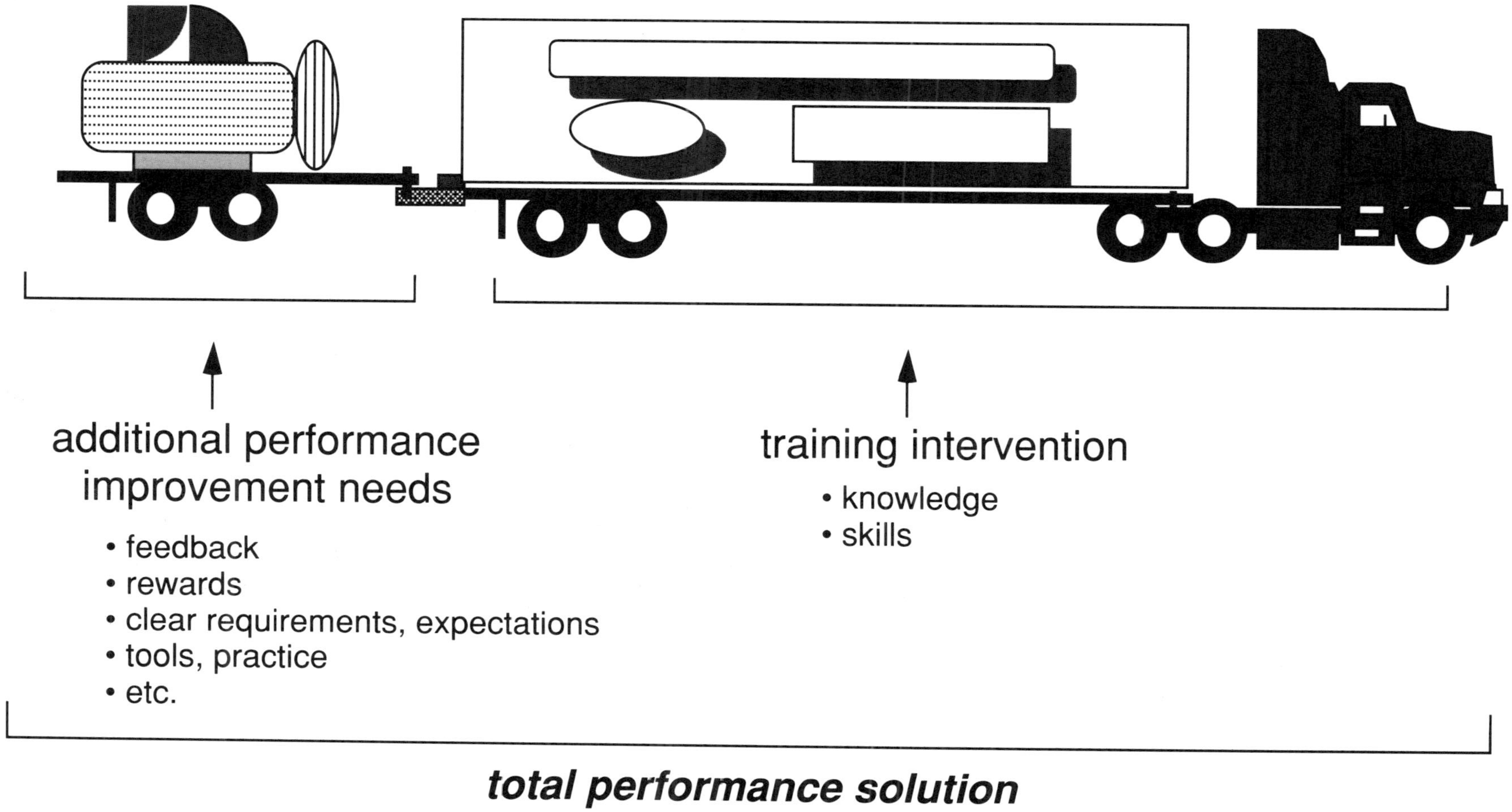

Figure 2.2. Components of a total performance solution. The solution to a performance problem must include *all* of the appropriate factors, not just training. Providing only training is like delivering part of a load of equipment to a customer—all the needed equipment must be present for the customer's requirements to be met.

For the performance problem to be solved, that is, for the goal to be achieved from the current situation, the total solution must include *all* the necessary components. Figure 2.2 presents an analogy of what comprises a total performance solution.

The performance analysis process

When confronted with a problem, use the following steps to first conduct a performance analysis:

1) State the desired performance or goal.

2) State the current situation or performance.

3) Describe what the desired performance really is and how an expert does it.

4) Examine the current situation or performance with the seven categories in mind:

- Capability *(Do people have the capabilities to safely and effectively perform the task?)*
- Job/task design *(Can the process / job / task be done better, more simply?)*
- Desired performance/expectations *(Do people understand what is expected of them?)*
- Feedback *(Are those performing the job / task provided positive feedback when they do the job / task correctly? Are they given negative, constructive feedback when they do the job / task incorrectly?)*
- Rewards *(Are there incentives for people to do the job / task correctly the first time? Are there disincentives [punishments] for doing the job / task correctly? Are there incentives for doing the job / task improperly? Are there disincentives for doing the job / task improperly?)*
- Tools and resources *(Are people provided with the physical and informational tools and resources that the job / task requires? Are there other tools or resources that, if provided, allow the job / task to be done more safely, effectively? Do they have opportunities to practice doing the task?)*
- Knowledge and skills *(Do people know why they are doing the job / task and the importance of doing it correctly? If*

their lives depended on it, could they do the job/task safely and correctly? [Mager and Pipe 1984])

5) Analyze the data citing specific evidence or examples in the above categories.

6) Propose recommendations taking into account all the above information.

7) Ask yourself, based on what you have learned, *"If I could do anything to affect the job or task so as to make it simpler or done more safely/effectively, it would be . . . "* Consider your response. Could it be a potential recommendation?

8) Review the recommendations yourself and with others. *What are the costs* (direct, indirect, hidden)? *What other effects might this have* (e.g., environmentally, upon the process or facility and their validation, regulatory-wise, socially, organizationally). *Do the benefits outweigh the costs? Do any additional changes have to be made* (e.g., revised validation exercise, a supplement to the NDA, ANDA). *Do they make sense? Will they create any unforeseen problems? Will they solve the problem?*

9) Review the recommendations with others and have them approved.

10) Implement the recommendations and monitor the results. Follow-up as necessary. (If there is a need for training because of the lack of knowledge or skills, use the instructional systems design process described in Chapter 7 and detailed in later chapters.)

11) Document your rationale for making the changes and the results. Include those who approved the changes and when they were implemented.

Example: State the goal and the current situation (Steps 1 & 2)

Most guides on problem solving recommend that you define early on where you want to be and where you are now. Both statements need to be factual, simple, clear, and not contain hidden solutions. For the situation described above, you write the following:

Desired Performance: All personnel complete the gowning process and enter the aseptic area with microbial counts below the action level.

Current Situation: 15 percent of the workers enter the aseptic area with microbial counts above the action level, as shown by periodic rodac monitoring.

Describe the current performance and how an expert does it (Step 3)

The first person you talk with is Dave. He has been identified by his supervisor as the best "gowner" in the department; his monitoring results have consistently been "no microbes detected." As Dave demonstrates putting on the gown for you, he points out some of the critical points that can lead to microbial contamination, such as the gown touching the floor or a bare hand or arm, not following the proper sequence in putting on the pieces of the gown, and so forth.

After talking to the expert, you have a very good idea of how someone can achieve the desired performance. Now you are ready to talk to people who, for some reason, aren't achieving the goal.

Examine the current situation (Step 4)

Four of the five people who were identified as not meeting the desired performance are available. You ask them to demonstrate putting on an aseptic gown and talk to you as they do it. During the conversation, you learn the following:

- Alice had never been told of the results of the recent or previous monitoring.
- Brad mentioned that since he had back surgery, putting on the gown has been much more difficult. He did not think it made that much difference if a sleeve of the gown touched the floor since the cleaning crew sanitizes the floor twice a day.
- Chris put on his head covering at a different point in the sequence than the others. He explained this was the way he always did it. He also said Donna, who was not available, is a relief person. She only gowned up and entered when the group was shorthanded, maybe once or twice a month.
- Ev went through the process very quickly, taking a shortcut here and there. She said she learned to gown so fast because she was always running a little late.

One last thing you need to do is review the historical data. You find that all five individuals had previously been trained (3–6 years ago) in aseptic gowning. In looking at the monitoring records, you see that all of the people had a number of samples taken that were below the action level.

Analyze the data (Step 5)

As you check your notes, you see that you have the following:

- The statement of desired performance or goal (what you want);
- The statement of the current situation (what you have);
- An example of the desired performance (how an expert can achieve it);
- Examples of the current situation (how the problem cases do it currently); and
- Documentation showing all five individuals had received training and passed several previous monitoring exercises.

Examining your notes of the conversations with the four people with performance problems, you begin to see some connections to the listing of barriers and supports described earlier and you create a table as shown in Table 2.1.

Table 2.1. Analysis of the current situation

Category of Barrier/Support Structure	Example/Evidence
Persons are capable of doing the job.	Brad's back problem presents difficulty in his of gowning.
The job or task is well designed.	
The desired/expected performance is clear.	Brad does not know why gown must remain aseptic and not touch the floor.
Appropriate feedback is provided.	Alice—no results of prior monitoring Brad—no feedback about gown touching the ground Chris—no feedback on wrong sequence
Appropriate incentives are in place.	Ev is rewarded by being counted "on time" even though she takes shortcuts in the gowning procedure.
Adequate and appropriate tools and opportunities to practice are provided.	Procedure exists; copy is not available in gowning room. Summary of gowning sequence is not available. Practice sessions with an expert are not available. Donna does not gown regularly; has problems.
Persons have the knowledge and skills necessary to perform the required task.	All persons have gowned successfully in the past. All persons have completed a prior training program.

Propose recommendations (Step 6)

As you consider your table of information, you wonder, "What can be done so that the people always meet the goal of desired performance?" You begin to form recommendations.

- Provide individual feedback to all personnel about their monitoring results, whether within or outside action levels.
- Provide coaching on gowning and some of the simple "tricks" involved in putting on the gown properly; include reasons why gowns must be put on in the proper sequence and not touch the floor; why shortcuts can cause problems. (Use Dave as the coach?)
- Post plastic-laminated photos or written sequence steps as reminders.
- Provide more practice or periodic coaching for those who only enter area on an infrequent basis.
- Provide extra, temporary microbial monitoring and feedback to these individuals.
- Communicate planned changes/improvements in staff meetings to all personnel affected and benefits to them/users of products.
- Review monitoring data; follow up as necessary.
- Supervision should reconsider if Brad is capable of performing the task; supervision should talk to Ev about punctuality.
- Document actions taken and date completed.

Modify the task (Step 7)

There is nothing you can suggest to simplify the task or make it easier or safer to do.

Review the recommendations (Step 8)

Your recommendations are quite specific and based on actual needs. You have discovered that there is no one, single "magic bullet" that can solve the problem, because, when you break it down, there are several different causes. The response was determined by a broad, systematic look at the whole situation.

One of the people you share the results with asks why training is not included. You respond that individualized coaching is part of the solution, but a formal training session was not recommended because it was not indicated from the information collected.

Present and implement the recommendations (Steps 9 & 10)

The manager who initially asked you to help solve the project invites you to her staff meeting to present the recommendations.

They approve the recommendations and also want to see how they can minimize the number of nonessential and "temporary" people entering the area. A senior supervisor was asked to report back in two weeks on the progress made.

Documentation (Step 11)

Not only is it a good business practice to formally document the improvements put in place and their results, it is something that a regulatory agency, such as the FDA, may want to see. This could arise if, during an inspection, the investigator saw out-of-limits data. A follow-up question would reasonably be, "*What did you do about this*?" Having a well-documented and systematic response to the problem would show thought and reasonableness. In addition, the investigator may also want to know if someone considered the ramifications of the changes upon process validation and the commitments made to the Agency in the drug application (NDA, ANDA, NADA, etc.) as well as who approved the changes and when they were put in place. (The formal approach to evaluating and approving potential changes is called *change control.*)

For more information

Analyzing Performance Problems, Second Edition by Robert F. Mager and Peter Pipe. Belmont, CA: Lake Publishing Company, 1984.

3

Training as a Way to Improve Human Performance

Knowledge is the only instrument of production that is not subject to diminishing returns.

—J. M. Clark

Goals

- Define training intervention.
- Distinguish performance-based training from other educational models.
- Identify two ways of improving how learning is applied back on the job ("transfer").
- Identify benefits in using performance-based training.

As you conduct performance analyses, you will undoubtedly find a situation where the people involved do not have the knowledge and skills necessary to perform the required tasks.

You could have a problem that is solved very simply by giving the person information by way of a tool or job aide. For example, if people do not know what number to call in the event of an emergency, attaching a highly visible sticker with the emergency numbers on each phone (and informing people the sticker has been added) could accomplish your goal.

Most of the knowledge/skill issues you encounter will not, however, be solved by a simple sticker. They will involve a training intervention.

Training interventions

A training intervention provides a person with the knowledge and skills necessary to meet a particular need. The training

"It's a fast track here, Herndon. Once you get through our training program."

interventions we will discuss and create in this book have several characteristics, including the following:

- Performance-based,
- Learner-centered, and
- Systematically developed.

Performance-based training

Performance-based training is instruction where the "learners perform in ways that approximate and progressively approach the ways they will perform on the job" (Brethower and Smalley 1992a). It has focus. It has utility. The content of the course and the ways the content is presented enable the learner to do something (i.e., meet the objectives) at the end that is important in the learner's job or task.

For example, you attend a course at a local college on the subject of auto repair. If it is taught by an engineer from General Motors who lectures and shows slides, tells you the theory of why it is done and how he approaches the issue, and talks a little on doing auto repair, the course is not performance based. It is educational.

On the other hand, if it is taught by a real mechanic wearing coveralls in an auto service center and you are told, "Prepare to get your hands dirty because by the end of today's class, you are going to be able to change the oil in your car," it is performance based. You will not know everything about repairing cars, but you will be able to change your oil successfully.

Performance-based training focuses on the "now"; educational instruction, while very important and useful in certain industrial situations, is more general and broader in scope and time frame.

Table 3.1 compares three models of instructional paradigms and how they differ from one another.

Learner-centered training

Learner-centered training relates to the learner's characteristics. (Knowledge and skill needs and specific audience requirements, are covered in the section below, *Systematically developed training.*)

This means taking into account the people to whom you are providing the instruction and taking advantage of what they bring with them.

Table 3.1: Overview of three instructional paradigms [Source: Brethower, D. M. and K. A. Smalley 1992. Reprinted with permission from *Performance & Instruction,* May/June 1992, Volume (31), Number (5)]

Paradigm	GENERAL EDUCATION Content-Based Instruction	VOCATIONAL EDUCATION Performance-Related Instruction	TRAINING Performance-Based Instruction
Purpose	Transmit cultural heritage	Transmit useful knowledge	Develop valuable performance
Models	Oral tradition	Apprenticeship	Master performer
Methods	Present, test, and promote those who pass tests	Present, guide, practice, test, and certify people who pass tests	Demonstrate, guide, practice, provide feedback, and certify competence
Content	Knowledge first: selected with deference to academic subject-matter experts, social philosophers, publishers	Skills first: selected with deference to practitioner subject-matter experts	Content secondary: selected with deference to accomplished performers
Teacher's Role & Preparation	Authority/evaluator presenter Extensive content preparation + brief instruction in methods	Mentor, presenter evaluator Extensive content preparation + experience + brief instruction in methods	Coach Experience in facilitating adult learning
Student's Role & Preparation	Recipient of truth Prerequisite courses	Recipient of useful information Prerequisite courses	Novice performer acquiring mastery Acquisition of learning skills
Scheduling	By clock and calendar with consideration of administrative needs	By clock and calendar with consideration of instructional needs	By instructional needs with consideration of clock and calendar
Problems	Enormity of scope. Time lags between learning and use. Integration of parts and wholes.	Breadth of scope. Time lags between learning and use. Integration of parts of wholes. Changing technology. Cost.	Narrowness of focus. Integration of parts and wholes. Cost.

In teaching cooking, for instance, the way information is presented and skills developed could be very different if the audience is children or if it is adults. Adults have much more experience that can be used, they have a different relationship to the instructor, and can evaluate to a better extent what they need to help themselves. (See also Chapter 6, How Adults Learn Best.)

Systematically developed training

You can provide a training program, have it performance-based and treat the adult participants as adults, but not really meet the needs of the people or the organization. An exaggerated example would be having people, who change oil in cars as part of their job, attend a cooking course. The cooking course does not meet the needs required by the task they need to perform.

Using a systematic approach in producing a training intervention is not simply meeting the real needs of the learner and the organization, but presenting the required knowledge and skills in ways to optimize the learning and performing. This means the information is selected, arranged, and delivered appropriately. (Chapter 7 gives an overview of the instructional systems design [ISD] process that is discussed in detail in later chapters.)

Another aspect of performance-based training is that it is concerned with transferring what has been learned to the person's job or task. Part of this involves examining the learning and transfer process by using an evaluation strategy. Another aspect means designing the course to maximize transfer.

Two simple concepts (Brethower and Smalley 1992b) used to maximize transfer are

- *Matching learning conditions to working conditions* by using tasks, tools, performance standards, feedback, and incentives in the training experience that are as similar as possible to those back on the job. If mechanics are required to wear gloves and goggles when repairing a piece of equipment in real life, they need to wear them during (at least part of) the hands-on portion of the training course. If operators get feedback from a visual display at their workstations, that should be done or simulated during training.

- *Matching instructional tasks to work tasks* by doing things in training that are done on the job. A mechanic learning to repair a capsule filling machine should learn by *doing* it, not only by hearing about it. Identifying the different parts of a respirator used to purify breathing air is not all that useful if the trainee simply needs to put it on correctly.

Teaching the "whys"

Does focusing on performance mean that learners are not given background information or reasons why something is important?

Not necessarily. Having an understanding of the reason why something is done a certain way and the potential outcomes if it is not done correctly are an important part of the training. *It must be kept in perspective*, however. If an objective of the lesson is to have the learners *apply* Current Good Manufacturing Practice regulations on their jobs, they may be more motivated in their application if they know something about what they are, their importance and legal status, and who wrote them. However, the focus of the course, as stated in the objective, needs to be on *applying* the regulations.

Benefits of performance-based training

The benefits of using a performance-based approach to training include a savings of time and money. Since only the things that need to be taught are presented, trainees spend less time sitting through unnecessary lessons. Increasing transfer from training to the job makes the training more effective.

4

Training and the Organization

If you think education is expensive, try ignorance.

—Derek Bok

Goals

- Discuss ways a training program can support the strategic goals of an organization.
- Describe pressures pharmaceutical firms face in the 1990s.
- List several of the short- and long-term benefits of a training program.
- List several of the direct and indirect costs of a training program.
- Describe how a business case is developed and used to justify a training intervention.
- Discuss the value of communication and integration of training and human performance activities to the organization.

For most, if not all of the things it does, an organization expects to receive direct or indirect benefits. Training is done because management expects something positive to occur when the training is completed.

If training is applied correctly, what can an organization expect as its return on the money and time invested in training?

We have previously seen that performance-based training is effective when it is matched with a problem where people lack the knowledge or skills required to perform their job or a task. Here we will look at some of the ways to justify the use of a training intervention.

(Chapter 23, Plan Evaluation Strategy, looks at more of the specific approaches that can be used to measure the training intervention's effect.)

Training can have short-term and long-term benefits. Sometimes, these are called "tactical" and "strategic" benefits, respectively.

"Strategic" means taking an extended view towards reaching a destination or goal. "Tactics" are the activities or steps used to implement the strategy. As you put together tactics, you need to keep "your eye on the prize," that is, the long-term view, or you may face situations where you win the battle (i.e., successfully complete a tactic) but lose the war (fail to implement the strategy).

Short-term benefits

If training is used to solve a particular, defined problem or need, such as teaching proper documentation techniques or providing people the knowledge and skills needed to use an electronic mail (E-mail) system, you can link the training to the results. There are tangible (measurable) AND intangible (very difficult to measure) benefits associated with the training; some examples are shown in Table 4.1.

The more clearly defined the problem, and the closer the match between the training program's objectives and the problem, the easier it will be to link the intervention with the desired results.

Long-term benefits

Most organizations have strategic goals describing their current mission and longer-term vision of where they want to be in the future. Training can be used to help meet some of these strategic goals.

In addition to the strategic goals of your organization, there are pressures facing all industries in the United States plus other, more specific ones confronting the pharmaceutical and healthcare industries (Table 4.2). As one who will implement, design, and deliver training interventions, you need to recognize that these pressures exist. More importantly, you need to anticipate them.

Table 4.1. Examples of tangible and intangible benefits of a training program

- reduced waste (e.g., raw materials, product, supplies)
- reduced time
- reduced labor
- reduced costs (e.g., substitution of less costly raw materials)
- decrease in deviations
- decrease in reworked materials
- improved performance
- increased reliability
- decreased job turnover
- improved attendance
- increased productivity
- increased sales
- increased customer satisfaction
- decreased complaints
- decreased returned goods
- smoother operations
- increased adherence to master schedule
- improved attitudes
- improved attitudes
- improved compliance
- increased quality
- increased flexibility
- improved motivation
- improved conformance
- increased durability
- improved service
- increased durability
- increased perceived quality

Assign value to hard-to-measure benefits

Some people complain it is difficult to measure the return on investment of a training intervention. Their problem is not finding an appropriate parameter to measure. Whenever possible, look for measurable changes and associate a monetary value with those changes. If the changes aren't directly observable, what *indicators* are there that can be used as substitutes?

For instance, "decreased complaints."

- How much does it cost to respond to a complaint?
- How much investigation time?
- How many people are involved and what is their time worth (in salary and benefits)?
- Does a replacement product need to be sent?
- What does the replacement cost, along with handling and shipping?
- What portion of customers complain with their dollars and never buy your product again?
- If it is a drug with a marketed generic equivalent, how much in sales and profit will your firm lose?

Table 4.2. Pressures confronting U.S. pharmaceutical and healthcare companies

Pressures common to U.S. businesses today.	• *Changing Technology.* By the year 2000, an estimated 5–15 million manufacturing jobs will require different skills compared to today's jobs. • *A Transitory Workforce.* "Modern college graduates can expect to change careers up to five times and hold twelve to thirteen different jobs" (Moskal 1992). • *Illiteracy.* Twenty million people in the U.S. are estimated as being illiterate, with another twenty million adults estimated as being marginally literate, i.e., reading at or below an eighth-grade level. 65 percent of the American work force reads below a ninth-grade level (*New York Times* 1991). • *A Changing Workforce.* The pool of young workers entering the labor force will shrink (Johnston and Packer 1987). About 30 percent of work-force entrants through the year 2000 will come from racial and ethnic groups that have the highest high-school dropout rates (Placek 1989). • *Time-to-Market.* Getting products out of research and development and to the user (or patient) is one of the newest and fiercest areas of competition, especially in high-technology industries (Stalk 1988). • *Quality.* Not only are consumers (individuals as well as businesses) pressing for goods and services that meet their needs and expectations, but national and international initiatives are instituting quality systems. The European Community's ISO 9000 series and U.S. ANSI/ASQC 93 have become quality standards and present an opportunity for evaluating supplier's goods and services consistently and uniformly, regardless of the location of the supplier (Jackson 1992).
Pressures on the pharmaceutical and healthcare industries	• *Cost pressures.* Congress, government agencies, consumers, and hospitals are putting pressure on firms to maintain prices or even provide discounts. Also, as name-brand drugs go off patent, generic competition can significantly erode the brand-name product's marketshare. Thus, there is incentive for the industry to find ways of improving productivity and efficiency (*Fortune* 1991). • *Increased enforcement activities.* The U.S. Food and Drug Administration has significantly increased its inspection and enforcement activities in the early 1990s. Inspections not only have a direct effect on the firm actually inspected, but cause a secondary effect in proactive firms who monitor FDA actions and who do not want to be found lacking in the same ways.

There may be some situations where there are several things associated with a change. For example, if there is a decrease in employee turnover in a packaging area and it is associated with improved wages as well as expanded training efforts, it may be difficult to say that your training program alone saved $25,000 associated with the hiring and training of new people. However, if you conduct interviews and find that 40 percent of the people rank training as the reason for their staying in the department, you may want to claim a certain percentage, perhaps a range of $8,000–10,000 of the savings as a result of training. If challenged on the point, you have the data collected to support your conclusion.

As a Harvard Business School accounting professor wrote,

> Although intangible benefits may be difficult to quantify, there is no reason to value them at zero . . . in an analysis. Zero is, after all, no less arbitrary than any other number. Conservative accountants who assign zero values to many intangible benefits prefer being precisely wrong to being vaguely right. . . . This may not be exact mathematics, but it does help put a meaningful price on . . . intangible benefits (Kaplan 1984).

Departmental and divisional goals

Frequently, divisions and departments have their own mission and vision statements describing what *they* will do to help support and actualize the parent organization's mission and vision. To be effective, these statements *must* be shared and understood by *everyone* in the organization who can help implement them.

For example, the vision statement of a firm may include this declaration:

> *The company is committed to the highest levels of ethics, integrity, quality, and customer service in all phases of its worldwide operations.*

The vision statement of the Quality Assurance Division may be:

> *Quality Assurance will use its resources to assure that products that meet all specifications and that are made according to good manufacturing practices will be released to the market as expeditiously as possible.*

Example: A "micro" approach

As the trainer in the Quality Assurance Division, what could *you* do to support the strategic goals of your division and corporation?

A colleague mentions to you during lunch that a product made at your firm's licensee in Kapacawaca will be tested in your central quality control laboratories because the licensee does not yet have the analytical device needed. You learn the turnaround time for getting the sample in, entered into the computerized system for tracking analytical samples, testing, getting the results reviewed and telexed back to Kapacawaca will take eight days. The big bottleneck is getting the sample logged into the computer and getting the results out and telexed to the overseas site. Your colleague wishes it could be reduced; there are significant customer service issues and costs for each day the product sits in quarantine awaiting the lab results required for its approval and release.

As you listen, you do a mini–performance analysis in your head:

The desired performance: Total turnaround time for product Q to be less than eight days.

Current performance: eight days.

Barriers:

- Data entry into computerized tracking system;
- Laboratory analysis;
- Obtaining results from computer system; and
- Telexing data to overseas site.

As your eyes start to glaze over, your friend asks what you are thinking. You give her the analysis so far. She gets excited and says, "If only I could enter the sample into the system and get the results out myself!"

Could she do the entry/retrieval if her life depended on it, you ask. "No," is the reply.

Aha! A problem that has a training solution to it—she needs knowledge and skills.

You and your colleague work together, and in the end, she is trained to enter the sample upon receipt so it immediately becomes part of the queue. She is also trained to get the results out, review them, and send them to the site. She comes up with a way, using a facsimile machine hooked into her desktop microcomputer, to bypass the telexing step. Not only does that save time, but there is less chance for typing errors. She then develops a one-page flowchart showing how this all happens, something that can be used in the future as a training tool for others.

The solution has a training component to it, as well as task simplification. It is an integrated solution. When put into place, it saves three days of the process and has a significant financial savings. You have helped your division and the company meet a goal important to them. You have linked training with a strategic goal and can rightly claim some of the savings that are now occurring. Congratulations!

This example shows a "micro" approach involving training and human performance—a particular problem is solved.

Use a "macro" approach

Another way to use training to achieve the long-term vision of an organization is to use a macro approach. This means designing an integrated system for instruction design and delivery from the top down. A macro approach would be implemented by following the instructional systems design (ISD approach) for all positions in the organization. This is the best approach for a new facility, division, or processing line; however, it could prove more difficult to effectively implement in an existing situation where there are daily pressures, problems, and a scarcity of resources.

Consider today and tomorrow

These pressures not only speak to the need for effective programs and courses, but also about how they are designed for the learners. For instance, if you design a course on statistical process control for packaging personnel that will involve considerable reading, do not think only about the reading levels of the *current* employees. Think about those who will be coming into the area in the *future*, i.e., the next several years. Consider flexibility in the design and how it will add value to the course and extend its usefulness.

Also think of how courses will be delivered in the next few years. Will your firm have a cadre of qualified instructors who can teach, or does it make better sense to use a computer-based or video medium for delivering the instructional material?

Not costs, but investments

A goal for the programs and courses you design, develop, and deliver should be that they just not cost something, but are investments for the future. Financial decisions and investments have short-term and long-term implications; programs and courses have them as well. By using instruction as a solution *only* when it is *really* called for, and designing it so it will have a measurable effect, instruction can be an *investment*.

One major incentive in using an ISD approach for the design and development of programs and courses is that you are looking for measurable changes (improvements, we hope) from the very beginning of the process.

Items that make up the investment

The Association for Training & Development (ASTD) released a "Consensus Accounting Model" for identifying and organizing costs associated with training (Carnevale and Schulz 1990). The model was developed with the assistance of leading experts and practitioners of industrial instruction and accounting in the U.S.

The Consensus Model consists of four steps:

1. Establish an organization-specific definition of training,
2. Determine all training costs categories,
3. Calculate training costs, and
4. Code costs.

Step 1

Establish an organization-specific definition of training.

What does your organization consider "training"? While some people consider "learning as part of living," you might not want to take that broad of view. One possible definition (used by the ASTD) is

> a structured program with identified objectives and learning plans to improve the knowledge, skills, and attitudes of trainees for use in their current and future job assignments.

There is a tradeoff: As you expand what is defined as "training," you potentially increase the difficulty in calculating accurate costs. For instance, it is fairly easy to count the costs in sending personnel to a seminar on computer validation. It is more difficult to get a good grasp of the costs involved in providing on-the-job training to summer personnel who load trucks.

You need to do what makes sense and is doable in your situation. It may be better to start out measuring the costs for one particular program or course and then expanding it, with modifications as needed, to others.

Step 2

Determine all training cost categories. The ASTD model categorizes costs as direct, indirect, and miscellaneous. These categories will apply to each phase of the design, development, and delivery activities, for the life of the program.

As you will see later, some subcategories will only be used once (e.g., the direct costs of producing a videotape), while others (e.g., the direct cost of renting a large screen video projector) must be considered each time the course is given.

The detail you put into identifying categories and acquiring the specific costs will vary; it will depend on how you (and your management) will use the numbers as well as what is important to you. It may be helpful to work with a financial analyst (perhaps one assigned to your department). Also, when you identify a particular category, identify the source(s) of the data you will use in Step 3.

Tables 4.3 and 4.4 give examples of direct and indirect costs. Indirect costs are generally harder to measure and track.

Step 3

Calculating training costs. With the categories and data sources identified, you can begin to compile and calculate costs.

As mentioned earlier, some costs are one-time, while others are recurring.

Examples of one-time costs include:

- personnel expenses of graphic artist used to produce trainee notebooks
- consultant fees during design phase

Examples of recurring costs:

- each time the course is presented:
  - instructor's salary, including preparation and teaching time (if using part-time instructor)
  - equipment rental
  - room or facility rental

Table 4.3. Direct costs associated with training programs

Categories	Subcategories and examples
personnel	• salaries and benefits of training personnel • salaries and benefits of other personnel assisting in training (e.g., part-time instructors, subject-matter experts) • salaries and benefits of training participants • outside personnel services
outside goods and services	• purchased program materials and supplies • audiovisual, video production costs • equipment rental or lease • equipment purchases • consultants (includes fees and expenses, if any)
facilities	• room/facility rental or lease • food and beverage service
travel, food, lodging, and incidental expenses	• training personnel travel • training personnel food (or per diems) • training personnel lodging (or per diems) • other training personnel expenses • participant travel • participant food (or per diems) • participant lodging (or per diems) • other participant expenses

- per participant
  - salary of time involved in pre/post-course activities, course
  - travel/food/lodging
  - course materials

The costs are then totaled:

The cost of a course = (one-time costs*) + (recurring costs*)

where recurring costs* = [(per session costs* × number of sessions)] + [(per participant costs* × number of participants)].

*Costs include direct, indirect, and miscellaneous categories

Table 4.4. Indirect costs involved with training programs

Categories	Subcategories and examples
overhead	• office supplies and materials • telephone • equipment capitalization • equipment maintenance and repair • office and facilities
general and administrative	• travel and expenses charged to overhead • management and staff salaries
miscellaneous costs	• as desired or needed

(Some categories and examples taken from Carnevale and Schulz 1990).

Step 4

Code costs. This means classifying the various costs according to the accounting categories (e.g., account numbers) used in your organization. This helps with recordkeeping and consistently tracking and comparing costs over time.

Justify the investment

At a conference of pharmaceutical training professionals in 1991, the manager of training at one of the larger U.S. firms mentioned that he recently received a memo from the Chief Executive Officer (CEO) of his firm. The CEO said he was behind training 110 percent, but that in the future, every new program needed to have a justification describing how the investment would further the strategic, or long-term, goals of the company.

Other firms in other industries are requiring similar documents.

The business case

One way you can answer the question is by using a "business case." Each organization may use something a little different, but it generally consists of the following:

- Project title and description;
- Areas affected;
- Why the proposed project is needed;
- What the proposed project consists of;

- Expected increases or decreases in personnel (full-time equivalents or overtime);
- What the proposed project will cost to implement;
- How the costs are spread out over time;
- Paybacks from the invested cost and when they will occur;
- Financial calculations based on standard models (ROI, ROR, etc.); and
- Strategic implications.

Some firms only require a formal business case for expenditures over a certain dollar value; however, if you do this (or a simplified version) for any significant project, it will add clarity to your understanding.

How you answer the cost/benefit question, either informally or as part of a more formal business case depends, in part, on how your organization views training. If training is viewed as a necessary evil, something that has to be done because of "requirements," or as a limited tactic to solve a particular problem, chances are that you will need a case that has some very hard numbers attached to it. Short-term savings/returns on investment would be important.

On the other hand, if your management takes a longer, more strategic view of training, numbers are still valuable, but other aspects, such as how the program or course will further the organization's strategic mission, can be emphasized.

In the past few years, more and more people are talking about changes needed to the conventional accounting systems in use, with such statements as "corporate management accounting systems are antiquated for the modern work environment" (Carnevale and Schulz 1990), and "if there is a time to ignore conventional return-on-assets calculations, it's when your long-term goals are at stake," (J.T. O'Rourke, CEO of Allen-Bradley) (Kirrane 1986).

The real acceptance of these last ideas is still a long way off; there is a lot of training to do in the meantime. You need to know what information your customers want. Sometimes you may need to have answers from *both* the short-term and long-term perspectives prepared, because of the different viewpoints various individuals take within an organization.

Use the business case in making decisions

An additional use of a business case is as information to make decisions and set priorities.

Management may not be persuaded by your business case if the benefit to investment ("bang to bucks") ratio is not high enough. They may have other projects where the need is greater and the cost is less.

If you find yourself in this situation, it can be discouraging, especially if you have invested a large amount of time and yourself in the project. Consider what improvements can be made to your business case, but *do not* go back and try to make more dramatic, unrealistic claims for your project or use an inappropriate design.

The importance of integrating training efforts

In large organizations, with many people involved in different aspects of training and performance improvement, operations training professionals sometimes feel like they are continually having courses thrown at them from corporate offices. These courses may vary considerably in design and production quality, assistance available to trainers, and, frequently, have short periods of lead time.

Personnel *receiving* the training are also overwhelmed by the information—many pieces and few threads providing a structure or framework that the pieces can be connected to.

Training and human performance is not an island in the corporation's world of operations and functions.

No matter what other programs (e.g., Total Quality Management, Quality Improvement Program, worker empowerment, etc.) are in place or will be in fashion, training and human performance will play a major role.

It is important that all people share an understanding of how training and performance fit into these other programs, so that they are viewed as integrated, and not just as islands in the middle of the sea.

Communication between training groups and personnel

Communication and collaboration between training professionals and their customers are very important, not just to save time and money, but more importantly, for people to feel (and actually be) involved in this critical organizational function.

Some ideas for improving communication within your organization include the following:

- *An electronic bulletin board service (BBS) or common E-Mail box* where people can ask questions, find out what is going on, become familiar with what others are doing, and so forth. Master schedules with course numbers, locations, times, and dates would be another feature of such a system.
- *Trainer's newsletter* that comes out once a quarter and goes to all training and management people describing what will be coming out in the coming months, a group doing something interesting, success stories, etc.
- *A training brochure or catalog* is a way to let others know what you are doing. General information, course descriptions, and scheduling information could be included.
- *Periodic workshops, meetings, and seminars for everyone involved in the training process.* Invite the CEO or president of your company to talk about people, training, and future trends. Perhaps an outside speaker from a university or another local industry can be brought in to talk about a particular topic of interest.

5

Regulatory Compliance: The Minimal Goal

The FDA concluded that [firm name] "failed to provide training necessary to assure that personnel have a thorough understanding of their jobs."

—from an article in *The Wall Street Journal,* July 1992

Goals

- Give examples of several regulatory agencies with training requirements.
- Differentiate between explicit and implicit training requirements.
- Discuss the FDA's requirements for training.
- Describe expectations an FDA investigator may have regarding training.
- Discuss reasons why documentation of training and instructional materials is important.

In previous chapters, we saw situations where training could be an effective tool:

- To solve performance problems where there are knowledge and skill deficiencies;
- In implementing the short- and long-term goals of an organization; and
- As a response to pressures on business in general and the pharmaceutical industry in particular.

There is another reason why training is needed for persons involved in the development, manufacture, control, and distribution of drug products and medical devices, as well as those who directly support such operations—*it is required by law.*

For professionals in industrial instruction, this last reason has some irony to it; some of us owe at least *part* of our careers to the need to comply with regulations. (A colleague who is an industrial hygienist, with health and safety training as one of her responsibilities, said that management does not always understand what she did in trying to minimize worker exposure to toxic materials. She said they *did* understand when she explained that her job was to keep the company out the courts, management out of jail, and the CEO off *60 Minutes*.)

With most managers you can use the "carrot" aspects of training; however, on others you may need to use the "stick" side—compliance.

Who are the regulators?

The pharmaceutical and medical device industries are two of the most regulated industries, both in the U.S. and internationally. Among the U.S. agencies who have special interests in activities related to the manufacturing, control, and distribution of pharmaceutical and medical device products are the following:

- Food and Drug Administration (FDA),
- Drug Enforcement Administration (DEA),
- Nuclear Regulatory Commission (NRC),
- Occupational Safety and Health Administration (OSHA),
- Environmental Protection Agency (EPA),
- Department of Transportation (DOT), and
- Equal Employment Opportunity Commission (EEOC).

There may be other international agencies expecting compliance of U.S.-based facilities, such as the European Community (EC). Producers of products sold in the EC must comply with the "Rules Governing Medicinal Products"; the portion on EC training requirements is found in Appendix A.

Explicit and implicit requirements

Some regulations explicitly say that training is required (i.e., the cGMPs for Finished Pharmaceuticals [Part 211.25]). They may or may not be specific about the content of the training that is required.

On the other hand, some regulatory agencies and regulations do not mandate training; however, people still must know about the processes and activities a firm or department uses to meet the requirements. The Drug Enforcement Administration does not have specific training requirements for pharmaceutical manufacturing personnel, but it does have a number of requirements for reporting, drug diversion, labeling and packaging, and so forth. People need to meet these requirements; training would be part of a total performance solution.

This chapter is not written to include a complete list of agencies and regulations with which you need to comply; regulatory activities are changing too rapidly. In addition, many states and localities have their own, additional requirements. However, several major agencies are discussed, with a heavy emphasis on the U.S. FDA requirements for drug manufacturing and control.

Training requirements of the U.S. FDA—drug manufacturing

The Current Good Manufacturing Practice regulations (cGMPs) cover all aspects of manufacture and control of drug products that are used by people or animals. Both prescription and over-the-counter (OTC) human pharmaceuticals are included.

There are other FDA regulations that also mandate training; some of these are discussed below.

The word *current* in the title means that the interpretation of the regulations periodically change, based on industry practices and advancements in technology. In addition, the cGMPs are the *minimal* standards. Strictly complying does not mean an operation is superlative.

The sections of the cGMPs that specifically speak about training are in Subpart B, Organization and Personnel, of Part 211. Covered are employees who are involved in all aspects of "manufacturing"—operations, supervision, and consultants. The importance that the FDA places on people as a resource and training as a tool is evident by the subject's position within the cGMPs; only several paragraphs about the scope of the cGMPs and the responsibilities of the quality control (QC) unit come before the training requirements.

The requirements are:

§ 211.25 Personnel qualifications.

(a) Each person engaged in the manufacture, processing, packing, or holding of a drug product shall have education, training, and experience, or any combination thereof, to enable that person to perform the assigned functions. Training shall be in the particular operations that the employee performs and in current good manufacturing practice (including the current good manufacturing practice regulations in this chapter and written procedures required by these regulations) as they relate to the employee's functions. Training in current good manufacturing practice shall be conducted by qualified individuals on a continuing basis and with sufficient frequency to assure that employees remain familiar with CGMP requirements applicable to them.

(b) Each person responsible for supervising the manufacture, processing, packing, or holding of a drug product shall have the education, training, and experience, or any combination thereof, to perform assigned functions in such a manner as to provide assurance that the drug product has the safety, identity, strength, quality, and purity that it purports or is represented to possess.

§ 211.34 Consultants.

Consultants advising on the manufacture, processing, packing, or holding of drug products shall have sufficient education, training, and experience, or any combination thereof, to advise on the subject for which they are retained. Records shall be maintained stating the name, address, and qualifications of any consultants and the type of service they provide.

!!! A key word in the training regulation is *performance*. This is the outcome the FDA is wanting and the firm should be seeking.

When the final cGMP regulations were published by the FDA on March 28, 1979 (there have been several changes since then), they were accompanied by a "Preamble." The Preamble discusses the comments made to the FDA's Commissioner during the period when industry, interest groups, private citizens, and so forth, had the chance to react to the agency's proposal. (168 respondents were heard from.) Some of the comments caused the agency to modify or clarify; others required a brief response by the Commissioner and were dismissed.

The comments and responses related to training are included below to provide some insight into the agency's intentions on the subject.

> 107. Many comments questioned the frequency of the "continuing training" required in §211.25(a), asked for a definition of the word "continuing" and questioned who should receive what type of training.
>
> The requirement that training be on a continuing basis is intended to mean, for example, that a single training course at the time an employee is hired, with no subsequent training activities, is not sufficient. Subsequent training should be sufficiently frequent to assure that employees remain familiar with cGMP requirements. The Commissioner does not believe it would be prudent to specify time intervals for training in view of the broad nature of the drug industry and [the] wide range of employee functions covered by these regulations. The Commissioner believes this section is sufficiently clear in identifying "who should receive what training" in stating that each person engaged in the manufacture, processing, packing, or holding of a drug product must have training in current good manufacturing practice that relates to the person's functions in the firm. The requirements of §211.25(b) contain an additional requirement for supervisory personnel.
>
> 108. Numerous comments pointed out that paragraphs (a) and (b) of §211.25 are not consistent in that §211.25(b), but not paragraph (a) contains the phrase "or any combination thereof" following the phrase "education, training, and experience." Most argued that §211.25(a) should also contain this phrase.
>
> The intent of the requirement is that a person have a sufficient mix of training, education, and experience to perform his or her job adequately. What is adequate in regard to each of the criteria depends on the job. It may be that a person can adequately perform a particular job with very little or no previous experience, or limited education, or with minimal training, depending on the demands of the job and the qualifications of the person. Because the intent of

> this section has been misinterpreted, §211.25(a) is revised to include the phrase "or any combination thereof" and be consistent with paragraph (b).
>
> 109. One comment questioned how much education, training, experience, or combination thereof, qualified a person to be a supervisor under §211.25(b).
>
> The Commissioner believes it should be understood that broad regulations such as these could not reasonably quantify the degree of education, training, and experience necessary. It is left to management's reasonable judgment as to what constitutes sufficient background in these criteria so that supervisors can perform their assigned functions in a manner to provide assurance for the quality of drug products within their purview.
>
> 110. One comment on §211.25(a) and (b) said it would mean little for some individuals to be instructed in the legal and technical language of the regulations. The respondent indicated that it is more important that personnel be instructed in the principles of good manufacturing practice relevant to their particular tasks.
>
> Section 211.25 requires training in current good manufacturing practice as it relates to an employee's function. The Commissioner intends that training be meaningful to the employee, not a formalistic but useless exercise to satisfy a regulation. The requirement is written to provide reasonable latitude to a firm as to the extent to which technical and legal instruction will be given.
>
> 111. A number of comments said the requirement in §211.25(c) for an "adequate number of personnel" does not belong in the section on personnel qualifications. The Commissioner is revising this paragraph in the final regulation by inserting the word "qualified."

Recent FDA enforcement activities, formal presentations, and informal conversations with agency investigators and management do not vary dramatically from the agency's original intent, although it has broadened.

For instance, "supervision" should not simply be viewed as line supervisors or department heads. It should include middle, upper, and senior members of management as well. A senior special investigator told a meeting of pharmaceutical training professionals: "It's more important to train management than anyone else in the plant" (Tetzlaff 1991).

Evidence from investigations, specifically FDA Form 483 (the standard form on which an FDA investigator records observations of practice not in keeping with the cGMPs), show training as an important activity:

> Untrained employees performed quality assurance and production functions for more than six months prior to receiving any training. None of the employees have completed the planned training program (GMP Trends 1991a).
>
> There was no program for training employees in GMP concepts and procedures. The GMP requirements for each position or function have not been established in writing, including the degree of supervisory oversight needed to assure employees are knowledgeable of each phase of their duties and that they maintain a satisfactory level of performance (GMP Trends 1991b).
>
> There was no documentation of the formal retraining of personnel associated with the filling of [product name] in terms of microbiological and GMP concerns although this action was ordered by the (batch) failure investigation (GMP Trends 1991c).
>
> There was not a formal documented GMP Training program for QC, QA or laboratory personnel . . . The QC unit lacked an active GMP training role, and GMP training requirements for particular job functions had not been defined. There was no documented system of review, evaluation, or approval of the adequacy of training for particular employees . . . There was neither a written SOP (standard operating procedure) nor documented review and approval of the firm's corporate training program by the QC unit. GMP training requirements for various positions or functions had not been established and written GMP training manuals or outlines were not available . . . There was no written requirement that GMP training be reviewed or approved by management or supervisory personnel . . . . (FDA 483 1989).

Table 5.1 shows particulars as to what the agency is looking for in the early 1990s, based on these observations.

Expectations of an FDA investigator during an inspection

Training programs are not usually the first thing an investigator examines when conducting an inspection. Training is typically looked at because there is a problem in another system or an observed deficiency in a skill or performance of a task.

Table 5.1. Inferred FDA training requirements for the pharmaceutical industry

Requirement Inferred From Observation	Commentary on Requirement
an SOP describing the firm's training program	The SOP would include most of the items described below; it would need to be reviewed and approved.
a written, planned program describing what courses a person must take and when they should be taken	A learning plan or curriculum map would be suitable.
a listing of what a person needs to know (and do) as part of his/her job	The FDA observation specifies GMP regulations and procedures but could reasonably be expanded to include other related skills and tasks; listing required knowledge and skills would indicate that one has made a systematic job/task analysis.
adherence to the SOP and planned program documentation of training and retraining	"Having and following" is an important and often repeated theme in the cGMPs. In the eyes of the agency, if it isn't written down, it didn't happen.
use of training as a tool to solve problems, deviations	If you say you will take certain action, you are expected to comply with these internal commitments; you should have data to show that training will solve a problem before prescribing it.
instructional materials available: outlines, etc.	Not only do course objectives and outlines document what was covered, they are essential in developing a quality course.
review, approval, and sign-offs by QC unit	The QC unit (quality control and/or quality assurance) is intended to have a knowledgeable yet detached view; it is expected to review the program/course and determine whether it meets the SOP requirements and is adequate. Any exceptions or deviations should be corrected and these should be reviewed and approved.
review, approval, and sign-offs by supervision, management	The management of an operation should review, approve, and sign-off on the plan and materials.
review by management of who has been trained	Management should periodically review the documentation of who has been trained and compare this to what was planned to take place. If discrepancies are seen, they should be investigated.

> *!!!*
>
> While walking through a facility, an investigator observed aseptic operators performing with very poor aseptic technique (reaching over open vials, spending too much time within the critical zone, using fingers instead of forceps, etc.). During the following days of the investigation, FDA personnel audited the firm's GMP training program. At the end of the investigation, the lead investigator told management that seeing the poor performance of aseptic operations personnel prompted the FDA team to review the training requirements and documented courses for each aseptic operator.

Investigators expect records, reports, and materials to be "readily accessible." Instantaneous access is preferred by some FDA personnel, but they will wait a reasonable amount of time. It is critical that you have a *useful* system in place and can explain that system. In one instance, the investigator asked for a listing of all those attending a particular skills course; the list was computerized and the only two people who could obtain the list from the computer system were out of the plant for several days—there was no recent hardcopy backup available. The investigator concluded that the records were not readily available; if management needed to check on someone's training history, they would not have been able to do so. Documentation and records are not solely for the investigator; they are tools for training professionals and management to get a job done correctly and effectively.

The plans, procedures, documentation, and materials related to training programs and courses must not only be readily available, they must be part of a system. When your training process and program are looked at by an outside pair of eyes, does it all fit together? Does the information have integrity? If there are missing dates or signatures, have you discovered them and noted what happened? Do the pieces "hang together" when looked at closely and also from a distance? You do *not* want to be criticized for having a program where "there is less to this than meets the eye."

Who needs to be trained? What topics do they need to be trained upon?

These questions are *yours* to answer. For cGMP-related training, a simple answer is **anyone and everyone directly and indirectly involved in the manufacturing, packaging, control, support, and distribution of bulk drug substances and finished drug products.** A job and task analysis is a method to systematically find out what the person needs to know and be able to do to safely and effectively perform the job and task. Once you have the information, you can eventually include this into a learning plan (with the plan reviewed and approved by QC and line management). If you have a good rationale for deciding who attends what course, you should have a good case if questioned by an investigator.

What about others?

While it is easy to draw a circle around those areas needing extensive cGMP-related training (i.e., those directly and indirectly involved in manufacture and control of components and raw materials), what about other areas of the organization?

Biochemical / bulk drug substance manufacturing. According to the FDA's *Guide to the Inspection of Bulk Pharmaceutical Chemicals*, the agency does not specifically state there are differences in regard to training personnel involved with bulk and finished drug products; therefore, it would use the previously discussed sections of the cGMPs (Part 211.25) as the requirement.

Development and pilot-scale production. The Pre-approval Inspection Program was begun as a way of integrating field inspections with the review of New Drug Applications (NDAs) and Abbreviated New Drug Applications (ANDAs), as well as establishing a more systematic, consistent, and national approach for approvals (*Federal Register*, January 28, 1991, 56(18):3180–3183). In this program, investigators visit a facility early on in the approval process and scrutinize, among other things, SOPs (having and following), reprocessing procedures, and label control. It is obvious that in order to perform properly, people involved in new drug development and the production of clinical trial and stability lots need some sort of training.

Equipment and facility maintenance and repair. An FDA inspector was touring a manufacturing site and writing down all the names of people he encountered. He went back to review the training records on each person. Two people who were found in the area were not trained because, the department head said, they were not production personnel. They were crafts people (e.g., electricians) called into the area to repair a piece of equipment. These people were there when open product was present. They could affect the equipment, adjusting it so it was outside of the validated range. In aseptic operations, it is even more critical to have maintenance personnel fully aware of how they can cause contamination of the area and what they can do to prevent it.

Distribution and wholesale personnel. The FDA's Prescription Drug Marketing Act "prescribes minimum standards for the storage and handling of prescription drugs for human use" (*Federal Register*, September 14, 1990, 55(179):38012–38026). These regulations require that

> personnel employed in wholesale distribution have appropriate education and/or experience to assume responsibility for positions related to compliance with state licensing requirements.

The preamble to the act states,

> *The agency believes that it is reasonable and appropriate to require that personnel involved in the handling, recordkeeping, and distribution of prescription drugs be competent to perform these important tasks.*

A job/task analysis will provide details on what "competent" means in a particular operation.

Outside or third-party personnel. In the push for more "outsourcing" of tasks, firms are using temporary or outside personnel. Sometimes these people perform "noncritical" tasks; other times they work side-by-side full-time workers and their activities are indistinguishable. In both situations training is indicated, the content to be determined by analysis. Some firms require the agency providing the workers to provide training—the content of which should come from the pharmaceutical firm.

Human Resources personnel can make a business case for hiring "temporary" people. Frequently, training is not considered as part of the equation. The business case may not be as persuasive if training is included, especially when the actual turnover rate for temporary personnel is taken into account.

For outside personnel entering an area to repair an instrument or facility, their training requirements may be reduced if they are accompanied by a departmental person, knowledgeable with the area. A firm might also use a checklist to review policies with the outside person or use a brief videotape to describe requirements of the area.

In all cases, documentation must be kept.

Nonmanufacturing personnel (e.g., human resources, financial, marketing, etc.). While the cGMPs do not require nonmanufacturing personnel be trained, you can make a strategic case for it. These people make decisions that can help, or hurt, the good manufacturing practice and training efforts. Most people in these positions have no idea of the systems and practices needed (and required by the FDA) to develop, manufacture, and distribute a product. A well-designed course could provide an understanding that following good manufacturing practice is a continuing journey involving, to some degree, everyone in the organization.

Other training requirements of the FDA

There are other FDA regulations calling for training in addition to the cGMPs and the Prescription Drug Marketing Act. These include the following:

- Good Laboratory Practice for Nonclinical Laboratory Studies (21 CFR Part 58.29)

  (a) Each individual engaged in the conduct of or responsible for the supervision of a nonclinical laboratory study shall have education, training, and experience, or combination thereof, to enable that individual to perform the assigned functions.

  (b) Each testing facility shall maintain a current summary of training and experience and job description for each individual engaged in or supervising the conduct of a nonclinical laboratory study.

- Good Manufacturing Practices for Medical Devices (21 CFR Part 820.25)

  Each manufacturer shall have sufficient personnel with the necessary education, background, training, and experience to assure that all operations are correctly performed.

  (a) *Personnel training.* All personnel shall have the necessary training to perform their assigned responsibilities adequately. Where training programs are necessary to assure that personnel have a thorough understanding of their jobs, such programs shall be conducted and documented. All employees shall be made aware of device defects which may occur from the improper performance of their jobs. Quality assurance personnel shall be made aware of defects and errors likely to be encountered as part of their quality assurance functions.

Comply with other regulatory agencies: DEA

Drug Enforcement Administration (DEA). Manufacturers producing controlled or scheduled substances must follow strict rules for security, and reporting of diversion, accountability, and employment practices (21 CFR 1301). Training is not called for directly, but in order to perform according to the regulations, training would be part of the total solution.

NRC

Nuclear Regulatory Commission (NRC). Radioactive materials are used in a variety of situations in the pharmaceutical industry, including:

- Gauges in biochemical operations;
- Sealed-source detectors in laboratory equipment;
- Low-level emitters (e.g., tritium) used in biochemistry laboratories;
- Laboratory animals injected with radioactive isotopes;
- Waste materials;
- X- and gamma-ray equipment; and
- Radiopharmaceuticals.

Properly conducted and documented training is a requirement of the facility's license to use radioactive materials. If an organization fails to train or does not properly document, handle, account for, and so forth, fines can be levied and, even more seriously, permission to use radioactive materials revoked by the NRC. Such an action could seriously affect an organization's research, production, and control activities.

Organizations using radioactive materials are required to have Radiation Safety Officers. This person would be an important resource for the specific requirements affecting your facility and personnel. In addition to outside consultants, universities may have staff or graduate-level students who could provide assistance.

OSHA

Occupational Safety and Health Administration (OSHA). OSHA was established in 1970 by the Williams-Steiger Occupational Safety and Health Act. A few states are regulated by federal OSHA, but most have their own state plans (e.g., Cal–OSHA, I[Indiana]–OSHA). State agencies usually adopt federal OSHA standards; however, they have the prerogative to set state standards more stringent than the federal ones.

Training requirements are included in various OSHA–promulgated rules, such as Hazard Communication, Respiratory Protection, and so forth. However, the OSHA–Act requires that the employer be ultimately responsible for the safety and health of his/her workers. For example, if a researcher uses a biological safety cabinet as a means to protect herself, it is up to the employer to make certain she knows how to use it, even though training on the device is not a specific requirement of an OSHA standard.

Frequently, health and safety topics are covered as part of departmental or shift meetings. Documentation of the topic, instructional outlines, and employee participation are just as critical as for more formalized courses.

!!!

An industrial hygienist was called by Plant Security early one morning: There had been a small solvent spill during the night in a manufacturing department. Instead of cleaning up the liquid according to the procedure, the employee on duty went to another department and borrowed an electric floor scrubber/vacuum. The device, which was not constructed to be used in a flammable atmosphere, was effective in cleaning the spill, but when shut off, emitted a spark that ignited the solvent vapor. The operator was seriously burned in the resulting fire and was taken to the hospital.

Investigators discovered that the topic of the previous month's departmental meeting was electrical safety; the supervisor's notes showed that use of proper electrical equipment in designated areas was discussed; others present confirmed it. The operator, who later died from the burns, had signed the attendance sheet as being present.

This example shows the critical need for having instruction that is transferred back and used on the job and the need to try and make it as difficult as possible to make a mistake. To prevent the situation from happening again, caution labels were put on all similar cleaning/vacuum equipment and the floor scrubbers were secured by locks.

> Another important point in this example is that training records and materials can very quickly become documents used as part of an investigation to determine what people were taught and who was present or absent. The accuracy, clarity, and integrity of all your work as a training professional is critical.

For more specific details on OSHA requirements, contact the industrial hygienist or safety engineer for your site. Additional information may be obtained through your local or state OSHA office.

DOT

Department of Transportation (DOT). Protecting the person and the environment while transporting materials is the responsibility of the DOT. A particular, complex aspect is the classifying and labeling of materials for transport, whether in company-owned vehicles or via common carriers.

EPA

Environmental Protection Agency (EPA). One of the most complicated areas for training involves environmental law; a separate volume could be dedicated to it. Some of the more important legislation that could affect pharmaceutical manufacturing and control operations includes the following:

- Good Laboratory Practice Standards,
- Clean Air Act,
- Clean Water Act,
- Safe Drinking Water Act,
- Resource Conservation and Recovery Act (RCRA),
- Superfund (CERCLA),
- SARA Title III (Community Right to Know), and
- Toxic Substance Control Act (TSCA).

In regard to hazardous waste, OSHA, DOT, and the EPA all have specific interests and different requirements. An example is in the area of removing asbestos (frequently used as insulation around older fermentation tanks, steam lines, etc.).

An example of where two agencies have virtually identical training requirements are the Good Laboratory Practice regulations of the FDA and the EPA (FDA—21 CFR §58.29; EPA—40 CFR §792.29).

With all the regulation-required training that must be done, it is easy to understand why some organizations cynically call themselves "government training centers." Instead of simply training for compliance, think how much better of an investment it would be to have people understand and *perform* in their jobs better so that it has a *real* effect on the firm's needs and goals, of which regulatory compliance is a part.

For more information

- *Training Requirements in OSHA Standards and Training Guidelines (OSHA Publication 2254).* U.S. Department of Labor, Occupational Safety and Health Administration, Washington, D.C., 1988. (This publication is updated periodically and available from your local OSHA office or the OSHA Publications Office, U.S. Department of Labor, 200 Constitution Ave., N.W., Washington, D.C., 20210.)

6

How Adults Learn Best

When I was a child, I talked like a child, I thought like a child, I reasoned like a child; when I became an adult, I gave up my childish ways.

—St. Paul

Goals

- Define andragogy.
- Describe the differences in the teaching practices appropriate for children and adults.
- Discuss and provide examples of various learning styles.
- List five rules of thumb for designing, developing, and delivering instruction to adults.

As a training professional, you will have several different customers to satisfy. Besides your management, the supervision and management of the people you are involved in training, you have the learners. Unless you can address *their* needs and satisfy *them* so they have and can *use* the knowledge and skills to safely and effectively do their jobs, neither their management nor your management will be happy.

Children as learners

We all have experienced teachers and education as children going through the school systems. We can think of the eighth grade teacher who traumatized us on the subject of algebra or the college professor who taught organic chemistry, receiving applause at the end of a lecture after bringing seemly disjointed facts into a harmonious arrangement. In these cases, and hundreds of others like them, we were taught using the principles of *pedagogy*, the art and science of teaching children (Knowles 1989).

In western culture, schools evolved out of the cathedrals and monasteries in Europe, which focused on the educating of boys for the priesthood in the Roman Catholic Church. The curriculum was strongly rooted in the Greek and Roman traditions of grammar, logic, rhetoric, arithmetic, astronomy, geometry, and music, plus an emphasis on religion. A set of assumptions or guidelines gradually developed into a body of knowledge called "pedagogy." As public schools began to be developed in the eighteenth century, the pedagogical method became more and more established, and has continued, with relatively small refinements, ever since.

Adults as learners

As children progress into young adults, and then into adulthood, the person is changing not only physically and mentally, but emotionally. They become more and more independent. As they learn and experience more, they gradually become differentiated as individuals, with their own unique combination of knowledge, experiences, interests, and values.

To be successful in teaching adults, you need to make use of all that they are and what they bring into the learning situation.

Andragogy is the art and science of teaching adults. Although the term had been used in Europe earlier in the twentieth century, it was Malcolm Knowles who gave the concept more substance, based on his research and decades of experience in teaching adults. His work is based on contributions made by John Dewey, Carl Rogers, and others.

Table 6.1 compares pedagogical and andragogical approaches.

Carl Rogers, a psychologist, studied adult learning and described ways of making it more effective (Rogers 1969).

- The learner must perceive the relevance of the subject matter.
- Learning involves a change in self-perception.
- Learning occurs when the self is not threatened.
- Learning is facilitated by doing.
- Learning is facilitated when the learner actively participates in the process.
- Self-directed learning involves the whole person (Cranton 1989).

Table 6.1. Comparison of pedagogical and andragogiocal models (after Knowles 1989)

How Children Are Traditionally Taught	How Adults Learn Best
• Teacher makes all of the decisions; students accepts this.	• Adult wants to know *why* they need to learn material.
• Teacher considers all students dependent on him/her; students believe and accept this.	• Adults have the self-concept that they are adults, want to have control over their lives, and wish to be viewed as being capable of self-direction.
• Learners have little experience to contribute as a resource to learning; experience they have is not valued.	• Adults have considerable experience of many different types—some are positive, some are negative that can get in the way of learning.
• Learners are ready for the next level when the teacher says so.	• Adults are ready to learn when they can apply the knowledge or skills to a real-life situation.
• Learning experiences are organized according to subject matter units and the logic of the subject matter.	• Adults are "life" centered; learning is arranged around tasks or problems that the learner encounters.
• Learners are primarily externally motivated (by teachers/parents approval/disapproval).	• Adults are motivated both externally (supervision, promotions, more money) and internally (satisfaction, responsibility, etc.); internal motivators are considered to be more potent.

Preferred styles of learning

In addition to some common characteristics of adult learning based on the fact that adult learners *are* adults, there is evidence to show that *how* people learn can be a function of their own preferred style.

I recently conducted an admittedly unscientific piece of research with friends when I asked, "When you purchased your first microwave oven, what did you do?"

The responses were something like this:

- "I unpacked it and made a batch of popcorn. Most of it burnt the first time."
- "I called my sister who has one and she gave me a quick and dirty way to set it up and start using it."
- "I carefully read the instructions before plugging it in."
- "I skimmed through the instructions, looking at the pictures that weren't all that great."
- "My son showed me what I wanted: I just boil water and defrost food with it."
- "I took a 3-hour course at the local continuing adult education center on how to cook using a microwave oven."

Most of us can identify with one of these replies. When faced with a particular challenge, some of us jump right into it, while others collect data and analyze. Some of us use formal or informal people-resources to assist us. Still others use a combination of methods.

This all has to do with the insights we have (usually unknowingly) learned about ourselves—a particular method of learning has typically worked well for us in the past, and we have become adept at using it. If someone were to force us to use another style, say jumping into a situation when we usually studied it in detail first, we would become frustrated or even panicked and we would find learning difficult.

!!! Adults who have a particularly well-developed learning style can become very frustrated when forced into another one. If a learner is adept at receiving information visually, he or she can be bored, angry, and nonreceptive if obliged only to listen to it.

There is no one right or wrong style. Each of us is simply different. We may sometimes use an alternate style depending on the situation. For instance, if we come across a problem very different from anything in our experience or it has some potentially serious consequences for an incorrect performance (e.g., "This looks like a real complicated waste control system. If I turned the wrong valve, it could cause a real mess. Maybe I should get some help . . . "). One researcher who has extensively studied learning styles suggests that as one grows older, learning styles evolve and then integrate (Kolb 1984).

Another view of learning styles looks at the preferred learning conditions that people have. They are grouped into four categories (Dunn and Dunn 1977):

1. Immediate environment (temperature, light levels, music present or absent, ambience).
2. Sociological need (working alone or in pairs or groups; working with instructor present).
3. Physical needs (preferred time for learning—e.g., morning or afternoon, length of time to sit in one place, preferences for eating/drinking).
4. Emotional aspects (motivation, need for structure—e.g., deadlines or lack of pressure).

There are various tools or tests available (Dunn and Dunn 1977; Kolb 1984) to measure learning styles, if desired; however, there is a debate whether knowing the learner's styles is of any real benefit.

Critics of adult learning and learning-preference theories

While these ideas and theories are now generally incorporated into the practice of adult education (Cranton 1989), there are critics who say the comparison between andragogy and pedagogy is difficult to maintain (Cross 1981). Knowles himself admits there are times, such as in safety training, where indoctrination should be used instead of a self-directed approach (Knowles 1989).

Other published articles challenge the learning styles concept: "There is no research to support the premise that matching learning styles to teaching styles improves learning performance" (Davidson 1990). Others describe the difficulty in trying to take into account the various styles and creating a program that meets the "preferences" of everyone (Cranton 1989).

Rules of thumb for adult learners

The important point about andragogy and learning-style theories is the guidance they provide as we design, develop, and deliver effective courses and programs. Some rules of thumb to use regarding adults as learners include the following:

- *Involve the learner during all phases of course production and delivery.* Talk to at least some of the potential learners as you design and develop a course. Try out ideas and concepts and consider the comments. Ask operators or quality control personnel to collect data about deviations as part of the needs assessment process. Let them help write objectives. Not only does this provide some ownership in the program, but it shares some of the work load. Involve the learners who are attending your programs. Challenge them with questions. Let them challenge *you* and the other participants with questions. Think "interactive," whether the course be computer-based or it involves an instructor.

  If you are developing a computer-based course, have selected learners try out pilot versions at the earliest possible stages. Their input is critical in creating interfaces and screens that are intuitive, simple, and consistent.

- *Let the learner become a* partner *in the training process.* Use the expertise of those who are doing the job. Very few instructors have strong technical credibility across the breadth of subject matter taught in the pharmaceutical industry. If you do not know an answer, reflect the question back and try to have someone else answer it. Even when you do know, see what their answer will be (it provides feedback to you about their understanding) and comment on it. Ask them to provide examples—positive ones and also negative ones, when things went wrong. Let the learners decide when to take breaks in longer sessions. Consider their input as you fine-tune the course. If people describe blocks to their performance or structures that could make performance better, discuss these ideas with the area's supervision.

- *Respect the individual.* As an instructor, you need to maintain an environment of openness and respect. Nonparticipants should be encouraged, not harassed. If you seek examples, be sensitive so personalities and feelings are not hurt. Begin and end the session on time; if more time is needed, ask the group to help you with more time or in finding another time to continue. Be honest. Encourage. Support.
- *Focus on real-life.* Use problems the learners are familiar with or case studies learners can relate to. If you are teaching a group from various disciplines, use a variety of examples from their areas. If you need to use jargon or abbreviations, have a reference sheet or glossary to help newer personnel.
- *Include the "whys."* Do not focus only on the hows. Look at the possible outcomes if the job is done correctly or incorrectly. Let the learner safely examine how these outcomes could cause rewards or repercussions in the future. Do not threaten; present the facts.

Considering learning styles

Incorporating learning-style preferences (e.g., reading versus listening) into your program design and development can be more difficult since various people have different preferences.

Why then even bring the subject up? One reason is the "Golden Rule" may *not* apply in this case. Handing a beautiful workbook to learners to complete in five days, just because *you* learn best that way does not necessarily mean your learners or *customers* will respond in kind.

Although the following statement in a recent Carnegie Foundation report originally focused on delivery technologies (videotapes, teleconferences, etc.), it makes a valid point for us here as well in regards to learning styles:

> The all-important point is to select a combination of methods that promises to be most effective for the purpose or goal of the course.... Analysis of the various means leads to one conclusion: a mix of technologies is best (Eurich 1990).

In practice, this may mean that there are optional ways available to cover the same material. For instance, a course on Stability Testing may be given in a self-study format as well as in a leader-led session. Participants cover the same objectives in each version; *they* can choose which one they want.

In the 1990s, multimedia technology is exploding into the world of education and training. One of the many reasons for its success and effectiveness is its ability to simultaneously affect several learning styles. (See Chapter 59, Using Multimedia Technology.)

For example, one particular multimedia program includes the following:

- A "talking-head" narrator who introduces each topic;
- The narration duplicates words on the screen;
- The learner controls the pace at which information is given;
- The learner can obtain more background information on topics he or she is interested in; and
- Data is presented using tables and graphical animations.

Another way of considering various learning styles is to have a course that incorporates different ones. For example, an introductory, leader-led course on Good Manufacturing Practice may include the following:

- An instructor providing an overview of the course and the expectations and objectives;
- A 13-minute videotape;
- A five-minute interactive summary-review of the videotape with the instructor and learners;
- Individual exercises;

- Small-group discussions;
- Large-group discussion using information gathered in small-group discussion; and
- Individual reflective exercises.

Not only does the course in this example utilize the expertise people bring into the session, but there is something to appeal to most of the participants, whether they like to simply observe or enjoy the interaction with others.

Learning styles, and the specific way(s) they are addressed, are considered when instructional methods are selected during the design phase.

One more way to meet the varied preferences of your learners is through a *variety* of courses. Be creative! Do not let your catalog of courses become carbon copies of each other. Do not use the same, tired, old format topic after topic, course after course, year after year. Not only will the variety meet the various wants and needs of your customers, it will keep you and others involved with training interested and vital.

7

Overview of the Instructional Systems Design Process

Education must have an end in view, for it is not an end in itself.

—Sybil Marshall

Goals

- Define instructional systems design.
- Compare the approaches used in instructional systems to those of traditional instruction.
- Describe the instructional systems design model.
- Identify the five phases of the instructional design process and give examples of activities in each phase.
- Discuss the advantages in using a systematic approach to produce training (or instructional) interventions.

Every month, a consultant I know receives a phone call that is almost always the same:

Client: "Our management wants a training program to be given to ten groups over ten days covering the FDA's Good Manufacturing Practice Regulations. They want each session to be a full day and include fifty people per session."

Consultant: "What do you want people to do at the end of the session?"

Client: "Well, you know, understand the cGMPs. Management wants to do something right away. Are you available to do this two weeks from now?"

Consultant: "But what do you want the people *to do* when they are finished with the program? Apply cGMPs in their job? Be able to recite a certain paragraph? Do their jobs differently? What is the goal of all this?"

Client: "I'm having a little problem with what management wants as well . . . "

Consultant: "There's a new product on the market called GMP Compliance Spray. You bring the employees into a training room and have somebody with good credentials spray the stuff. After that, everybody signs a list saying they were present and were sprayed. Is this what you'd like me to use?"

It is difficult to convince people to use a more involved, complicated, costly, and time-consuming process when they *think* they want training sprayed on their people.

The critical question is, *What do they want as the return on their training investment?*

No matter what sort of training is done, there is a cost involved (time for each participant, room rental, coffee, donuts, etc.). If you train just for the sake of training, you have very little to show for the receipts. If you want to train for results (like those in Table 4.1, page 29), you need to plan and produce a training intervention to get those results; what you spend will be an investment.

Producing a training intervention to effectively meet a goal involves using a systematic process to

- Identify the problem,
- Design a solution, and
- Implement the solution.

The solution must also be effective and efficient (Van Patten 1989).

In the area of education and training, the process used is called *instructional design*. Other terms, each with their own subtle differences used by various practitioners in the field, include *instructional systems design* (a term that seems to have its roots in the military), *instructional technology*, and *educational technology*. For our purposes we will consider them equivalent and use the term *instructional systems design* (ISD) to emphasize the systems approach.

What is instructional systems design (ISD)?

Instructional systems design is a process with which to

- Identify as goals what people need to know and do,
- Set out to achieve those goals, and
- Understand whether or when the goals have been achieved (Johnson 1989).

Further, ISD emphasizes the needs of the individual learner and his/her unique needs (after Reiser 1987). (This concept is stronger with those having roots in the technology side of the ISD house.)

ISD is the result of the integration of various disciplines and technologies, such as social science, information science, management science, and engineering. Professionals in the field typically have advanced degrees in areas like education, instructional design, instructional technology, and management.

While ISD is a systematic process, in practice, it is not a rigid one. It is a creative, flexible, dynamic, fluid, and responsive process (Johnson 1989), especially when used by an experienced professional. Principles, guidelines, and rules of thumb help give people new to the process a methodical approach that will yield good results.

ISD compared to traditional instruction

There are two major differences between an ISD approach and the more traditional instructional approach (Johnson 1989).

The first difference is that ISD is driven by the needs of the audience (or "customer"), whereas traditional instruction is driven more by the instructor and the instructional content.

For example, questions like, *What does the learner need to know and be able to do? What else needs to occur for the learner to use this knowledge and skill on the job? are found in ISD.* Traditional instruction would ask questions like, *How does this subject fit into the larger discipline? What is important about the content?*

By focusing on the needs of the audience, training can be more uniform throughout a diverse organization.

The second difference is ISD follows a systematic approach to optimize the delivery and transfer of information while traditional instruction does not. A college professor, who is considered to be a successful teacher, may have a grade distribution fitting a bell-shaped curve, with an equal number of students excelling (receiving an "A" grade) and failing (receiving an "F"). However, a performance-based course produced using an ISD approach would be successful when *all* the learners meet the performance objectives. Its goal is for none to fail.

The ISD model

Different variations on the basic ISD model exist, some with four, five, ten, or more "phases." The model used in this book uses five phases, each having a number of tasks and subtasks.

The five phases in this ISD model are

- Analyze,
- Design,
- Develop,
- Implement, and
- Evaluate and Maintain.

The ISD process builds on the work done in preceding phases and tasks. Some tasks are iterative, that is, they are repeated several times until a manageable unit of instruction is developed or the same steps are used on different areas of content. Figure 7.1 shows the phases and tasks associated with the ISD model.

A feature of the ISD process is that "deliverables," that is, pieces of the process—reports, outlines, storyboards, etc.—are produced. In addition, data (from job, task, and audience analyses) are retained for historical or future use.

This benefits the organization in several ways:

- Documentation is produced on how the problem was solved and the training intervention developed.
- Documentation is available in the event of a compliance inspection.
- Material developed by an accepted, systematic process can make it easier for someone else who needs to complete a project originally begun by another instructional designer.

Analyze

Data is collected and analyzed during the analysis phase (sometimes called "front-end analysis") to

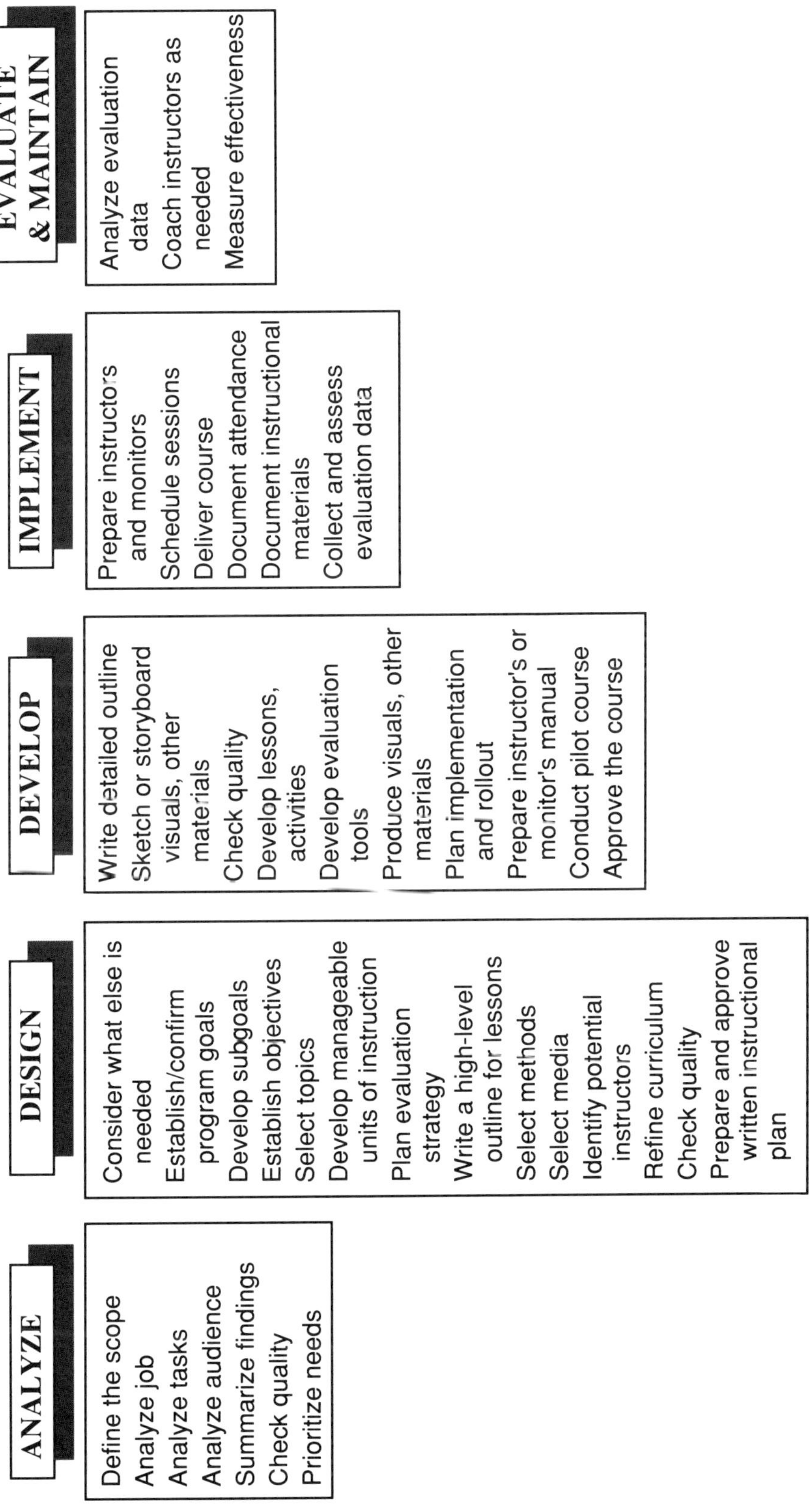

Figure 7.1. Phases and tasks included in instructional systems design

- Describe the job and task(s),
- Define the problem(s),
- Quantify the problem(s),
- Identify the audience(s),
- Identify knowledge and skill needs, and
- Prioritize the solutions.

Analysis is started after a performance analysis (or its equivalent) has pointed to a skill or knowledge deficiency.

The solutions generated during the analysis phase sometimes include more than just training interventions. Other performance-related factors, such as increased feedback from supervisors, job aides, and so forth, may also be required for the training to be effective and transferred back to the job.

Analysis is a complex and time-consuming process that can expand almost infinitely unless it is approached carefully with its scope defined at the outset. For example, instead of defining *all* the tasks a quality control representative does in his or her job, it may be desirable to define the two or three most important, critical, or frequently performed tasks.

Analysis is a critical part of the ISD process if the instruction is to be part of comprehensive solution to the problem.

Design

The design phase uses data collected and decisions made during the analysis phase to establish a blueprint of what the training intervention will look like and consist of. The blueprint, more formally called the *instructional plan*, includes

- Goals;
- Objectives;
- Requirements, constraints;
- Strategies for instruction, delivery, and evaluation; and
- More closely defined costs and benefits.

Manageable, modularized instructional units are designed for maximum flexibility, ease of implementation and future modification. Objectives describing what the learner will be able to do, in clear, observable terms are written. Content is organized and sequenced so the learner can progress into more advanced levels after successfully completing the lower ones.

Strategies for evaluating effectiveness of the training intervention are selected, ranging from how the learner reacted to the lesson or course to measuring the impact on organizational goals.

Also selected in the design phase are methods for presenting and vehicles for delivering the instruction. Factors such as content, audience characteristics, location, numbers, and future needs are considered when method and media decisions are made.

Develop

In this phase, the instructional intervention is produced, based upon the details and specifications found in the instructional plan. Products of the development phase include the following:

- A detailed outline with instructional content and activities;
- Sketches, storyboards, and so forth that are reviewed before final production;
- Instructional materials, (e.g., visuals, videotapes, printed items, computer-based instructional modules, etc.);
- Evaluation tools;
- An instructor or facilitator's manual;
- A pilot course with modifications made as needed; and
- An approved course ready to be delivered.

Implement

This is the phase traditionally associated with "training"; this is where the instruction is actually delivered to the learner(s).

The exact nature of implementation depends to a large degree on the vehicles for delivery. It will usually involve

- Preparation of instructors, facilitators, or monitors;
- Course delivery;
- Documentation of learner participation;
- Documentation of instructional materials; and
- Collection and assessment of evaluation data.

The scope of the implementation effort is related to the size and location(s) of the audience, the number of instructors or training stations (e.g., simulators or computer-based training devices) available, and the number of instructional units that need to be given.

Whereas the most visible spending of funds typically occurs in the development phase (and to a lesser extent in the design and analysis phases), the implementation phase can be extremely costly when the learners' and instructors' time is considered. This is often "invisible" or not considered by the firm. If the instructional design has been a good one, only the important, "must-have" skills and knowledge will be taught using the most effective and efficient instructional methods and media, thus reducing the learner's time to a minimum.

It is frequently seen that instructional media that are relatively costly to design and develop (i.e., interactive multimedia programs), can have substantial cost savings over the life of the program, when compared to more traditional delivery media.

Evaluate and maintain

Based upon the information gathered with the evaluation tools, instructional content, methods, and media may need to be fine-tuned to more effectively and efficiently meet the objectives and goals. (This type of evaluation is sometimes called "summative.") Also, a "follow-up" evaluation may be desired months after the training is given to look for long-term changes and program success.

If there is content that changes with time (e.g., regulations, interpretation of the cGMPs, industry practices, etc.), this will also need to be updated.

Instructional systems design is based on scientific and technological methods and tools, but it requires people who can ask the right questions at the right time to define the needs and who take this information to create and craft an effective and efficient solution. The ISD practitioner needs not only knowledge, skills, and creativity, but a perspective focused on the learner.

The ISD process tends to be a collaborative one: learners, subject matter experts, graphics artists, and other professionals are involved at various steps, each adding value and richness to the finished program.

II

Analysis Phase

8

Introduction to the Analysis Phase

How did I get here?

Analysis is the place to start when you have a problem or need that is, at least in part, due to a skill or knowledge deficiency.

You should have discovered whether or not there is a knowledge or skill deficiency as part of a performance analysis (such as described in Chapter 2) or another problem solving methodology.

Purpose of the analysis phase

You use the analysis phase of the instructional systems design (ISD) process to

- Define the problem; and
- Identify, describe, and quantify parameters to be considered when designing and developing the solution.

What you will be doing

Figure 8.1 presents the tasks, their descriptions, and the output generated during the analysis phase. The results of the job, task, and audience analyses, and the prioritized lists of instructional and performance solutions are all important foundations for the work done in the design and development phases.

Analysis Phase

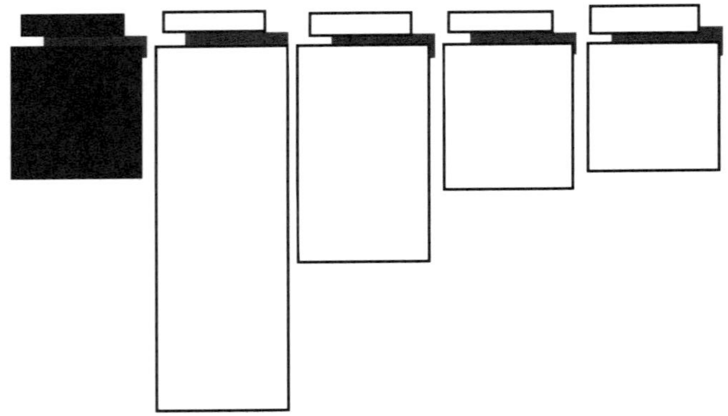

Task	Description	Output
1) Define the scope	Set boundaries on project (jobs, areas, etc.).	Definition of project
2) Analyze the job	Describe what the person does in the course of his/her job.	Functions, duties Tasks performed for each duty Background/qualifications
3) Analyze the task	Identify tasks for each job; knowledge, skills needed.	Task steps and substeps Sequence; performance requirements; when/frequency of task; tools, resources, information needed
4) Analyze audience characteristics	Describe parameters of audience related to learning.	Education, literacy, age, special needs, influence groups, past courses
5) Summarize findings	Analyze data and develop information.	List of training needs List of performance improvement needs
6) Check quality	Review information for completeness, accuracy, clarity.	Reviewed (and modified) needs lists
7) Prioritize needs	Prioritize items to be included in training program.	Prioritized training needs Prioritized performance improvement needs

Figure 8.1. Tasks associated with the analysis phase

9

Define the Scope of the Project

Description

Set boundaries for the work to be done for this and future phases.

Why do it

The scope of the project is defined in order to

- State the need that the training intervention will be designed to meet;
- Formally identify the target group(s) who will receive the training intervention;
- Help manage a complex project;
- Communicate to management and others what is going to happen;
- Minimize the chance of getting side-tracked on other issues; and
- Develop the program's goal (in the design phase).

Who is involved

Management and the analyst are involved in defining the scope.

Output

A "needs statement" related to training and a "scope statement" are produced in this task.

Comments

Here's a quick summary of how you got to this point:

- There was a performance problem.
- You conducted a performance analysis that showed deficiencies in the skills and knowledge of people involved in the task.
- The performance analysis included training in the recommendations as (at least part of) the solution.

Now, you are ready to say, in general terms, what needs to be done and who will receive the training.

How this differs from a goal. The goal of the program, developed at the beginning of the design phase, is much more specific and focused on what the outcome of the training intervention will be; the goal can be written more specifically because of the information obtained during the analysis phase.

The scope statement is partially derived from the needs statement which is written first and is an interim step.

How it is done

1) Write the needs statement. It should include
   - Who the training will be directed at and
   - The intended result of the training intervention.

2) Write the scope statement, based on management and organizational input. It should include
   - Who the specific audience(s) is that the training will be directed at,
   - Where the audience(s) is located,
   - What the training results will be,
   - Why the training is being given, and
   - When the training intervention should be ready to be implemented.

The scope statement does not need to be more than a few sentences.

Example

In the earlier example explaining performance analysis (Chapter 2), you focused on existing employees who entered the aseptic manufacturing area with microbiological counts on the their gowns that exceeded the action limits.

Your solutions to that problem were so successful that management is now asking you to look at *new* employees entering the area.

While there are similarities, there are also differences between the two situations. Therefore, you conducted another performance analysis that showed the following:

> *Desired performance:* New employees enter the aseptic manufacturing area with microbiological counts below the action limit.

> *Current performance:* New people have counts greatly exceeding the action limit (they do not enter the aseptic area).
>
> *Recommendations:* Provide new employees appropriate skills, knowledge, practice, and coaching.

You write the needs statement based on what you understand needs to happen.

> *Needs statement:* New employees who will work in the aseptic area need skills, knowledge, and practice in order to have microbiological counts (on their gowns) below the action limit.

Next, for the scope statement, you answer the questions a reporter asks: who, what, when, where, and why. You use information found in the needs statement, as well as other input from supervision and management.

> *Scope statement:* All new employees entering the aseptic area of the Blue Island Aseptic Manufacturing facility must have the skills, knowledge, and practice necessary for correct gowning so that products and the aseptic area are not contaminated. The training intervention will be available for use in 30 days.

Broken down into its parts, you can see the various elements:

- Who: all new employees entering the aseptic area.
- Where: Blue Island Aseptic Manufacturing facility.
- What: skills, knowledge, and practice necessary for correct gowning.
- Why: so products and the aseptic area are not contaminated.
- When: training intervention will be available for use in 30 days.

You share the written statements with management who agree with you. You are now ready to begin the next tasks in the analysis phase.

How it is used

The scope statement puts limits on the project. In the example above, you are including all new people who will work in the area—operators, supervisors, maintenance, quality control, and so on. You also know the training solution will be used at the Blue Island facility, not in your company's facilities in Europe, Asia, or Puerto Rico. (As the scope statement is developed, you should check this out with management, since factors like this have a major affect on how the course is designed.)

As you progress through the analysis phase and beyond, you can check your activities with the scope statement to be sure you are on target. If management would ask in the future why certain groups were included/excluded from the scope of the project, you have a written, agreed-to definition of the project.

10

Analyze the Job

Definition

Develop a description of what a person does in the course of his or her job.

Why do it

Job analysis is done as a prerequisite to a task analysis. It provides a clear understanding of the job. The documentation of duties provides important baseline information that is refined and detailed in subsequent tasks.

Who is involved

Job analysis involves

- The analyst;
- Persons currently doing the job, preferably individuals who are considered "experts" at what they do; and
- Supervision.

Output

For each job analyzed, a list is developed of the

- Functions/duties,
- Tasks performed for each function/duty; and
- Relevant background and qualifications of persons currently performing the job.

Comments

As you learn more about the job, you can begin forming questions that can be used in developing the *audience characteristics analysis.*

There are a number of methods that can potentially be used, each providing a slightly different perspective of the job. To increase the reliability of the data collected, two or three methods should be used and their resulting data pooled. These methods include

- Standardized job analysis data,
- Observation of an "expert" worker,
- Interviews with an "expert" worker,
- Interviews with a small group of workers,
- Interviews with supervision, and
- Questionnaires.

How it is done

1) Select the appropriate analysis method(s).

2) Develop the tools required by the methods (i.e., write the questionnaire, interview questions, etc.). Experiment with two or three people from the target audience and test the tools for clarity.

3) Ask supervision to identify several people who are experts in a particular job (the "content experts" or the "subject matter experts"). They might not be the ones with the longest time in the area. You are looking for those who are the *best* performers.

4) When you ask the subject matter experts to help you, explain what you are doing and why you are doing it.

5) Use the tools. Give out the questionnaire, conduct the interviews, and so forth.

6) If interviews or questionnaires are used, observation should be used to validate the results. Investigate any discrepancies with the experts or supervision.

Example

You are doing a job analysis for the position of formulations operator, and you have decided to use the interview method. You first ask the supervisor who the best people in that job are. With three of these people, use the questions you developed and tried out earlier, including

- What are the duties you perform in your job?
- What part of your job (e.g., percentage of time spent) is doing each duty?
- What is your educational background? Did it contribute to your ability to do your job? What training have you had?
- What job experience(s) have you had that contributes to your ability to do the job well?
- What training have you *not* had that might have helped you to do the job better?

- How long have you had this job?
- What is the most difficult part of your job? Why?
- What is the most critical part of your job? Why?
- What job did you have previous to your current one?
- What job could you have in the future?

Ask other questions for clarification, as needed. Look for consistencies or themes as well as inconsistencies between the experts.

After the interviews, you use a second method, observation. You watch another "good" performer as he or she does his or her job and note any deviations to what you had been told earlier.

Develop a "standard" list of duties, tasks, resources, and the like. Show this list to the area's supervision for concurrence and for an accuracy check. (Again, note any discrepancies between what you observed.) Also discuss with the supervisor the typical worker's progression to various jobs or levels within the department, in part, so that you can understand how people are rewarded for good performance. When finished, share the information with other interested parties, such as your management, human resources, recruiting, and so forth.

The completed job analysis may look something like this:

JOB TITLE: Formulations Operator

DEPARTMENT NAME: Dry Products Manufacturing

JOB DUTIES:

- Clean and prepare equipment for use (50 percent of time),
- Check in raw materials and assemble in staging area (15 percent of time),
- Assist Senior Formulations Operator in setup of manufacturing equipment (15 percent of time), and
- Assist Senior Formulations Operator in operation and teardown of equipment (20 percent of time).

OTHER CRITICAL JOB REQUIREMENTS:

- Must react quickly to equipment problems,
- Must be able to read at a tenth grade level, and
- Must pay attention to details.

DIFFICULTIES IN THE JOB:

- Frequent schedule changes and
- Not knowing what extra equipment parts are required and need to be prepared.

EXPERIENCE OF WORKERS (length of time in job): Two–eight years.

EDUCATIONAL BACKGROUND: High school graduates (required); some have one year of college experience.

EXAMPLES OF PREVIOUS JOBS HELD: Service operator, QC clerk.

TYPICAL NEXT ASSIGNMENT: Formulations Senior Operator.

11

Analyze the Tasks

An expert is one who does not have to think. He knows.
—Frank Lloyd Wright

Description Task analysis is the process of breaking down the functions or duties of a job into tasks. Knowledge and skills necessary to perform each task are also identified and rated.

Why do it The task analysis

- Identifies what the job duties include and what they do not include, thus making the actual training focused on the important elements;
- Divides the task into a step and substep sequence that can be developed into a standard operating procedure (SOP); and
- Can discover how various individuals perform a task differently, which could be combined into the one best way, producing more consistent results.

Who is involved A task analysis is conducted by

- An analyst (frequently more than one is required in a project);
- Persons currently doing the task, preferably individuals who are considered "experts" in the task; and
- Supervision.

Output For each job there will be a list of the tasks to be performed. Then, for each task there will be a *task description*, a listing that includes the

- Steps and substeps (if needed) of the task;
- Sequence in which the steps and substeps are to be performed;
- When the task is performed;
- Frequency that the task is performed;
- Performance requirements (e.g., rate, tolerance specifications, etc.);
- Degree of criticality in performing the task correctly;
- Consequences of not performing the task correctly;
- Tools, resources, and information needed;
- Safety, health, and environmental considerations involved with the task;
- Skills necessary to perform the task;
- Knowledge necessary to perform the task;
- Differentiation between "must-know" and "nice-to-know" topics;
- Difficulty in learning the task; and
- Suggestions on training that would be helpful.

Additional outputs

- A flowchart that graphically describes the inputs, activities, outputs, and decisions involved in the task.
- A *standard operating procedure* for the task may be required for cGMP compliance. The data collected above can easily be used in writing one. (See Chapter 55, Having and Using Procedures.)

Comments

Task analysis is a very time-consuming process. Conducting a task analysis on all of the activities a person does can be overwhelming; there *may* be a very important business reason for doing so. However, you may want to consider doing a task analysis *only* on the tasks that were identified in the job analysis as

- Critical,
- Difficult, and
- Frequently performed.

Alternatively, the performance analysis may indicate certain specific tasks requiring additional knowledge and skills for which a task analysis is appropriate

Existing SOPs may contain some of the information needed for the analysis; however, it is not uncommon for a written procedure to be different from the "way we *really* do it."

As you collect information, have the learners help you sort it. For instance, as they describe skills and knowledge necessary to perform a task, ask them if it is a "must-know" item (you cannot perform without it) or if it is a "nice-to-know" item (it may provide more efficiency or other benefits). This will be helpful as you determine the instructional needs.

There is a possibility that you may collect too *much* data and be overwhelmed by it. As you prepare for the interviews or develop the questionnaire, ask yourself, *"Why do I need this information? What am I going to do with it?"* Consider the trade-off between asking too much and asking too little and going back for more.

The remaining design and development activities will be based on the results from the task analysis. If not done properly, much time and money can be spent without obtaining the desired results. If using a systematic design process is new for you, consider starting on a very small scale or working with someone who has successfully performed one. Another option would be working with an outside consultant, where you are the consultant's "trainee" or where the consultant continually reviews your work. Design for yourself a learning experience where you *will* succeed.

Cautions!

The task analysis should examine what *is* being done and what *must* be done to complete the task. You may find nonessential steps are being performed that add no value to the product or information being processed. "Re-engineering" or eliminating these unneeded steps can simplify the process and reduce the training required. However, **before eliminating or changing anything, consult the appropriate supervisory and quality control (QC) personnel.**

If you (or others) feel that you are not making progress due to all the data that has been collected, pause and see if you are becoming bogged down in this step. As mentioned above, consider what you will do with all the information.

How it is done, part one

1) Select the appropriate method(s).

As with the job analysis, there are a number of methods that can be used. In addition to people, documents and records give a good, objective view of what has and is currently occurring. A combination of methods will provide a broader perspective on how the task is performed as well as produce more accurate and reliable information.

Types of methods

- *Review of records and documentation.* Pharmaceutical manufacturing involves more than producing medicines; documentation is also produced describing the exact process used to manufacture, control, and release the drug product. Deviation records shed light on problems (many of which must be solved using other interventions than training). For example, if the need is for a course on documentation techniques, reviews of batch records will indicate particular types of problems, such as illegible writing, missing initials, and so forth.
- *Observation of an "expert" doing the task.* Watch a person do the task. As he or she does it (or afterwards, if necessary), ask the person to describe what they are doing and why they are doing it. Notice if they refer to a procedure or document or ask the advice or assistance of another person. Ask them about the decisions they make and how they arrive at the "correct" answer.
- *Interviews with "experts."* If used as a follow-up to an observation, ask the remaining questions (such as knowledge or skills required, etc.). Ask for clarification as necessary. If observation was not used earlier, ask the "expert" to go through the sequence step by step. Ask for details about any decisions they make and what they base those decisions on.
- *Interviews with a small group of "experts."* Gather a group of people who do the job best and ask them to verbally list each step and substep. Write their responses on wall chart paper. If the group members have alternate approaches, first list the approaches and then go back to each, trying to reach consensus on the best way to do the task. Ask for other information in a similar way, collecting it first, then going back to clarify and add or eliminate.

A small group can provide a lot of good information in a short period of time. A second benefit is that one response might prompt another group member to think of something he or she might not have otherwise remembered. It is helpful to have an additional person, with no content to contribute, write down the information so that you can act as a group leader and facilitator.

One thing to be careful of is "group think," when everybody starts nodding their heads in the same way. When this happens, group cohesion is so powerful, no one inside the group will want to challenge what is being said. The results can be inaccurate data and/or very poor decisions. If someone does not bring up a different opinion or play a devil's advocate role, you should.

!!!

As you watch or talk to different people, you may find that there are differences in the way they each approach and perform the same task. Some of these differences may not be significant; others may be quite important.

An instructor was watching pharmaceutical warehouse personnel as they received incoming goods. She noticed that none of them performed the task in the same way. In individual interviews, she had each person write out on wall chart paper the steps they performed. Then she brought all of the people together to agree on the best way to do it. The group recognized there were good points to each of the methods and pooled the best of each to come up with one standard method. This became the basis of the SOP. In addition, each person felt as though he/she made significant, individual contributions to improving the performance of their department.

How it is done, part two

2) Develop the tools required by the methods selected. Write questions and develop questionnaires or forms to be completed when examining documents and records.

3) Work with supervision to provide documents and identify the people you will talk to or observe.

4) Apply the chosen tools and collect data.

Whenever possible as you observe and interview, use several different people to supply their understanding and approach to the task.

5) Review the results . . .

— *With supervision.* Show your preliminary information to the area's supervisor for his or her input, corrections, additions, and clarification. This step is highly recommended for quality reasons as well as for keeping supervision built into the process.

— *With quality control personnel.* Many tasks have elements that are GMP-related. QC can make sure that the appropriate checks, verifications, and documentation are included in the task description. If there are any steps that might be changed, discuss it with QC.

Example

You have gathered three quality control representatives together to conduct a task analysis on one of their duties, specifically on how they approve a batch of raw materials for use. The three QC representatives were chosen because of their experience in the job.

You start by explaining what you are doing, why your are doing it, and what you want to achieve at the end of the small group session. In preparation for the meeting, you have written each question on the top of a separate piece of wall chart paper. You ask the following questions and record the responses.

- What is the first step in approving a raw material for use?
- What do you do to accomplish this first step (i.e., the substeps)?
- What is the second step?
- How is this second step accomplished (i.e., the substeps)?

(Continue until all the steps and substeps are listed. If there are differences in the steps used, reach an agreement on the best way; if it makes no difference, reach agreement on the way that a new person should be taught.)

Next, you ask the QC personnel other questions about the task.

- How frequently is this task done?
- Are there any performance requirements for the task, such as so many lots or batches approved per day?
- On a 1 to 4 scale, with 1 being not important and 4 being very important, how would you rate the importance of doing this task correctly, based on the examples?
- If an error is made, which of the following will occur?

  (1) It will be immediately caught and corrected.

(2) It will not be caught, but the consequences are minimal.
(3) Product quality will be affected; significant rework will occur.
(4) Serious consequences will probably occur, such as GMP violation, consumer safety issues arise, or product recall.

- What are the consequences of doing the task incorrectly?
- What tools, resources, or information are used as you complete this task?
- Where do you do this task?
- What do you have to know to be able to do this task?
- What skills must you have to do this task?
- On a 1 to 5 scale, with 5 being high, what is the difficulty in learning this task?
- What makes learning the task difficult?
- What would make doing or learning the task easier?
- What type of training course would you suggest?
- What topics would it include?
- What training courses or topics would be helpful for a new person doing this task?
- How would the information be best presented?

For a complicated task, you may only be able to complete one description in a session. Be sensitive to time and that doing a good job takes considerable mental energy of all the members of the group.

When tasks for all of the duties have been completed, summarize your findings, perhaps in a spreadsheet format. An example is shown in Table 11.1, where the task, step, and substep are indicated with “1.1.1” notation, in that order.

Additional suggestions from QC representatives:

- Train new people on HPIS *before* they begin approving raw materials.
- Having an “expert” nearby is very helpful for handling “oddball” situations.
- Teach people the “tricks” and shortcuts once they know what they are doing.

Table 11.1. Example of a task description

Job: Quality Control Representative **Duty: Approval of materials**

Task/Step/ Substep	*Frequency*	*Performance Requirements*	*Importance rating/ Consequences*	*Tools, Info Used*	*Where Done/ Safety, Health, Environmental Concerns*	*Knowledge, Skills Necessary*	*Difficulty in Learning and Performing*	*Suggested Improvements*
1. Approval of raw materials	• 25 times per day	• within 1/2 day of completion of lab data • 100% accuracy	• criticality: 4 • If not done correctly, items not neeting specifications could be used, product would then not be approved or, if released, product could be recalled.	• HPIS computer system • item specification sheets • QC department head (for questions) • item referral and rejection forms • **(verification of the results of this task made during final lot review by prduction QC)	• QC office • no special equipment used • no chemicals handled	• *how to log on and operate HPIS computer system • *how to interpret specifications • *cGMPs and how to apply them • general policy on raw material handling and storage • *definitions and implications of terms: "approved," "not approved," "pending," "preliminary approval"	• rating: 3 • sources of difficulty—poor instructions for using HPIS, difficulty in identifying who in laboratory is running a test	• develop a one-page user's guide to HPIS • develop a listing of lab tests, and responsible person and phone number
1.1 Check computer listing of "Materials received needing approval."								
1.1.1 Use HPIS† computer transaction "Mat I."								

Table 11.1. Example of a task description (continued)

Task/Step/ Substep	*Frequency*	*Performance Requirements*	*Importance rating/ Consequences*	*Tools, Info Used*	*Where Done/ Safety, Health, Environmental Concerns*	*Knowledge, Skills Necessary*	*Difficulty in Learning and Performing*	*Suggested Improvements*
1.1.2 Select option P to highlight unapproved items and lots.								
1.2 Select an unapproved lot with cursor.								
1.3 Check lab data for lot.								
1.3.1 Use F5 key to check lab status.								
1.3.2 If status is "complete," view data by using F6 key.								
2. Approval of containers and closures etc.	• 4 times per day	• within 1/2 day of completion of lab data	• criticality: 4 • If not done correctly, items not meeting specifications could be used, product would then not be approved or, if released, product could be recalled.	• same as task 1.	• same as task 1.	• same as task 1. plus differences between plastic and glass types	• same as task 1.	• same as task 1.

* "must-know" items
† HPIS—Howdy Pharmaceutical Information System

12

Analyze Audience Characteristics

Description Audience analysis is the process of identifying and describing the important parameters of who the learners are.

Why do it Identifying and understanding the characteristics of your intended audience will

- Guide your decisions as you select instructional methods and media;
- Influence your selection of examples;
- Alert you to special needs learners might have that, if not addressed, will prevent the training from being successful; and
- Assist as you develop instruction to secondary or peripheral groups who influence and support the performance of the primary learners.

Who is involved Conducting an audience analysis involves

- An analyst,
- Members of the learner population,
- Supervision,
- Human resources representatives (as needed), and
- Other instructors who have experience with the audience (as needed).

Output When completed, an audience analysis should be a description of the primary characteristics of the learners including the following:

- Educational levels completed (average and range);
- Literacy (reading, arithmetic) status of the learners;

- Examples of instructional courses, and materials that the learners have benefited from in the past;
- Examples of courses, and materials that have *not* been successful in the past;
- Age and sex of the learners;
- Situations where learners have special needs; and
- Groups or persons who could influence the learner as he or she performs the tasks.

Comments

(Additional information on adult learners is found in Chapter 6.)

Analysis of audience characteristics is not specific to the objectives of the particular course(s) you are developing.

There are several differences between doing a job or task analysis and an audience analysis. A job/task analysis involves a detailed look at the best performers in a position, usually just a few people. An audience analysis looks at a large number of people—the learners—in a way that is as all-inclusive as possible.

If you are very familiar with the learners, you may be able to conduct an analysis with a minimum of assistance. If you do this, have someone else confirm your understanding of the audience. For courses or programs specific to newly hired workers, consult with someone in your firm's human resources group to understand who the new workers will likely be in the next several years.

It is not uncommon for people developing or delivering instructional courses to discover workers with literacy problems. These are very delicate situations where the worker's self-esteem could easily be destroyed. People with literacy problems tend to develop other skills and behaviors to compensate for their weaknesses. For example, a maintenance person may have exceptional observational skills and, once he or she sees a task performed, be able to repeat it flawlessly. Others with reading problems, to fit in, may carry around a newspaper or magazine. In such situations, your effective use of interpersonal skills and diplomacy will be put to the test. Consult with selected members from human resources and line management for assistance.

Some people in your learning audience may be hearing or visually impaired; others may be learning disabled. Discuss these situations with supervision. As you approach the design and development of training and instructional materials, strive for being as *inclusive* of all personnel as possible.

There may be implications for trainers as your firm complies with the *Americans with Disabilities Act (ADA).* Talk to someone in your human resources department familiar with the ADA and its requirements.

!!!

The training group of one pharmaceutical firm knew that hearing impaired people worked in various manufacturing areas. The group made the commitment that all videotapes they produced be "open captioned," that is, the words spoken in the video would appear in the lower portion of the television screen without the need for special equipment. Those who were hearing-impaired felt like their special communication needs were being considered. Additionally, the training group was commended for showing their commitment to training all employees, and the firm's international affiliates used the videotapes in teaching English to their employees.

How it is done

1) Select the appropriate methods. Observation, interviews, and questionnaires are some of the ones used to gather information on audience characteristics.

Try to use unobtrusive methods first, such as human resources data and talking with supervisors and other instructors who have worked with the particular group. Then confirm your findings with surveys and observations.

As with previous data-gathering activities, you should use at least two or three methods to increase the accuracy and reliability of the data.

2) Develop the tools called for by the methods.

Questions typically asked of the audience include the following:

- How long have you been doing this job?
- What level of education have people typically completed? (Note: this question is sometimes better answered by supervision or human resources.)
- What was your high school or college major?
- What is the gender and range of ages of people in this area (or doing the job)?
- How many years have you been in this job?

- What training experiences or courses have you been through where you felt you really gained something? Why?
- What training experiences or courses have you been through where you felt that they were a waste of time? Why?
- What position or type of person has a positive or negative influence on how you do your job?
- What is the location of your workplace (e.g., site or specific plant location)?

Questions that should be directed to supervision or others who know the audience include the following:

- Are there any people who have difficulties learning or reading?
- Are there people who have (U.S.–English, Spanish, etc.) as a second language?
- For this training course (or program) to be effective, are there other people who need to be involved? If so, who?

3) Identify people to talk with.

4) Use the tools. Conduct the interviews, utilize the questionnaire, and so forth.

When looking at examples of past instructional courses, find out *specifically* what made the course useful or not useful. It may be helpful to break this down as shown in the example.

Example

Personnel in the product distribution warehouse will participate in a safety training program for which you are analyzing needs. As you conducted the job and task analysis, you were also collecting data on the learners. You now compile the data but notice there are several questions you still have. For this information, you consult with others who know the trainees, such as a representative from human resources and a GMP trainer who recently conducted a training session there. Your summary sheet of audience characteristics is as follows.

AUDIENCE: Operations personnel

DEPARTMENT: Product Distribution Warehouse

NUMBER OF PEOPLE: 15 full-time, 3 part-time

AGE RANGE:

18–20 years (3 part-time students)
21–30 years (6 full-time)
31–40 years (2 full-time)
41–50 years (4 full-time)
51–60 years (3 full-time)

YEARS EXPERIENCE IN JOB:

0–1 year (3 part-time; 4 full-time)
2–3 years (4 full-time)
4–5 years (3 full-time)
6–10 years (2 full-time)
11–20 years (1 full-time)
more than 20 years (1 full-time)

EDUCATION LEVELS: All high school grads, a few with some college (not counting students in college now).

SPECIAL CONSIDERATIONS: Two personnel with English as a second language (Spanish as their first language); all personnel have good arithmetic skills.

LOCATION: All learners located at Central Distribution Warehouse; (similar facilities in Atlanta, Connecticut, San Francisco not included in the scope of this project).

TRAINING CONSIDERED AS BENEFICIAL: Fire extinguisher (hands-on use); Corporate orientation (includes tour of facilities); Good Documentation Practices (positive results of training seen immediately by all; good story in video).

TRAINING CONSIDERED AS NOT BENEFICIAL: Personnel polices (does not relate to problems experienced by older employees; "dull" lecture); Hazard Communication (too technical).

Instructional Elements Beneficial

— hands on involvement
— story people could "relate" to
— met real need

Instructional Elements Not Beneficial

— too much lecture
— content learners could not apply

THOSE WHO MAY INFLUENCE PERFORMANCE: "Old-timers," supervision

!!!	The differences age make . . . The age of a person can influence (or be associated with) how a person prefers to learn as well as motivational factors. A person who is young in her career may be motivated by the potential for advancement. A person nearing retirement may be more motivated by leaving a mark in the department by helping to train younger people coming in.

!!!	You may find that there are individuals who hold significant influence over the way your learners perform on the job. For instance, if you are teaching personnel the correct way to wear a respirator as protection from potentially toxic dusts or vapors, there may be others who give strong, conflicting messages by what they say or do. One person may laugh at others who wear the device properly; another person may wear the mask loosely because of concerns for his or her hair. As you consider how to make your training intervention effective, you must consider other factors that can influence performance and how they can be managed.

13

Summarize the Findings

Description Develop a list of the skills, knowledge, and tools necessary to perform the tasks and/or job.

Why do it Summarizing the data collected will

- Convert large amounts of data into useful information,
- Help identify trends and important issues,
- Uncover points needing clarification, and
- Provide the basis for developing goals and objectives.

Who is involved The analyst is primarily involved in summarizing the findings, with others, as needed, to provide clarification.

Output Based on what the learners and their supervision have said about their duties and tasks, you will develop a list of the

- Training needs
  - — knowledge that should be provided
  - — skills that should be developed; and
- Performance improvement needs
  - — tools, resources, information, job aides, and other support that should be provided.

Comments Achieving an accurate understanding of what the job and task analysis data means is one of the most difficult aspects of the analysis phase. It sometimes helps to reflect on all the data and ask, "What is all of this data trying to tell me?"

You may also discover relevant nontraining issues, such as process problems, management difficulties, hiring practices, and the like that need to be addressed. You may want to discuss them verbally with key individuals prior to including them in a written report.

It may be helpful to work with someone who has had experience in summarizing job and task data.

The results from the audience characteristics analysis will typically not need summarizing if it is already in a usable form (as shown in the previous task's example on page 99). These results will be used further in the design phase.

How it is done

1) Assemble the data in as integrated a form as possible. Methods include using spreadsheets, large pieces of paper, and so forth. Count how often a certain phrase or category comes up in the answers or responses to questionnaires.

2) Resolve conflicts and discrepancies. When there are apparent conflicts or confusion in the data, go back to those you talked with or who supplied the information. To be successful in the tasks that follow, *you must understand* and *be confident* of the information.

3) Look for

- Themes,
- Identical or similar responses,
- Patterns,
- Contradictions and inconsistencies,
- Ways of meeting needs that do not involve training, and
- Activities that add little or no value to the product or information being produced.

Note the frequency, difficulty, and criticality that are related to a particular task. This will be useful when tasks are prioritized.

4) Involve someone else. It may be helpful to show a colleague your work in progress and explain some of the trends you are finding and the resulting needs. He or she may see other trends or ask questions, forcing you to clarify your thinking.

Example

In the earlier task analysis, data was collected on QC representatives. You are now summarizing that and additional data collected on the duties performed by these people.

For each QC representative's duty, you have created a wall chart with all the tasks and steps listed (similar to Table 11.1).

You have combined the data gathered in small groups along with additions from the QC department head. Your work identifies eleven tasks that a QC representative performs in doing his or her job.

You note how often certain words appear in the "knowledge and skills necessary" column, such as "cGMPs" (11 of 11 tasks), "computers" (8 of 11), technical writing skills (4 of 11), and so forth.

Nontraining interventions, such as lists of contacts, a job aide (e.g., one-page summary of HPIS computer commands) are kept separately for inclusion under the heading of "Performance Improvement Needs."

When finished, your summary of the data looks like Table 13.1.

Table 13.1. Summary of training and performance improvement needs

JOB: Quality Control Representative

Training Needs

- Good Manufacturing Practice Regulations (cGMPs)*
- Operation of computer systems (HPIS, E-mail, personnel computing applications—Microsoft WORD 5.1, Microsoft EXCEL 4.0, Aldus PERSUATION 2.1)*
- Proper documentation techniques*
- Technical writing*
- Document review and approval*
- Process validation*
- Definitions of terms used in department and HPIS*
- Sampling procedures
- Equipment operation
- Statistical process control
- Resource people
- Corporate policies and procedures

Performance Improvement Needs

- One-page user's guide to HPIS computer system
- Cross-listing or directory of laboratory personnel, phone numbers, and assays
- Better access to SOPs
- Standardization of personal computing applications software used in department

* Identified by experts as "need-to know" information

14

Check Quality

I worry whoever thought up the term "quality control" thought if we didn't control it, it would get out of hand.

—Lily Tomlin

Description Review the information and materials developed to this point for completeness, accuracy, and clarity.

Why do it A check on quality at this point is appropriate because

- All further design and development will be based on the findings made during the analysis phase;
- Corrections are much easier at this point than later in the process; and
- The next step, prioritization, will be done with supervision and management; your credibility will be strengthened if your work is complete, accurate, and clear.

Who is involved Checking the quality will involve

- The analyst,
- One or two selected "experts" in the job,
- A member of supervision, and
- Others (as needed)—e.g., people familiar with job and task analysis.

Output A reviewed and modified (if needed) list of training needs and performance improvement needs.

Comments If you have been working closely with those expert in the jobs and with supervision, this quality check should be a rather simple activity.

While this review is an important checkpoint, it can be done rather informally.

How it is done

1) Review the *audience characteristics analysis* and the *summary of training and performance improvement needs* with those who contributed to your data collection. If the analysis phase is something new for you, you may want to describe the process you used with someone who has used the instructional systems design approach before. If you cannot find someone with experience, consider showing your work to a colleague or supervisor with good analytical skills.

Points to cover in your review of the results include the following:

- Completeness—Are you missing anything? You might have everything you were given, but the "experts" might realize something needs to be added.
- Accuracy—Are your interpretations of the data correct? Are the frequencies and criticality of performance correct?
- Clarity—Do your results make sense? Are they understandable? Are the results clear, simple, and direct?

If you encounter a lack of agreement among the reviewers, arrange a meeting where they can discuss their differences and then come to a consensus. Let them work out the problems. *Do not let yourself become caught in the middle!*

2) Review the process you used. Another aspect of your quality check is to reflect on what *you* learned. Did you collect too much data or too little? The next time you do an analysis, what would you do differently? How could you make the process work better for you?

Example

You reviewed the summary of needs for the Quality Control representative job with a long-time member of that group and then with the department head of the area. Each person had a question that caused you to clarify the wording of a need so it was more direct and understandable.

As you thought about the process you used, you think that the *next time* you analyze a group of professional people, you will introduce the process at a staff meeting a few weeks before starting to collect data. That way, people will have a chance to think more about what they do and how they do it prior to the data collection session.

15

Prioritize Needs

Description Arrive at an agreement about the priority items to be included in the instructional units that will be designed and developed.

Why do it Prioritizing needs is important in order to

- Make the best use of limited resources,
- Include management's perspective on how the training fits into other strategic goals and priorities,
- Obtain "buy-in" from the learners and those paying for the course or program,
- Share the performance improvement needs with those who can address them, and
- Identify issues that need to be resolved by management.

Who is involved Prioritizing needs is done by

- The analyst,
- A person currently doing the job at an "expert" level or someone who has expertise in the job,
- Supervision, and
- Management.

Output A prioritized list of training needs and performance improvement needs; agreement on who is to work on particular performance improvements; agreement to move on to the design stage.

Comments As you present the information to management, let it speak for itself as much as possible. Have the data used for the summaries available as reference material. Avoid pointing to particular individuals as sources of data.

How it is done

1) Call a meeting of the appropriate people to review the results of your analysis and to prioritize the data.

2) Prioritize the training needs before the meeting. The more critical and frequently done operations should have higher priority. Note your recommendations separately and take them to the meeting.

3) Show the group the agenda and goal for the meeting.

4) Describe for the group the analysis process, why it was done and how you did it, if the group is not familiar with it.

5) Show the group the summary of training needs with the "must-knows," criticalities, and frequencies noted. Since you have put the information through a quality check, you are not asking the group to modify or add anything. If suggestions are made, ask the job expert and supervision for their guidance in including or not including the changes.

6) Ask the group to identify the highest training need. If they do not pick your recommendation, discuss why they see it differently; share your reasons. Arrive at an agreement on the top training priority.

Continue down the "must-knows" until all have been prioritized. Then do the same for the "nice-to-know" items.

A useful technique is to put each topic on a card or piece of paper and tacked or taped in a way that makes it easy to arrange and rearrange.

7) Introduce the performance improvement needs by describing how these help the instruction be more effective as well as build more efficiency into performing the task correctly.

If an improvement need is outside the scope of your job, ask the group for assistance in solving it.

8) Identify any issue(s) that must be solved. Identify who will work on the issue(s) and when it will be resolved.

9) At the conclusion of the meeting, review the prioritized needs with the group and any other assignments made. Then, in general terms, describe how this data will be used in the design phase. Obtain agreement on proceeding to the design phase.

!!!

You may find that there are issues that need to be resolved. In some cases you can continue with the design phase in hopes that they will be resolved. In other cases, the design may have to be put on hold temporarily.

A training professional was analyzing the needs for new aseptic operators (located at various sites) regarding how to properly put on a sterile gown. During the prioritization meeting, the instructor became aware that one site allowed people to wear jewelry into the aseptic block. Another site did not. One site had specific instructions on not wearing makeup, whereas another had not taken a stance on the issue.

The group soon realized that these issues needed to be addressed before any work on the course content could continue. The design went ahead with the understanding that one consistent policy would be established. It was and the same policy was then incorporated into all the materials.

Example

You assembled a quality control representative and the department head and manager together to discuss the training needs and priorities for their department. You used the list developed earlier and, by the end of this meeting, you had a prioritized list as shown in Table 15.1.

Table 15.1. Prioritized training needs and performance improvement needs for quality control representatives

JOB: Quality Control Representative

Training Needs

High Priority:

- Good Manufacturing Practice Regulations (cGMPs)*
- Operation of computer systems (HPIS, E-mail, personnel computing applications—Microsoft WORD 5.1, Microsoft EXCEL 4.0, Aldus PERSUATION 2.1)*
- Proper documentation techniques*
- Document review and approval*
- Definitions of terms used in department and HPIS*
- Corporate policies and procedures*

Medium Priority:

- Technical writing*
- Process validation*
- Sampling procedures

Low Priority:

- Equipment operation
- Statistical process control
- Listing of resource people

Performance Improvement Needs *(and decisions made)*

- User's guide to HPIS computer system *(to be developed by HPIS systems personnel; QC manager to contact them.)*
- Cross-listing or directory of laboratory personnel, phone numbers, and assays *(joint QC / lab project; QC department head to develop.)*
- Better access to SOPs *(issue: How many extra copies and where to locate? QC department head to investigate.)*
- Standardization of personal computing applications software used in department *(QC manager / staff to decide along with QC representatives; to be decided within 3 weeks.)*

* Identified by experts as "need-to know" information

III

Design Phase

16

Introduction to the Design Phase

How did I get here?

Design begins when you know

- The scope of the project,
- The skills and knowledge required by the audience(s),
- Other performance improvement needs,
- Audience characteristics, and
- Details of the job and task.

Purpose of the design phase

During the design phase, you will be creating an *instructional plan* that is a blueprint or design manual to guide the later development and delivery of the training intervention. (Training intervention includes the training, instructional materials, etc., related to a need or goal.) The instructional plan will include the

- Goals,
- Scope,
- Objectives,
- Constraints,
- Requirements,
- Benefits,
- Costs, and
- Strategies for evaluating the success of the training.

Figure 16.1 shows the tasks, their descriptions, and the output generated in this phase.

The size of the final instructional plan depends on the scope and complexity of the problem you are trying to solve as well as the complexity of the training intervention.

Design Phase (Steps 1–7)

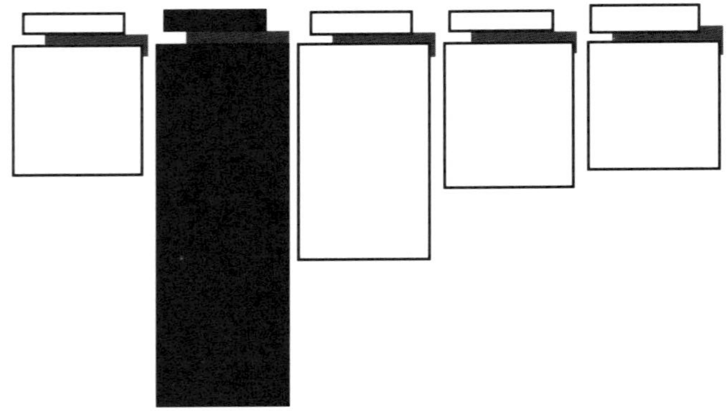

Task	Description	Output
1) Consider what else is needed	Review solution being developed; address any additional items, structures, barriers, or issues.	Revised list of performance improvement requirements
2) Establish/confirm program goal	Describe the intended ultimate outcome; have management confirm.	Specific, measurable outcomes
3) Develop subgoals	Divide program goal into smaller pieces.	Subgoals for each instructional unit
4) Establish objectives	Write objectives that the learner will be able to achieve after completing the instructional unit.	Performance objectives for each unit
5) Select topics	Choose the topics to include in the instructional unit.	Topics for each unit
6) Develop manageable units of instruction	Repeat tasks 3–5 until units (lessons) are on one topic and can be completed by the learner in one period.	Subgoals, objectives, and topics for each lesson
7) Plan evaluation strategy	Decide how the instruction and learner are to be evaluated.	Evaluation plan

Figure 16.1a. Tasks associated with the design phase

Design Phase (Steps 8–14)

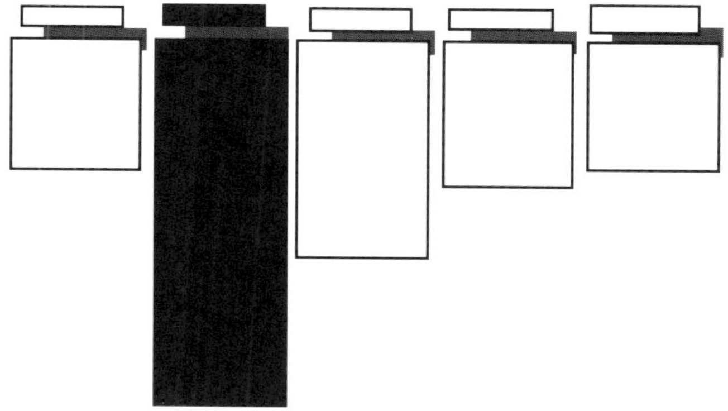

Task	Description	Output
8) Prepare a high-level outline	Analyze, sequence, and expand topics to include more content.	High-level outline of instructional content and events
9) Select the appropriate instructional methods	Choose the best techniques to accomplish the objectives, based on content, instructional events, and so forth.	List of instructional methods to be used
10) Select the appropriate media	Choose the best media to serve as vehicles for delivering the instructional content and events according to the methods identified.	List of media to be used
11) Identify potential instructors	If instructors are used, develop criteria for selecting them.	Criteria for selecting instructors, list of candidates who meet criteria
12) Refine curriculum	Finalize the arrangement (sequencing) of lessons, sections, and courses.	Curriculum map for the positions, jobs analyzed
13) Check quality	Review information and decisions for completeness, accuracy, and integrity of design.	Reviewed (and modified) decisions and output
14) Prepare written instructional plan and have it approved	Assemble all output into a blueprint from which instruction will be developed; have it approved by management.	Approved instructional plan

Figure 16.1b. Tasks associated with the design phase

The "instructional unit"

An instructional unit could be a course, a section or subsection, or a lesson. In the case of a course, the instructional unit might take three weeks for the learner complete; a lesson might take thirty minutes.

Each instructional unit includes three things:

1) The subgoal—a smaller, more manageable purpose that is derived from an earlier goal or subgoal.
2) Objectives—a set of performances, conditions, and criteria describing outcomes.
3) Topics—content subjects that will be covered in the instruction.

Figure 16.2 shows the relationship between different instructional units.

Lessons are instructional units that are focused on one particular topic and that can be completed by the learner in one sitting. It might be fifteen minutes; it could be two hours. You should choose the completion time that works the best for you and your organization. Figure 16.3 gives an example.

Lessons should be very flexible. You should consider them as modules that can be plugged in and out of a course. You may have two equivalent lessons covering the same objectives: one using a leader-led format, the other using interactive video. The specific lesson used would depend on the personnel and equipment available where the learners are.

Could you have a course with only one instructional unit? Yes, *if* you had a situation where the training to be delivered was on a specific topic and could be completed in one session.

To summarize, in the design phase of creating a program or course, you will be breaking down large instructional units into progressively smaller and smaller units, repeating the same basic steps until you have a lesson-sized unit. If the original program is broad in scope, you will probably have several courses, a few sections, and many lessons. If the course is focused to begin with, you may only have one course with several lessons.

Model

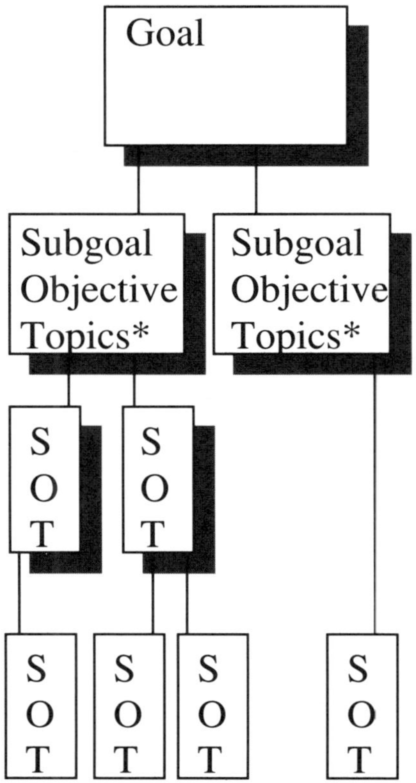

Instructional unit	Characteristics
Program	• Big, broad, extensive • Covers many topics • Takes long time for learner to complete
Course	↕
Section (subsections)	↕
Lesson	• Small, manageable • Covers one topic • Modular • Takes short time for learner to complete

*Optional if other, more specific instructional units are used that include topics.

Figure 16.2. Types of instructional units

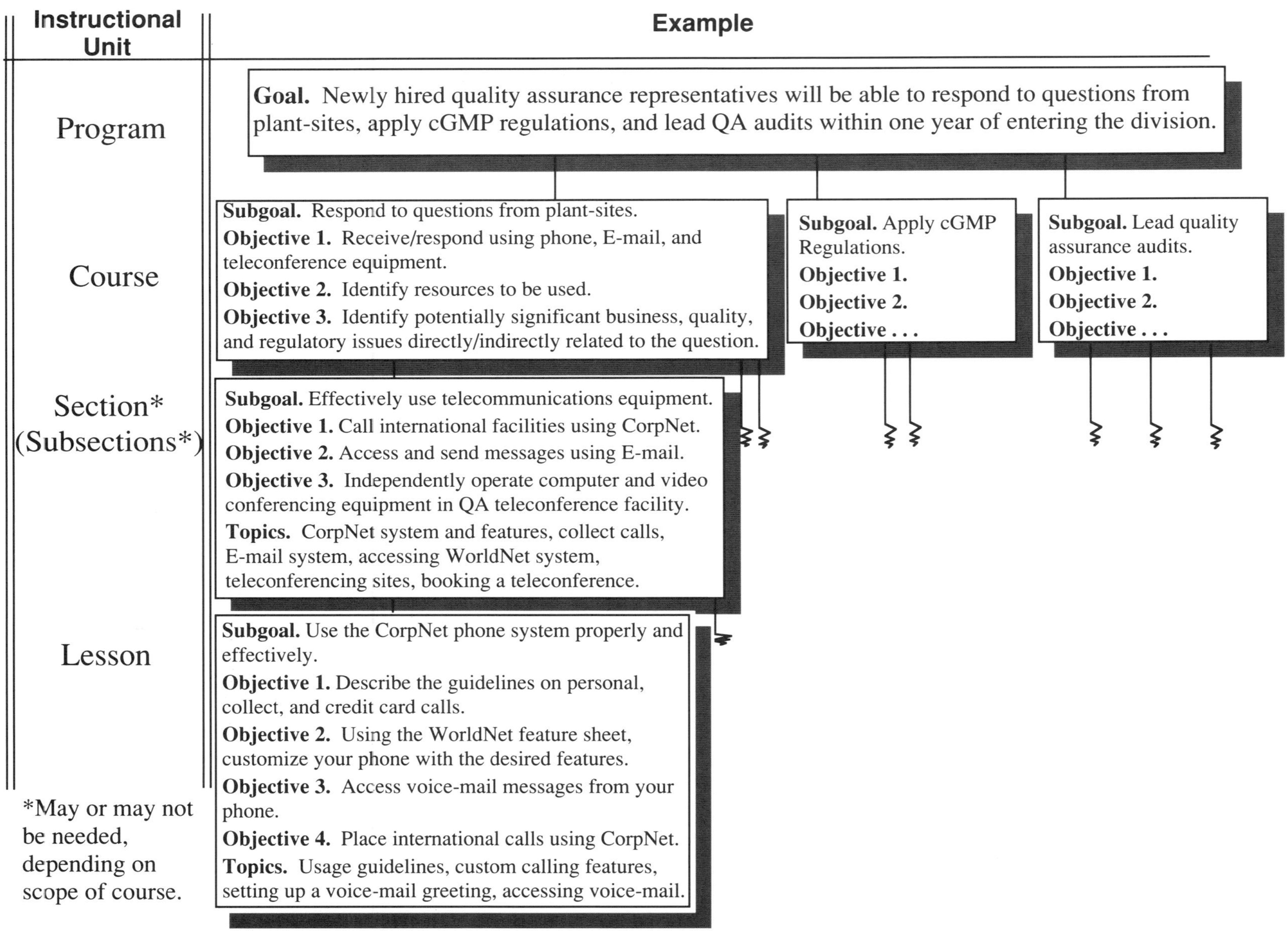

Figure 16.3. Examples of various instructional units

17

Consider What Else Is Needed

So much of what we call management consists of making it difficult for people to work.

—Peter F. Drucker

Note

One task that reoccurs *throughout* the instructional design process is the consideration of what is necessary to support the performance. You may want to make this a separate task, or better yet, constantly keep this requirement in mind.

Description

Review the solution being developed and determine whether any additional items, structures, barriers, or issues need to be addressed.

Why do it

Considering other elements required to meet the program and course goals are important because

- Reaching a performance goal typically involves more than simply training; and
- Additional data that has been collected may give the designer a better understanding of the issues, barriers, or structures that need attention.

Who is involved

Considering what else is needed involves the

- Analyst/designer,
- Subject matter expert,
- Supervision, and
- Management (as needed).

Output

A revised list of prioritized performance improvement needs (from the analysis phase). Also, a timeline for implementing them may be desired.

Comments

While this task may not add anything to your list of required performance improvements, it does give you the chance to reflect on the additional information you have been exposed to. At this point, you may have a deeper understanding of the situation, especially if it is a complex one.

How it is done

1) Look at the goals of the program and the training course. Also review the list of performance improvement needs that was developed at the end of the analysis phase.

2) Ask yourself, as well as subject matter experts and supervision, if anything else is needed for the training to be effective.

3) Follow up on issues and tasks identified at the prioritization meeting (analysis phase). Have the issues been resolved or are they still in progress?

Although *you* understand, those you work with must realize that training is not the only element in solving a problem. Supervision and management must help remove barriers and strengthen other structures, as needed, in order to get the most benefit from their investment in training.

Example

You are in the process of designing a course on the proper technique of documentation, including the topics of why it is necessary, how is it done, correcting errors, and so forth.

One of the particular points involves recording the time of day, such as when a mixing operation begins and ends. You notice that the manufacturing areas record time using the military method (i.e., a 24-hour clock with no need to differentiate between "A.M." and "P.M."). You wonder if 24-hour clocks are currently used in the areas; this would simplify the documentation of time.

You gather a supervisor and some experienced personnel from quality control and the manufacturing areas. After showing them the goals and the topics to be covered in the documentation course, you ask if anything else is needed for technical and operational personnel to perform as desired.

The group looks over the material and finds it to be satisfactory with nothing else needed. You raise the issue about telling time and the availability of 24-hour clocks. Not only does the group agree that these devices would be helpful, but states there are some processing rooms where there are no clocks at all.

As the discussion evolves, you ask, "How do people know what the date is?" The reply is, if a person does not know, he or she frequently asks someone who has a newspaper at their workstation or in their back pocket. In other words, there is no "standard" for determining the date.

As you listen, someone says in jest, "If you have standard clocks, then they have to be calibrated. How are we going to do that?"

The group laughs, but the members realize there is truth in the comment. The supervisor volunteers to have someone walk through the area on a quarterly basis making sure the clocks all read the correct time. (The SOP written to define this activity would designate an "official" clock or time source and describe how a portable, electronic clock would be taken from room to room.) Also, it is decided to request from the management 24-hour clocks that also have date displays, for use in several locations. Existing 12-hour clocks will be gradually replaced with the new type.

!!!

While the example above may sound odd and rather "picky," FDA investigators have been known to ask about the source for time and date information.

Having a standard source for time and date information is particularly important when an operation, say mixing, extends beyond one shift or if more than one person is involved. The concern is, not all watches show the same exact time. If two different watches are used in timing the operation, it is very possible that a five-to-ten minute timing error could occur, resulting in a potential over- or undermixing situation.

18

Establish and Confirm Program Goal

The end is where we start from.

—T.S. Elliot

Description Describe in specific and measurable terms the intended ultimate outcome of the program and have it confirmed by management.

Why do it Setting goals is important because it

- Provides a "reality test" for the objectives and instructional plan that will be developed later;
- Takes into consideration other pieces that frequently are part of the total solution to a problem;
- Links training with its benefits;
- Links training with what the department or organization has established as important;
- Helps in the evaluation of program effectiveness;
- Allows developers, users, and sponsors of the training to be focused on outcome and achievements; and
- Reinforces the concept that training is used for a purpose.

Who is involved Goal setting primarily involves the analyst/designer, with the assistance of management.

Output A description of the intended outcomes of the training intervention, and how this will benefit the learner, the department, and the organization.

Comments

Setting the goals for a training intervention, whether it is on a small (micro) scale (to solve a particular problem) or on a large (macro) scale (an integrated curriculum for each person in the organization), is the first step in answering the question, "What will we get for our investment of training dollars and time?"

The program goal is slightly different from the course goal (described later in this section). The *program goal* is broader and tied to a particular problem or to the organization's goals.

Establishing the goal of a training program is connected to why you initially thought that training was needed. This can be related to the original problem or the desire to accomplish a departmental or organizational goal.

Goal statements must be specific and measurable. The next task (Chapter 19) provides information on correctly writing a goal statement.

How do goals differ from the needs and scope statements written earlier? The goal you will write now is more specific. It is more results oriented, and it is based on information you discovered during the job and task analysis.

How it is done

1) Review the needs statement developed at the beginning of the analysis phase (Chapter 9). *What affect will your proposed training program have on that problem?*

This question must be answered as specifically as possible, with benefits that can be observed and measured.

2) If the training intervention is a broad one or covers many jobs or departments, consider how the benefits relate to the short-term and long-term goals of the organization. Again, the goal you write should be as specific and measurable as possible.

3) Review the goal with colleagues to be sure it is not only specific and measurable, but also has significance to the operation and organization.

4) Share the goal with management. Have management confirm that this is what is needed. In certain situations it may be appropriate for them to sign off in agreement.

Example 1

You have been asked to see how training can be used to solve a problem in one of the warehouse areas.

Needs statement: *Forklifts have periods of long downtime due to costly tire and wheel repair.*

An earlier performance analysis shows vehicle maintenance is done by an expensive and unresponsive outside firm. Management would like to bring simple maintenance tasks in-house. (Tire and wheel repair is considered "simple.") The job and task analysis shows forklift drivers need more knowledge and skills about preventing problems before they become serious. Maintenance personnel need skills on how to change tires and repair damaged wheels.

From this and other information, you develop a program goal that is reasonable to the area's management: *Reduce forklift downtime by 25 percent and tire/wheel repair costs by 50 percent within six months by using training and performance tools.*

Example 2

Several experienced quality assurance representatives will be retiring or leaving their current jobs in the next two years. People who have recently been brought into those jobs report that the job has a long learning curve because of its complexity. All of the training is currently "on the job" with the experienced QA representatives. Management has asked that you develop a comprehensive training program for all new personnel entering the division.

Needs statement: *New QA personnel need to be effective and comfortable in their job in less than the two to three years it currently takes them to do so.*

The program goal you initially propose is as follows: *Newly hired personnel will become effective and comfortable in their roles within one year of entry into the division.*

!!!

Example 2 contains vague or "fuzzy" language (Mager 1984a), such as "effective" and "comfortable." These words need to be made more specific. While you occasionally are stuck with vague words, with a little work and an understanding of the job and tasks, you can usually make the goals more specific and measurable.

Example 2, revisited

You review the job and task analysis data collected for QA representatives and find that conducting audits, working as resources for manufacturing sites, and answering questions on the application of cGMPs are the primary tasks. You also look at the division's mission statement for a better understanding of what management thinks is important.

Your new program goal, which is more specific and measurable, is as follows: *Newly hired quality assurance representatives will be able to respond to questions from plant-sites, apply cGMP regulations, and lead quality assurance audits within one year of their entry into the QA division.*

19

Identify the Subgoals

Education must have an end in view, for it is not an end in itself.

—Sybil Marshall

Description	For each larger goal (program goal or other, larger subgoal) identify several smaller and more specific subgoals and the outcomes associated with each one.
Why do it	Subgoals are more manageable pieces of the program goal. They provide the designer, the developer, and the learner a more focused and limited area to be covered by instruction.
Who is involved	Identifying subgoals is done by the designer. Subject matter experts may be used as a resource.
Output	For each program (or larger subgoal), there will be two or more subgoals. For each subgoal that is identified, there will be one or more performance outcomes.
Comments	Figures 16.2 and 16.3 (pages 117 and 118) show the relationship between the program goal and the subgoals of different instructional levels. In identifying the subgoal and performance outcomes, it is very helpful to work with someone who is an expert in the area or in performing the task.
How it is done	1) Review the program goal (or larger subgoal). Make it more specific and easier to accomplish by breaking it into two, three,

or more smaller subgoals. Each resulting subgoal should be more focused. Taken together, all the resulting subgoals, if they are reached, should cause the program (or larger subgoal) to be accomplished.

2) Write the subgoal so it is specific and observable.

3) Identify the specific performances, that, if accomplished, indicate that the subgoal has been met.

More detail on properly writing a goal and subgoal

Mager (1984a) has a five-step process used to clarify and analyze goals. In the following, the word *subgoal* has replaced Mager's original word of "goal" for consistency's sake.

1) *Write down the subgoal.* It needs to be an *outcome*, not a description of how it is to be achieved. If the words used are "fuzzy," that is, the actions are not observable and specific, try to make them observable and specific before continuing.

2) List the performances that, if accomplished, would cause you to say that the subgoal has been achieved.

3) Review and clarify the list just developed. Eliminate duplications. Make sure each item is an *action*. If not, repeat steps 2 and 3 for that particular item. Rewrite your list.

4) For each performance item in the list from Step 3, write a statement that includes the specifications for that performance. This would include rates, degree of quality required, amounts, and so forth.

5) Test each statement written (in Step 4) with the question, "If a person has achieved or demonstrated each and all of these performances, would I say that the subgoal has been achieved?" If yes, the subgoal analysis is completed; if no, consider why not. Does something else need to be added? Go back and repeat the necessary steps above.

Example

You are continuing with a program for quality assurance representatives (Chapter 18).

The goal of the program is as follows: *Newly hired quality assurance representatives will be able to respond to questions from plant-sites, apply cGMP regulations, and lead quality assurance audits within one year of their entering the QA division.*

1. You review the program goal (or larger subgoal) and break it into three smaller, more easily accomplished subgoals.

Subgoals:

- *Respond to questions from plant-sites.*
- *Apply cGMP regulations.*
- *Lead quality assurance audits.*

You reread the subgoals to see if there are some "fuzzy" words; "respond," "apply," and "lead," are not "fuzzy" because they are specific and observable.

2. For the each subgoal, list the performances that, if accomplished, would cause you to say that the goal has been achieved. Your list for the second subgoal, "apply cGMP regulations" is as follows.

The QA representative will:

- *Discuss how they would interpret the cGMPs that apply to the facilities they work with.*
- *Identify situations that are not in compliance with cGMPs.*
- *Identify specific sections of the cGMP regulations that could be cited in the event of noncompliance.*
- *Describe how they would change a noncompliant situation into one that satisfies the cGMPs.*
- *Appreciate their role in the firm's activities in being compliant.*

3. Reread the list and clarify, eliminate duplicates, and make sure each item described is an observable action.

- You can hear and evaluate a discussion; a description of something could be written or verbalized.
- "Identify" is action-based, but you may want to clarify it by saying "list" or "circle," and so forth.
- "Appreciate" is not something that can be observed. What do you really mean by that? You want to know how someone would behave if they *appreciated* their role. What behaviors would they exhibit? What behaviors would someone in QA exhibit if they did not appreciate the cGMPs? You then come up with a new performance: *List ways quality assurance representatives can support the adherence to cGMPs; list ways a quality assurance representative can hinder adherence to cGMPs.*

4. Write full descriptions for each of the performances, including the nature, amount, or quality of performance that you feel demonstrates achievement of the goal.

Quality assurance representatives will:

- *List five examples of activities performed by the areas they support that are covered by cGMP regulations and the specific section of the cGMPs that apply to each activity.*
- *Identify whether given situations are in or not in compliance with cGMPs.*
- *If a situation is not in compliance with cGMPs, cite the specific section of the cGMP regulations and what would need to be changed to bring the situation into compliance.*
- *List, within five minutes, three ways they can support personnel in complying with cGMPs and three ways they could potentially hinder compliance with cGMPs.*

5. Test each statement. If a person does these things, would you agree that he or she has achieved the goal?

Yes . . . if a person can do these things, he or she can "apply" the cGMP regulations.

20

Establish the Objectives

Description

Based on the subgoal, write objectives that the learner will be able to accomplish after successfully completing the instructional unit.

Why do it

Objectives are used by the course designer and developer as well as the learner. The *designer/developer* uses objectives to

- Design and select instructional content and how it is presented (i.e., the methods, materials, and media);
- Specify outcomes of the instruction;
- Determine if the instruction has been successful; and
- Communicate to management and others about the content of the course and lesson.

The *learners* use objectives

- To organize and focus their efforts on what is considered to be important in achieving the goal and
- As a standard to which his or her performance can be compared (Hannum and Hansen 1989).

Who is involved

Objectives are written primarily by the designer, with the review and input from those doing the tasks and their supervision.

Output

Several (typically two to seven) objectives are written for each subgoal.

Comments

Objectives describe *outcomes*, not the process used to achieve the outcome.

A very useful question in developing objectives comes from Mager (1984b): *What should the student be able to do at the end of the course* [or instructional unit—Vesper] *so all that stands between the student and skilled performance is practice?*

There are a variety of "objectives" discussed in educational and training literature, such as "learning objectives," "course objectives," "behavioral objectives," and so forth. In this book, we are looking at *performance* objectives (which are sometimes called "behavioral objectives") whenever the word *objectives* is used.

A well written objective usually has three parts:

1) **PERFORMANCE.** A description of what the learner should be able to do. Performance is *action* based. It should be observable and measurable.
2) **CONDITIONS.** The important conditions under which the activity is to be performed. This could include tools or references that can or cannot be used.
3) **CRITERION.** The quality or level of performance that is expected of a successful performer. This specification may be in units per hour, errors allowed, and the like. (This is sometimes called the *standard*.)

Examples of several objectives, with their parts identified are as follows:

- Given the required change parts and tools *(conditions)*, the learner will be able to change over the New Jersey labeler to run 10 mL-size vials *(performance)* within 1 hour *(criterion)*.
- After completing this course, and with coaching and feedback from group leaders and supervisors *(conditions)*, you will be able to document your work *(performance)* according to corporate requirements *(criterion)*.
- Given the cGMP regulations and an FDA-483 *(conditions)*, the participant will be able to identify sections of the cGMPs applicable to the 483 observation and discuss the impact of the observation on the product's purity *(performance)*.

!!! The last example above does not include a standard because, in the view of the objective writer, there is no reason to have one—the task analysis indicated the person has no specific

time frame to get this done. As he or she becomes more familiar with the cGMPs (i.e., practice), it is reasonable to assume that the time required to do this would decrease.

Objectives may not always include conditions and standards; however, there should be a very good reason for NOT including them.

Objectives have the characteristics of being *observable* and *measurable*. They should also be as *simple* and *clear* as possible.

!!! *Real-life linkage.* The closer you can make the objective to what and how the learner performs back on the job, the higher the probability of "transferring" the learning back to the work environment.

How it is done

1) An objective consists of a performance, conditions, and criterion; use the performance that has already been described (in the preceding task). You now only have to develop the conditions and the criterion.

2) Identify the conditions that are appropriate.

3) Identify the criteria that are appropriate.

4) Review the completed objective. The three parts should be clear and make sense. They may or may not form a "complete" sentence.

Example

In developing an instructional unit for quality control representatives, you list possible conditions and criteria for the first performance description:

Goal: Develop skills in order to communicate using the corporate E-mail system.

Performance Descriptions:

1) Log-on and log-off to the E-mail system.*
2) Retrieve, reply to, and delete a message sent to you.
3) Send a message to others.
4) Use several of the "special features" available in E-mail.

* Log-on and log-off to the E-mail system.
Possible conditions:
- — using standard QC computers (Macintosh)
- — given a user ID and password
- — from memory?
- — using a "cheat-sheet" or job aide?

Possible criteria:
- — within 2 minutes
- — without an error message

You examine the four possible conditions listed and consider each one:

- Macintosh equipment is standard in QC and is used to enter the E-mail system; other areas in the company use IBM-type computers; you feel this is a valid condition.
- All mainframe ("host") computer users are required to have an ID and password; you consider this condition to be redundant and do not include it.
- As the user has more practice, he or she will memorize the process of logging on and off; therefore, you don't feel it is a necessary condition for performing.
- Using a job aide may help people who are apprehensive; they are available and even some experienced people use them on occasion; you decide that this is a valid condition.

You do the same with the possible criteria or standards:

- There is nothing magical about "two minutes" in the way someone performs in real life; you eliminate this as a standard. You expect, with practice, the time needed to send a message will decrease.
- Error messages occur when a mistake has been made. You want the learner to be able to do it without a mistake; therefore, you keep this as a standard.

As a result, your first objective is as follows:

> Using a Macintosh computer and a job aide (if desired), the learner will be able to log-on and log-off the E-mail system without an error message.

You do the same for the other performance descriptions and come up with the remaining objectives for the course:

- Using a job aide (if desired), the learner will be able to retrieve, reply to, and delete a message sent to him/her without an error.

- Using a job aide (if desired), the learner will be able to send a message to three other users and a copy to one other user.
- With the on-line help system (if needed), use the *forward*, *status*, and *locator* commands without an error message.

The last objective is slightly different from the performance description. You changed it so it would be more specific because these commands are representative of the others available.

!!!

Writing good, usable objectives depends, in part, on how well the desired performance has been described. The key to this is using action verbs that can be seen, heard, or "observed" in some other way.

Examples of verbs that should and should not be used are given in Table 20.1.

Table 20.1. Examples of acceptable and unacceptable verbs used in performance objectives

Acceptable				Unacceptable
apply	disassemble	load	select	appreciate
approve	discriminate	match	set up	become
assemble	discuss	measure	spray	desire
clean	dissect	order	suggest	feel
compare	distinguish	prepare	tell	improve
complete	document	recognize	test	know
connect	draw	record	wash	learn
correct	gown	repair	wrap	understand
describe	label	report	write	value
design	list	review		

Additional comments

In selecting an action to be used in an objective, consider how it relates to the actual task being performed. If an operational person is required to make a judgment about the adequacy of a sterilization cycle, your performance description might be something like, "distinguish between an acceptable and unacceptable cycle," because that is actually what the person is doing on his or her job.

For some activities, like the one above, you may need to use performance "indicators." You cannot readily observe a person distinguishing. You can ask them to mark or separate the acceptable from the unacceptable. This could be stated as, "distinguish between an acceptable and unacceptable cycle by marking records with an 'A' or 'U'."

For more information

Preparing Instructional Objectives by Robert Mager. Belmont, CA: Lake Publishing Co., 1984. (A very useful guide to writing performance-based objectives.)

21

Select Topics to Be Included in the Instructional Unit

Description — Choose the topics that are important and reasonable in an instructional unit.

Why do it — Selecting the topics is needed to

- Identify the appropriate instructional content,
- Serve as the basis for the later selection of instructional methods and media,
- Make sure topics support the goal and subgoals,
- Confirm that topics are important,
- Determine if the topics can be covered in a reasonable amount of time,
- Group several related topics into one particular course, and
- Identify a similar topic and goal that crosses across two or more curricula.

Who is involved — The analyst/designer is primarily involved. A content expert may be used as needed.

Output — A listing of the topics relating to the subgoal and the objectives.

Comments — A goal of selecting topics, in addition to assuring the necessary topics are included, is to make sure the resulting course or lesson makes the most efficient use of the learner's time by including *only* the things that are needed.

If you are working on an instructional unit that is very large and you will be breaking it down into smaller units, you may skip this step for now, adding the topics when this task is repeated.

How it is done

1) Look at the subgoal and the objectives for the instructional unit. Go to the prioritized training needs (from the analysis phase) and select those closely related to the subgoals and objectives.

2) Are there other topics that must be included or considered to enable the learners to perform? (You may want to determine why they were not on the prioritized list. Were they missed? Intentionally omitted?)

Example

A lesson is being designed for new manufacturing supervisors regarding preventative maintenance.

Subgoal: Supervisors in each department will utilize the plant-wide preventative maintenance (PM) program.

Objectives:

- List five reasons why PM is important.
- Describe how equipment is placed on the PM program.
- Using the MaintNet computer system, demonstrate how the PM status of a piece of equipment can be checked.
- Demonstrate how to report a piece of equipment that is not in compliance with the PM program.

1) After reviewing the subgoal and objectives, you select the appropriate topics from a list of prioritized training topics that had been developed in a recent analysis. (Selected items are marked with a check mark.)

Equipment selection criteria
Equipment requirements
Knowledge of process, equipment
✓ PM schedules for equipment
✓ What is involved in a PM
✓ Identifying additional equipment needing PMs
Change control
Equipment expectations
Equipment capabilities
✓ PM basics
Knowledge of materials
MSDS availability
Using an MSDS
Quality systems
Approving procedures

2) One other topic that needs to be covered to enable the learner to meet the objectives that is *not* on the list is *use of the MaintNet computer system.*

The final list of topics that needs to be included in the lesson is then as follows:

- PM schedules for equipment,
- What is involved in a PM,
- Identifying additional equipment needing PMs,
- PM basics, and
- Use of the MaintNet computer system.

(The remaining training topics will be incorporated into other lessons.)

22

Develop Manageable Units of Instruction

Description

Repeat the previous steps of identifying the subgoals, establishing the objectives, and selecting topics to be included until the instructional unit covers one major topic and will take the learner fifteen minutes to three hours to complete.

Why do it

Creating "chunks" of instruction helps to make the process of development and learning less overwhelming. It permits easier scheduling (several hour sessions, for example, rather than one day-long endurance test). Smaller units also give more flexibility in the way the material is used and allow for changing content or methods more easily.

Who is involved

The analyst/designer is primarily involved. Content experts or supervision may be called in as resources.

Output

For each instructional unit, there will be:

- A subgoal,
- Objectives (typically two to seven), and
- Topics (content) that enable the objectives to be met.

Comments

As mentioned in the Introduction to the Design Phase (Chapter 16), this is an iterative process. The same basic process is used several times until the subgoal, objectives, and topics are of a manageable size.

There are no exact specifications as to what "manageable size" means; there is considerable room for judgment. Generally speaking, the more focused and compact you can limit the unit of instruction, the better, as this increases its modularity and flexibility.

You may want to set your own limits on time; three hours may be too long as an upper limit. Do what makes sense in your situation.

If there is consistency and coherence between the units, such as a unifying theme or idea, there is no problem in "stacking" two or more lessons together.

!!!

How long should a lesson last? It's an easy question with no single answer other than, "It depends."

The main issue is to not lose the learners. You want to keep their attention and involvement. Any time spent after the learners turn off the lesson because they are tired, bored, hungry, distracted, etc., is wasted—no learning is taking place. Experience indicates people mentally "leave" after 45–50 minutes.

Some designers have a rule of thumb that every 15 minutes something new or different must happen.

The longer the lesson, the more variety is needed in the instructional methods and media in order to keep people involved. Alternatively, if one particular method is used, people should be able to take a quick break at least once every 50 minutes.

How it is done

1) Look at a given unit of instruction. Is it on one particular, major topic? Can it be accomplished by the learner in a period of fifteen minutes to three hours? If it is, move on to the next task of planning the evaluation strategy.

2) If not, return to the earlier task of developing the subgoal. Then continue with establishing objectives and selecting topics.

3) Again, look at the instructional unit you just created. If it is on one major topic and can be accomplished in the right amount of time, move on to the next task.

23

Plan the Evaluation Strategy

Description — Select and develop the approach to be used in measuring the effectiveness of the instruction.

Why do it — To integrate various evaluation perspectives into the training intervention and the accomplishment of the goal.

Who is involved — The designer is primarily involved in this task, with input and assistance from supervision and management.

Output — A written plan for evaluating the course and, perhaps, initial sketches of the methods that will be later developed and used.

Comments — Evaluation is one of the more complex issues in training. On the other hand, using a systematic approach to identify real needs and performance problems makes it much easier to accomplish.

One way of looking at this task is as if you were designing an experiment. You are wanting to show the difference that training can make.

Measuring how "good" a training intervention is depends on what you mean by "good" (Gordon 1991). It has a large range:

- Total department hours spent in training;
- Hours per student in a training session;
- Number of course evaluation forms rating the session good to excellent;
- Number of people tested with scores of 80 percent or higher;

- Decrease in problems after the training as compared to before the training;
- Decreased waste or product loss;
- Increased efficiency; and
- Increased company profit.

If you and your management are satisfied with a report of "hours spent in training," you have an indicator that is simple, fast, and relatively worthless. (Why are you reading this book when you could be out training people?) If you want to show training is an investment and is having a positive effect, you need to link the training with something that is important and measurable to the organization.

The goal of the training intervention is critical. The more measurable and specific it is, the easier it is to select the appropriate strategy.

Caution!

Evaluating a person's learning and/or performance has a number of serious legal, regulatory, and organizational implications. Before tests or performance evaluations are implemented, it is critical that representatives from human resources, legal, and management thoroughly discuss such tools and how they will be appropriately and effectively used.

Levels of evaluation

There are four levels of evaluating training interventions, originally proposed by Kirkpatrick (1975). Each level increases in rigor and in "quantitativeness." All go beyond the "body-count" method of measuring training. The four levels of evaluation are as follows:

- Level I—Trainee reaction
- Level II—Trainee learning
- Level III—Trainee performance
- Level IV—Business results

While each level can provide useful information, one level really cannot be used to predict success at the next level (Gordon 1991). An evaluation strategy may incorporate methods from each level.

Level I

Trainee reaction. The method most frequently used is a questionnaire filled out by participants at the end of a session. Some training professionals call them "smile sheets" and dismiss their use. They are a very proper way of collecting information; they can be thought of as indicators of how satisfied (one set of) the "customers" of a training program are. If the learners are not satisfied or happy with the course, they probably have not have learned or will not use what they have learned. Their negative reactions will influence the expectations (and attendance) of others (Robinson and Robinson 1989).

Be careful in reading the evaluations; even the best program, be it instructor-led or computer-based, will have a few negative comments over time. Look for those comments that are specific and provide a user's insight into the training intervention.

Using Level I evaluation. If you ask questions that can help you improve the course or the way or setting in which it is delivered, you can obtain useful information. Ask questions that might produce responses that are challenging and might be negative.

Reading too much into the comments and responses is a problem as well. If you ask a question like "will you use the skills back on the job," you cannot say they were actually used there; you were not measuring for use, only for the learner's *prediction* of using the skills on the job.

Level II

Trainee learning. Did the participants learn the knowledge and skills you wanted them to learn? Did they meet the objectives of the course? Is he or she able to identify, discuss, select, and so forth? This usually involves a test (pen and paper or integrated into a computer-based program) or a demonstration of the skill.

For information-domain objectives, written or oral tests are good methods. For intellectual and motor skills, it is best to have the person show their competency (i.e., that they can do it) by way of simulation or demonstration.

Using Level II evaluation. Results from the learning evaluations could be used to see if the learner is ready to progress to the next stage of training or if he or she needs specific remedial help. If results from many of the learners are unsatisfactory, it can indicate part of the instruction needs improvement.

Even though the person has learned the knowledge or skill does not mean that they will transfer it back to their job. You cannot assume that this will happen.

Level III

Trainee performance. Here you determine if people are applying (or have "transferred") what they learned back at their job and tasks. Are they making fewer documentation errors in the batch records or laboratory notebooks they write in? Are they following procedures?

This level of evaluation also looks at how supportive (or not) the work environment is for the learner to apply the new knowledge and skills.

Performance can be observed directly (observing a worker putting on a sterile gown before going into an aseptic manufacturing area) or indirectly (taking Rodac samples to see if they have contaminated the gown with microbes while gowning). Another way is to interview or provide questionnaires to the learners, supervisors, or their internal or external customers.

How Level III differs from Level II. Level II determines if the person *can do* something. Level III determines if the person *is doing* it back on the job; it looks at the performance in real-life circumstances.

Using Level III evaluation. If people are not using the knowledge and skills they (supposedly) gained from the instruction, there may be reasons, *unrelated to training*, that it is not being transferred back to the job. If documentation problems exist (writing in log books using blue ink instead of the required black ink), it *could* be because no black pens are available.

Level IV

Business results. This level of evaluation looks at the impact the training intervention is having on the organization. You are looking for evidence that training is linked to changes that occur (pretraining versus post-training), or between trained versus nontrained personnel.

Using Level IV evaluation. You are designing a course for labeling and packaging operations where there have recently been a number of discrepancies. If there are fewer labeling discrepancies, because people use newly taught skills in their jobs, how does this affect the department? It could mean fewer deviations or discrepancies that need to be investigated and discussed (savings of time, resources), less time for a product to be "on hold" while the problems are being resolved (shorter cycle time, better service, less "work-in-process" inventory), fewer recalls, and so forth.

"Our late Chairman, Eli Hanson stood four square behind our training program! And his old man before him old Asa Hanson stood four square behind our training program and our founder old Asa's old man Abraham Hanson also stood four square behind our training program! Now who said our training program is outdated?"

Decreasing the incidence of deviations, recalls, and so forth is a good measurement, but an even better one is how much money you have saved the organization.

!!!

In 1992, a major firm reported at a pharmaceutical engineering conference that their average cost of investigating and reporting on one deviation was $1355. This cost considered *only* the time and expense incurred by their quality control department.

How it is done

1) Consider what questions you (and your management) want to answer and what you will do with the information once you obtain it.

2) If you are considering Level II or III evaluations, are there minimal requirements that might have ramifications? For instance, if you give someone a test (a Level II evaluation), is there a passing score? Is it pass or fail? What happens if the learner does not "pass"? Can they go back to their job? Do they get immediate remedial training or coaching? Are they assigned to work with a partner who *has* passed? What does this mean to the products they are involved with? What if you observe a person not performing adequately (a Level III evaluation)? Again, what do you do? Do you document this as a deviation? (These are all difficult but important questions to answer. Answering them is a little easier if you are focused on performance, and not solely regulatory compliance.)

3) Select the combination of evaluation levels appropriate for your situation, consider the methods, and how you will acquire the information. Can it be obtained during the instruction? For example, if you are using a computer-based training (CBT) program, can it ask content-related questions and provide feedback? Can a person do a simulation before moving on to the next lesson?

(Your strategy may include the use of more Level I evaluation at the beginning, to help fine-tune the instruction and then, after the program is running smoothly, only use trainee reaction evaluations for occasional monitoring. Level III evaluation might be used throughout.)

Example

You are working with the manufacturing division in designing a course that is part of an effort to minimize the time filled vials of a certain drug product are out of the chillroom. (If they are out of the chillroom for more than seventy-two hours total, samples of the batch must be analyzed to see if the active ingredient is within the specified potency and purity profile.)

The course is rather simple: It should take less than an hour and be divided into two lessons. In addition to the training intervention, there will be time/temperature monitors to measure the actual time out of the chillroom.

The subgoal for the course is as follows:

> There will be a 75 percent reduction in the number of lots that are referred due to their exceeding the limits for being out of the chillroom.

The objectives for the course are as follows:

- Describe two reasons why it is important, in terms of the patient using the product, to minimize the time the product is out of the chillroom.
- Identify three business reasons for not exceeding the time limit.
- Using a model of the process, identify at least five points that contribute most to exceeding the time limit.
- Name three actions the learner can take in his or her job to help minimize the chance of exceeding the time limit.

1) Questions you want to have answered are as follows:

- Is the course delivering the appropriate content to the learners?
- Does the course need to be improved? How?
- Are people putting into actions what they said they will?
- How much money could this course save the company if it is successful?

2) You and the supervision in the area are trying to make this program as positive as possible, with operations personnel understanding how they, the patients, and the company are affected by this issue. You collectively decide that anyone not scoring 100 percent on a written or oral test will be coached individually. The supervisors will observe worker performance and coach those who are not meeting expectations. (All of the area's supervisors have completed the *Supervisor Coaching Program.*) All future incidents will be studied to determine what went wrong and how it can be avoided in the future.

3) Obtaining the information could come from a combination of

- Trainee reaction evaluations at the end of course;
- Tests at the end of the course;
- Follow-up; and
- Comparison of pretraining and post-training incidents and costs; data will be obtained from deviation reports and divisional financial analyst.

Additional information

Training effectiveness is frequently written about in such journals as *Training* and *Training and Development.*

- *Training for Impact: How to Link Training to Business Needs and Measure the Results* by D. G. Robinson and J. C. Robinson. San Francisco: Jossey-Bass Publishers, 1989.
- *Measuring Instructional Results (or Got a Match?)* Second Edition by R. F. Mager. Belmont, CA: Lake Publishing Co., 1984.

24

Prepare a High-Level Outline

Description Topics in each lesson are analyzed, sequenced, and expanded to include more content.

Why do it Writing the high-level outline for each lesson

- Arranges the information into a logical instructional sequence, and
- Identifies the instructional content and events.

In addition, the high-level lesson outlines can be assembled into the course outline.

Who is involved The course designer and a subject matter expert are involved in this task.

Output When this task is completed, you will have

- A sequenced list of topics to be covered in each lesson,
- Topics expanded with more detail of the content,
- Content organized in a way that helps the learner, and
- Instructional events selected in a way to facilitate learning.

Comments *Instructional content* is the facts, ideas, concepts, skills, and so forth that are reflected in the objective. *Instructional events* are the features of the lesson that help facilitate learning (Hannum and Hansen 1989).

Up until this point, we have not needed to distinguish between different types or *domains* of learning. However, we now need to select, arrange, and present the instructional content to best fit how people learn. To do this, we first must look at the various domains of things people learn.

This is not as complicated as it might sound. Think of how *you* best learn different types of things. For instance, compare learning how to swim and learning the names of the states and their capitals.

Swimming is a *motor skill*. It involves coordinated, physical actions. Sitting in a classroom, reading books, or watching videos will not help you very much. Getting into the water and having someone more experienced show and coach you will help you learn to swim. You would start out by learning to holding your breath, float, developing correct breathing patterns, and so forth before moving on to particular strokes and more complex movements. The environment—a pool or lake—is important to the learning process. You (and your coach) will know you have reached the goal of learning to swim because you will be able to *do* it.

Learning states, capital cities, and other *facts* is another type of learning. This can very easily be done in an environment *unrelated* to the subject matter. To be successful, the information must be structured in a way to help you mentally organize it in a meaningful way. This could be alphabetically or by geographic region. You (and your instructor) will know you have learned the facts because you can *tell* someone the capital of Montana or *write* the states and capitals down on paper.

Types of learning

Research has shown that people learn five basic types of things (Gagné 1985). These categories or *learning domains* are as follows:

1) *Motor skills*—executing simple or complex movements such as throwing a ball or driving a car.

   A person can demonstrate they have learned the skill by performing it.

2) *Information*—knowing facts or statements. Telling someone your address or identifying the parts of a complicated machine are examples of having learned information. (In this context, "telling" means more than simply speaking. It also can mean writing, typing, pointing to, or drawing factual information.)

Someone can demonstrate they have learned the information or facts by using them in a conversation or writing them down on paper.

3) *Intellectual skills*—using symbols or concepts that can range from the very simple to the extremely complex. A "simple" skill would be distinguishing between an acceptable and unacceptable item. A complex skill might be solving a problem or applying a series of rules and guidelines.

   A person demonstrates their intellectual skills by showing they can apply the skills in one particular situation or in a variety of different situations.

4) *Attitudes*—acquiring the mental state to make a choice for personal actions. These can involve a combination of personal, ethical, legal, or moral values. Examples include deciding whether to listen to classical music or jazz, doing homework or watching TV, driving at the speed limit or driving fifteen miles per hour above it.

   A person demonstrates their attitudes by the choice(s) they make in a particular situation.

5) *Cognitive strategy*—skills that people develop for learning, remembering, and thinking. For instance, writing reports in the morning rather than in the afternoon because it is easier for you is a cognitive strategy. Another example is one's use of a mnemonic device in remembering someone's name based on a physical characteristic (e.g., "Tim is thin," "Sheryl is short").

   Someone can show they have learned a cognitive strategy by using it to solve an unfamiliar problem.

NOTE: In the remainder of this book, we will be focusing on the first four types of learning; the fifth, cognitive strategy, was included in the list above for completeness.

How it is done

1) Look at each objective and *identify the learning domain* that it best fits.

2) For each objective, *identify what the learner must know and be able to do* to meet that objective. What you are discovering

is the *instructional content*. Recommended approaches are found in Table 24.1. Data from the task analysis are used.

3) *Organize the instructional content* for the objective based on the model shown for the objective's domain (identified in Step 1). Recommended models for the different types of content are shown in Table 24.1.

4) For each objective, *organize the instructional events* using the appropriate model. These are also described in Table 24.1.

Additional definitions

Table 24.1 uses two terms that may be new.

Advanced organizer—a framework or outline that is provided to the learners early in the lesson to give them an idea of what is to follow. For example, if the topic is contamination of sterile products, the advanced organizer would outline the ones you are going to talk about and how they are related: viable (microbial) and non-viable (pyrogenic, inert, etc.).

What's in it for me—a basic reason for learning the information or skill. This intends to be a motivator for learning. It could range from "if you don't do it right, you will not get your merit increase" to "would you want your son or daughter to use products that were not made according to good manufacturing practice?"

!!!

Where is "on-the-job training" or OJT?

OJT is an instructional method that, when done properly, includes several of the methods shown in Table 24.1.

In Britain, OJT is called, "sitting next to Nellie," which, unfortunately, describes how it is sometimes done: the trainee is assigned to a more experienced worker with the trainee expected to sit by, watch what is going on, and passively learn.

OJT is a powerful technique when used properly. It needs to include:

- A trainee with the appropriate prerequisite skills and knowledge;
- A demonstration of the task or process;
- Explanations of the task's what and whys;

- Explanation of the performance expectations; and
- Practice, *with feedback*, beginning with the subskills or movements and continuing through the entire task.

The expert worker (or mentor who is instructing the trainee) needs to understand and be able to fulfill his or her role as a mentor. Not all people are interested in doing this; not all can do it well.

If OJT is used, use a structured approach with skilled mentors who have been instructed in the OJT process.

Examples

For each of the following examples, identify the learning domain to which they best fit:

- Given the data and the goal for how it will be used, select the most appropriate graphical form for presenting and interpreting the data.
- When working in the freeze drier mechanical room, the learner will wear the required safety equipment.
- Describe the general activities of the U.S. Food and Drug Administration.
- Using a car with an automatic transmission, the learner will be able to safely drive the car around the school parking lot.

Tables 24.2 to 24.5 consider each of the objectives above. Examples are given that identify and organize instructional content and events.

Table 24.1. Recommended models for identifying and organizing instructional content and events
(based on Gagné 1985)

Domain	*Content Identification*	*Organization of Instructional Content*	*Organization of Instructional Events*
Information	1) Identify key idea or theme.	1) Show the key idea or theme (the "big picture").	1) Inform learners of desired outcomes. • objectives • why it is important to know • what can happen if information is not known • "what's in it for me?"
	2) Find supporting details related to key idea.	2) Show supporting details for the key idea.	2) Summarize previous knowledge; provide "advanced organizer" as an introduction; give a structure that information will be built around.
	3) Find subdetails to support the previously identified details.	3) Show the subdetails.	3) Present key idea. Then give supporting information.
	4) Find the structure for how all the pieces fit.	4) Show how each piece relates to the other pieces and supports the key idea.	4) Provide concrete examples and applications relevant to learners.
			5) Ask learners to repeat what they have learned.
			6) Provide feedback to learners. Coach. Amplify previously given information.
			7) Assess learner's performance.
			8) Provide opportunities for learners to practice "telling" information in a variety of situations.
			9) Provide continued feedback to learners.
Intellectual skill	1) Identify skills and knowledge required to reach the lesson's objective(s); these are the prerequisites.	1) Teach the most basic skills and knowledge first.	1) Inform learners of desired outcomes. • objective(s) • demonstrate the intellectual skill or how it is used • why is important to do this • what can happen if not done correctly • "what's in it for me?"

	2) Continue to identify prerequisites and skills and knowledge needed to reach the prerequisites. 3) Arrange skills and knowledge in a hierarchical fashion with the most basic skills and knowledge taught first.	2) Once learners have achieved mastery, move to the next skill or knowledge in the hierarchy.	2) Recall prerequisite rules and concepts already covered. 3) Describe features, symbols, tools used. 4) Show examples, nonexamples, applications. 5) Have learners do it and demonstrate their use of the intellectual skills. 6) Provide feedback to learners. Coach. Amplify previously given information as needed. 7) Assess learner's performance. 8) Provide opportunities for learners to practice "telling" information in a variety of situations. 9) Provide continued feedback to learners.
Motor skill	1) Break the skill down into smaller subskills or individual movements. 2) Identify the specific sequence of how the skill is performed.	1) Teach each subskill or individual movement in its naturally occurring sequence. 2) Once learners have mastered the subskill, move to the next subskill or movement in the sequence.	1) Inform learners of desired outcomes. • objective(s) • demonstrate the motor skill • why it is important to do this • what can happen if not done correctly • "what's in it for me?" 2) Show subskills or individual movements. 3) Show conditions at the start of the operation. 4) Learner practices subskills in sequence, with feedback. 5) Learner demonstrates complete skill with feedback, coaching. 6) Assess learner's performance.

(Continued on next page)

Domain	Content Identification	Organization of Instructional Content	Organization of Instructional Events
(Motor skill, continued)			7) Learner continues to practice and apply skills to other situations. 8) Provide continued feedback to learners.
Attitudes	1) Identify the behaviors a person with the "correct" attitude would display. (Follow the goal analysis process described in Chapter 19.)	1) Find a person the learners respect or with whom they can identify.	1) Inform learners of desired outcomes. • objective(s) • why the attitude/correct choice is important • what can happen if correct choice is not made • "what's in it for me?"
		2) Put the person (from Step 1) into a situation where they are forced to make a choice relating to the attitude.	[NOTE: Gagné (1985) suggests there may be times when providing the objectives may be counter productive. If objectives or the desired outcome is NOT shared with the learners, there should be a valid and specific reason for not doing so.]
		3) Show person making the correct choice.	2) Introduce human model.
		4) Show the person receiving positive feedback.	3) Recall situation or action.
			4) Human model demonstrates or describes choices. 5) New situation is provided to learner; learner provides choices, makes choice. 6) Learner given feedback on choice. 7) Assess learner's performance. 8) Learner given other situations and practices. 9) Provide continued feedback and reinforcement to learners.

!!!

When using a "respected person" to help teach and form attitudes, be certain the *learners* respect the chosen individual.

One firm, when trying to change attitudes involving quality improvement, chose a very senior executive to help with the training. While management was comfortable with the choice, operations and technical personnel viewed this person as part of the problem. In the previous year, the executive turned down well-developed engineering and equipment proposals that were designed to solve several significant quality issues.

During the pilot course, it was discovered that using this executive was very damaging to the entire program. To correct the problem, learners were interviewed as to whom *they* most respected in the firm. This person then agreed to help with the training.

Table 24.2. Example of organized instructional content and activities—information domain

Content Identification and Organization	Event Organization
1) Key Theme: FDA protects the consumers of food, medical products/devices, and cosmetics.	1) Desired outcomes • Objective: Describe the general activities of the U.S. Food and Drug Administration • FDA protects us as consumers by regulating the pharmaceutical industry. • The future and profitability of our firm depends, in part, on maintaining regulatory compliance and good professional relationships with the agency. 2) Advance organizer: Examine what the FDA does by looking at some of the situations and events in the U.S. and abroad that established and strengthened the FDA. We will see how the FDA is trying to prevent future problems by writing and enforcing regulations.
2) Details: Legislative activities to establish and strengthen U.S. FDA, prompted by significant problems and events.	3) Present key theme: FDA protects the consumers . . . 4) Present details and examples. Problems and situations that have occurred and how Congress and others reacted.
3) Supporting subdetails a. 1906. Original Food and Drug Act passed; Meat Inspection Act passed same day. Shocking disclosures about meat packing industry (Sinclair's book, *The Jungle*) and cure-all claims for worthless and dangerous drugs were catalysts to these Acts. b. 1938. Federal Food, Drug, and Cosmetics Act passed by Congress. Requires new drugs to be shown to be safe prior to marketing. Was the result of public uproar after *Elixir of Sulfanilimide* tragedy, which killed 107 people, mostly children. c. 1962. Kefauver-Harris Drug Amendments pass Congress. Requires manufacturers to prove effectiveness. Prompted in part by *Thalidomide* tragedy.	5) . . . 6) . . .

Note: Numbered items used under each heading correspond to those in models shown in Table 24.1.

Table 24.3. Example of organized instructional content and activities—intellectual skills domain

Content Identification and Organization	Event Organization
1) A. Bar charts —examples —how they are used B. Complex bar charts —grouped (side-by-side) —stacked C. Proper/improper uses of bar charts 2) A. Pie charts —examples —how they are used B. etc.	1) Desired outcomes: • Objective: Given the data and the goal for how it will be used, select the most appropriate graphical form for presenting and interpreting the data. • Demonstration of picking the appropriate graphical form • Demonstration of what can occur if inappropriate one used 2) Previous related concepts covered: • Problem identification process • Data collection process 3) Graphical types: • Features of each • When to use, when *not* to use 4) Example: Picking a graphical form to show trends • Appropriate choices • Inappropriate choices 5) Learners select what they would use; repeat for all major categories. 6) . . .

Note: Numbered items used under each heading correspond to those in models shown in Table 24.1.

Table 24.4. Example of organized instructional content and activities—motor skills domain

<table>
<tr><th colspan="6">Identification and Organization of Instructional Content</th><th>Organization of Instructional Events</th></tr>
<tr>
<td>1. PREPARATION
a. Pre driving adjustments
1) Seat
2) Mirrors
b. Putting on seat and shoulder belts</td>
<td>→</td>
<td>2. START THE CAR
a. Insert key into ignition.
b. Place foot on brake pedal.
c. Check that transmission is in PARK position.
d. Turn key until starter sounds.
e. . . .</td>
<td>→</td>
<td>3. PUT THE CAR IN GEAR
a. Place foot on brake pedal.
b. Shift into DRIVE (or REVERSE for backing up).</td>
<td>→
Etc.</td>
<td>1) Desired outcomes
• Objective: Using a car with an automatic transmission, the learner will be able to safely drive the car around the school parking lot.
• Demonstrate the motor skill
• This opportunity provides learners an occasion to practice in a safe environment.
• When correctly done, learner will then do similar thing on a quiet public street.
2) Subskills demonstration and why this is important.
• Preparation
—predriving adjustments
—putting on seat and shoulder belts
• Start car
—insert key in ignition
—place foot on brake pedal
. . .
3) Conditions at beginning of sequence:
• Car is “off.”
• Car is in PARK.
• Someone else used car last.
4) Learner practices subskills
• Preparation
—predriving adjustments
—putting on seat and shoulder belts
• Start car
—insert key in ignition
. . .
5) Learner demonstrates entire performance, receives feedback and coaching.
6) . . .</td>
</tr>
</table>

Note: Numbered items used under each heading correspond to those in models shown in Table 24.1.

Table 24.5. Example of organized instructional content and activities—attitude domain

Objective: When working in the freeze drier mechanical room, the learner will wear the required safety equipment.

Content Identification	Content Organization	Event Organization
Performance/behaviors: Personnel will wear safety glasses and hearing protection.	1) Respected person: Mr. Tony Carneghi (now vice-president; started out twenty-five years ago as a chemical operator; well known, liked, and respected by all operational personnel) 2) Describe/show Tony entering mechanical area. 3) Describe/show Tony putting on glasses and ear protection. 4) Describe/show positive feedback.	1) Describe outcomes: • topic—choosing to wear safety equipment • why important—a choice *you* make to protect/not protect yourself • outcome—important to you *and* your family/friends. 2) Introduce Tony Carneghi. 3) Tony tells story of recent tour with engineers/operations people and how several of them did not wear safety equipment. Tony tells why he did. 4) Tony tells why he is so concerned over worker protection. 5) Tony questions learners—"What would you do in a situation like this?" 6) Tony gives feedback to learners. 7) . . .

Note: Numbered items used under each heading correspond to those in models shown in Table 24.1.

25

Select the Appropriate Instructional Methods

"Why," said the Dodo, "the best way to explain it is to do it."
—Alice in Wonderland

Description Choose the best techniques to accomplish the objectives and instructional events, based on the content, events, context, and the characteristics of the audience.

Why do it Some methods are better suited than others for effectively transferring information to the learners. In this task, you will choose the appropriate methods, based on the content and instructional events, in order to maximize the course's effectiveness.

Who is involved Selecting methods for the course is done by the designer with input, as needed, by subject matter experts.

Output Upon completing this task, you will have a final list of proposed instructional methods and notes concerning how they will be used and implemented.

Comments There are no standard, rigidly-adhered-to definitions for instructional methods and instructional media (discussed in the next section). The following two definitions are the ones we will be using.

- *Instructional methods* are the techniques used for presenting content to the learner.
- *Instructional media* are the means of delivering the instructional content and methods to the learner.

Figure 25.1 uses an analogy to describe both terms.

Six categories of instructional methods and examples are shown and compared in Table 25.1. The intellectual skill learning domain is divided into three categories.

Procedures primarily requiring decisions fall into the intellectual skill domain; procedures that are more physical and mechanical (e.g., cleaning, assembling) would be part of the motor skill domain.

Consider the comment by the former Director of Education (External Programs) at IBM: "The intent of the overall design is to make every ten minutes outstanding, so the student will maintain interest in the subject" (Bowsher 1989).

Cautions!

Take your time with this task. Talk to others with experience. Be forewarned, however, that many people (training professionals and management alike) have deep prejudices for or against certain instructional methods based on their own comfort levels, experiences, and fears.

It is not yet the time to say "videotape" or "lecture" or whatever media comes to your mind. First you must determine how to best get the knowledge or skill across to the learner (the methods). *Then*, as will be done in the next task, decide the best way for it to be delivered (the media).

Selecting the correct instructional methods is a major step in making your course or lesson a success. On the other hand, choosing inappropriate ones can result in a fast and very expensive failure.

How it is done

1) Find the suggested instructional methods for the particular learning domain (Table 25.1).

2) Identify the job/task context of the objective, that is, in what situation or environment is the objective performed? Are customer support technicians listening to product complaints over the phone? Are technicians reading letters where phone etiquette and instant answers are not required?

3) From the methods identified in Step (1), find the best instructional methods and specific techniques based on the context of the task and job. Note any special requirements

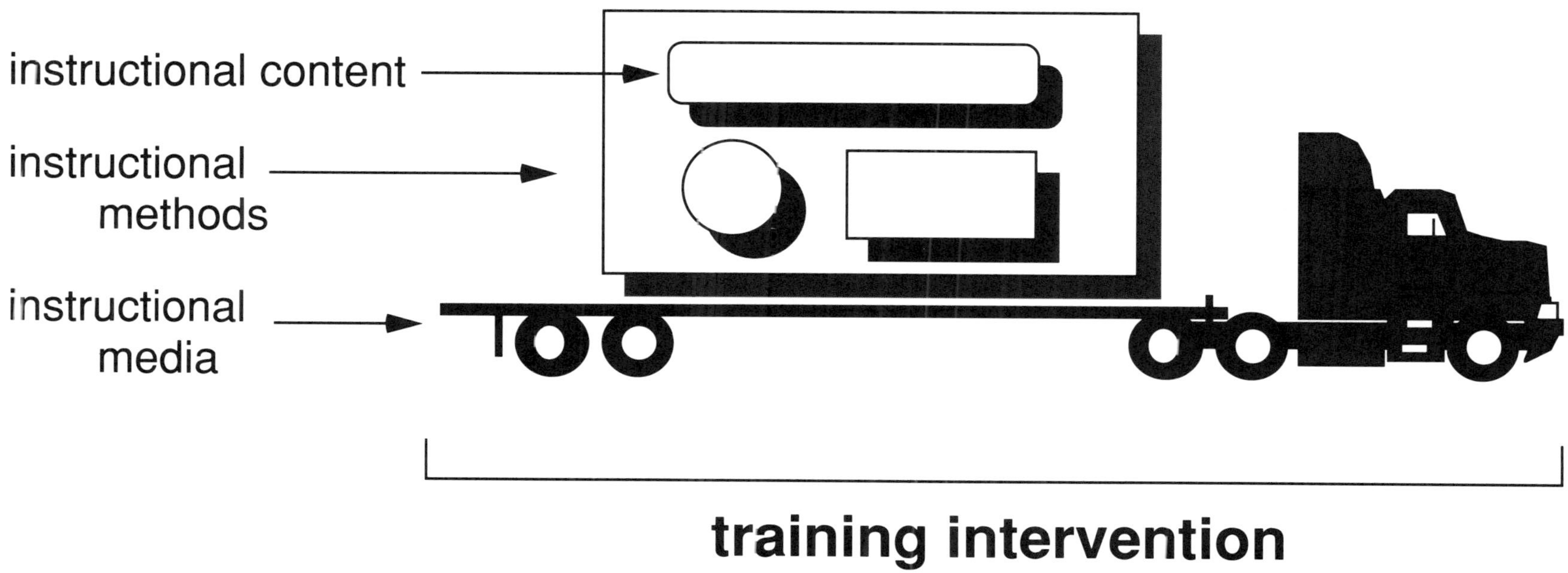

Figure 25.1. Components of a training intervention: an analogy. The training intervention consists of three major parts: (1) the instructional content (information), (2) the instructional methods (how the information is organized and techniques used for presenting it), and (3) the instructional media (the vehicles used for delivering the content and methods to the learner. For the training to have the optimal results, all three components need to be carefully matched.

Table 25.1. Learning domains and suggested instructional methods

Learning Domain	Suggested Methods
Information	*Tell* information to the learner. *Show* information. Have learner *read* information. Have learner *practice* using the information.
Intellectual skills	
Identifying differences	*Demonstrate* the differences with various examples. If situational differences, *discuss* the differences. Have learners *practice* making the distinctions between examples.
Concepts, rules, principles	*Show* the concept, rule, principle. *Tell* the concept, etc. *Demonstrate* the concept, etc. Have learners *read* about the concept, etc. Have learners *practice* using the concept, etc.
Procedures	*Demonstrate* the procedure. *Show* the procedure being done. Have learners *read* the procedure. Have learners *practice* using the procedure.
Motor skills	*Demonstrate* the motor skill. *Simulate* the motor skill. *Show* the motor skill. Have learners *practice* the motor skill.
Attitudes	*Show* someone behaving with the proper attitude. *Discuss* attitudes and behavior Have the learners *simulate* using the proper attitude.

(e.g., color images, callers expecting immediate satisfaction, etc.).

4) Consider how the methods can be optimized for the learner using the guidelines provided (Table 25.2), maximizing learner involvement. Also, provide the learner as many opportunities to practice as possible.

5) Eliminate potential methods after considering practical matters such as the following:

- Instructor requirements and availability (Is a subject matter expert needed to teach the course? Is the course to be delivered without an instructor? Do the events require a person with good facilitating skills? Etc.);
- Number of trainees and their availability;
- Number of locations to be covered;

- Development time available;
- Budget/funds available;
- Ease of use;
- Availability of equipment;
- Availability of facilities; and
- Expectations of learners and management.

6) Review the refined list of potential instructional methods with the lesson objective(s), instructional content, and instructional events to be sure the potential methods make sense. This then becomes the final list of proposed methods.

Example 1

Using the example from Table 24.2, the steps for selecting the appropriate instructional methods were followed with these results:

Objective: Describe the general activities of the U.S. Food and Drug Administration.

Learning domain: Information

Job / task context: Background information

Special considerations: Management wants program as soon as possible

Initial list of instructional methods to be used (from Table 25.1):

- Tell,
- Show, and
- Discuss/practice.

Specific techniques to be used (and ways to optimize) from Table 25.2):

- Presentation (visuals, questions to involve learners),
- Visuals (diagrams, still images, moving images), and
- Discussion/practice (questions/small group discussions).

Practical considerations: large number of participants (3,500); instructors might not be experts in FDA history/background; four different locations need to be covered with same program. People per class/session: 35–40. Sessions would be a mix of job types, organizational levels. Budget available: director says "be realistic" but funds are there. Management wants a program to show they believe FDA and compliance is important.

Table 25.2. Comparison of Instructional Methods

Instructional Method	Examples of Specific Techniques	Senses Stimulated	Active Involvement of Learner (relative)	Ways to Optimize
		Vision **H**earing **T**actile **K**inesthetic **A**ffective		
Tell (live)	lecture presentation panel discussion	H, A	low	Increase audience involvement. Combine with visuals.
Sound	play a recording generate	H, A	low	Increase audience involvement. Combine with live action, visuals.
Show	words/symbols diagrams still images moving images models	V, A	low	Combine with live action. If topic involves motion/changes, using moving images. Combine written words, symbols with diagrams, images.
Read	textbooks self-study books checklists	V, A	medium	Combine with diagrams, images.

Discuss	question/answers group discussions case studies	H, V, A	high	Combine with live action, visuals, written words. Use small-sized groups for maximum instruction.
Tutor	instructor/learner learner/learner technology assisted	H, V, A	high	Combine with reading, visuals.
Demonstration	real life	H, V, (T?, K?)	medium	Use actual equipment/environment if possible. Combine with practice.
Play/simulation	role playing games simulations case studies	H, V, A, T, K	high	Use actual equipment/environment if possible.
Practice	hands on practice with feedback case studies	H, V, T, K, A	high	Provide coaching.

Includes work of Allen (1967), Reiser and Gagné (1983), Romiszowski (1988).

Implications of considerations: Use instructors as facilitators; provide as much "canned" content as possible.

Final list of proposed methods, specific techniques, and notes:

- Tell: presentation (using visuals, questions to involve learners)—*instructors are not content experts;*
- Show: visuals (diagrams, still images, moving images)—*material needs to contain bulk of content;*
- Discuss/practice: discussion (questions/small group discussions)—*groups will be mixed; utilize the group's diversity;* and
- Read: reading (handouts for reference/review)—*keep to a minimum.*

Example 2

Using the example from Table 24.4, the steps for selecting the appropriate instructional methods were followed with these results:

Objective: Using a car with an automatic transmission, the learner will be able to safely drive the car around the school parking lot.

Learning domain: Motor skills

Job/task context: Real life—will be done each time car is driven.

Special considerations: Demonstration and practice requires car.

Initial list of instructional methods to be used (from Table 25.1):

- Show,
- Demonstrate, and
- Practice.

Specific techniques to be used (and ways to optimize) from Table 25.2):

- Visuals (flowchart),
- Reading (with diagrams),
- Demonstration (using actual equipment), and
- Practice with coaching from instructor.

Practical considerations: Small groups of learners (three to four per group); instructor has expertise; cars, practice space (large, empty parting lot) are available. Program must be available in four weeks.

Final list of proposed methods and specific techniques:

- Demonstration in car,
- Show flowchart with steps listed,
- Practice with coaching from instructor, and
- Supplemental reading and checklist provided.

26

Select the Appropriate Media

The form of the carrier of information is not neutral; it both dictates the kind of information conveyed and affects thinking processes.

—Alan C. Kay

Description

Choose the most appropriate media to serve as a vehicle for delivering the instructional content and events using the methods that have been identified.

Why do it

Some media are more effective vehicles than others for delivering particular instructional methods. Also, depending on the audience (locations, numbers of people, etc.) and how frequently the course will be delivered, when all the facts are considered, some media are *much* more cost effective than others.

Who is involved

The designer is primarily involved in selecting the media, along with the subject matter expert, supervision, and management.

Output

When this task is completed, you will have a list of the appropriate media to be used in each lesson of the course.

Comments

To help distinguish between instructional methods and instructional media, the definitions given earlier are repeated here.

- *Instructional methods* are the techniques used for presenting content to the learner.

- *Instructional media* are the means of delivering the instructional content and methods to the learner.

Figure 25.1 (page 167) uses an analogy to describe both terms.

Many of the same caveats discussed in the previous section on methods selection are appropriate here, as well as several others.

There is not a great amount of evidence linking instructional effectiveness with a particular type of media. Choosing the media for your particular situation is a judgment; there are tradeoffs and compromises involved. However, your choice *cannot be arbitrary.* You need to consider the best way to deliver the message and also receive feedback on how well the learner has understood and incorporated the information into his or her performance. Some media are much better at this than others.

Your choices will also be based on the opportunities, practical constraints, and limitations present in *your* own situation. (It is unusual when funding or resource availability is not a problem.) Linking the goals of the instructional program to what the organization feels is important, as we did in the early stages of analysis, can provide you the basis for a better cost justification.

One of the important trade-offs in selecting media is short-term versus long-term costs. Showing a video the first time is the most expensive use; after that, the costs per use and per student come down dramatically. This holds true for any program with high development and production costs, such as computer-based training (CBT), interactive video, and the like.

On the other hand, programs using "live" content experts generally *cost more over the life of the course*, especially if there are several teachers/facilitators involved. Availability of these specialized people can also limit the times when the course can be offered and present scheduling problems.

Studies conducted for the U.S. government and by several large corporations have shown using an interactive multimedia approach has a savings of 28–64 percent when compared to conventional instruction over a five-year time span (Macromedia 1992).

!!!	During World War II, the U.S. military purchased 55,000 motion picture film projectors and spent $1 billion to effectively and efficiently train large numbers of people from diverse backgrounds. After the war, the German Chief of General Staff said, "We had everything calculated perfectly except the speed with which America was able to train its people. Our major miscalculation was in underestimating their quick and complete mastery of film education" (Reiser 1989).

Caution!

You must consider the "handlers" of the media—the instructors or course monitors who will be using the tools you provide. If instructors are not comfortable using role-playing, for example, they may be reluctant to include it in the program; if role-playing is used, the instructors might not make the best use of it. Consider working with the instructors to help them become at ease with the media and instructional techniques. Train the trainer workshops can help with this.

How it is done

1) Review the data and information you have on

- Audience characteristics;
- How the course will be used (numbers of sessions, locations, etc.);
- Instructor requirements and availability (Is a subject matter expert needed to teach the course? Is the course to be delivered without an instructor? Do the events require a person with good facilitating skills?);
- Practical considerations;
- Development time available;
- Budget/funds available;
- Ease of use;
- Availability of equipment;
- Availability of facilities;
- Instructional methods (selected in the previous section); and
- Management expectations.

2) With the above factors in mind, consider the list of potential media for each of the planned instructional techniques, their advantages and disadvantages (found in Table 26.1), and how well each matches your needs. Select the media that will work the best.

Table 26.1. Media Selection Table

	AUDIENCE CHARACTERISTICS			CONTENT			DEVELOPMENT							USE				
Item	Delivered on Demand?	Senses Stimulated	Group Size	Category	Capable of Showing Motion	Content Stability	Cost	Cost Curve	Time Required	Ease of Development	Professional or Experienced Resources Needed	Ease of Distribution	Cost of Distribution	Setup	Role of Instructor	Special Equipment Needed	Flexibility of Use	Usability as Reference Tool
	Yes **N**o **P**ossibly	**V**ision **H**earing **T**actile **K**inesthetic **A**ffective	**I**ndiv. (1 or 2) **S**mall (3–14) **M**ed. (15–29) **L**arge (30–75) **H**uge (>75)	**T**ell (live) **S**ound **Sh**ow **D**iscuss **T**utor **Demo**nstrate **P**lay/**Si**mulate **Prac**tice	**Y**es **N**o	**N**ever changes **S**ometimes **F**requent changes	Low (**¢**) Med (**$**) High (**$$**) Expensive (**$$$**)	**I**nitially **R**ecurring	**I**mmediate **D**ays **W**eeks **M**onths **>4 M**onths	**E**asy **M**edium **D**ifficult	**N**one **S**ometimes **U**sually **A**lways	**E**asy **D**ifficult	Low (**¢**) Med (**$**) High (**$$**) Expensive (**$$$**)	**E**asy **M**edium **D**ifficult	**H**ost Content **E**xpert **F**acilitator **T**echnician **A**dvisor/Admin **N**ot Needed	**P**layer **S**ource **C**omputer **Sp**eakers **Ch**art **M**arkers **S**creen **P**rojector **TV** **M**onitor **Si**mulator	**L**ow **M**edium **H**igh	**L**ow **M**edium **H**igh
Lecture	P	H, A	S, M, L, H	T (S, Sh, D, Demo)	N	F	¢	R	D–W	E	N	E	¢	E	H, E		H	L
Panel discussion	P	H, A	S, M, L, H	T (Sh, D)	N	F	¢	R	D–W	E	M	M	$	E	H, E, F		H	L
Play a tape recording	Y	H, A	I, S, M, L, H	S, Demo, Prac	N	S	¢	I	I–D	E	S	E	¢	E	E, F, T	P	M	M
Generate sounds live	Y	H	I, S, M, L, H	S, Demo, Prac	N	F	¢	R	I–D	E	M	M–D	$–$$$	E–D	E, F, T	S	H	L
Generate sounds via computer	Y	H	I, S, M, L, H	S, Demo, Prac	N	S	$	I	I–D	M	U	E	$	M	E, F, T	C, Sp	M	M
Flip charts	Y	V	I, S, M	Sh	N	F	¢	R	I	E	N	E	¢	E	E, F	Ch, M	H	L
Blackboard	Y	V	I, S, M	Sh	N	F	¢	R	I	E	N	M	¢	E	E, F	M	H	L
Photographs	P	V	I, S	Sh	N	F	¢	I	I–D	E–M	S	E	¢	E	E, F		M	H

Overhead transpar-encies	P	V	I, S, M, L	Sh	N	F	¢	I	I–D	E–M	S	E	¢	E	E, F	Pr, Scr, M	M	M
35 mm slides	P	V	I, S, M, L, H	Sh	N	S	$	I	I–D	E–M	S–U	E	¢	E	E, F	Pr, Scr	M	M
Models	P	V, T	I, S, M	Sh	Y	N	¢–$$$	I	D–M	M–D	U	E	$–$$	M	E, F		M	M
Motion picture film (16 mm)	Y	V, H, A	I, S, M, L, H	Sh, S, Demo	Y	N	$$$	I	M–>4M	D	A	E	$$	M	F, T	Pr	L	M
Video—live	N	V, H, A	I, S, M, L*, H*	Sh, S, Demo	Y	F	$–$$	I/R	D–W	M–D	U	D	¢–$$	E–M	E, H, F, T	Mon	L	L
Video—tape	Y	V, H, A	I, S, M, L*, H*	Sh, S, Demo	Y	S	$–$$	I	D–M	M–D	U	E	$	E	E, H, F, T	P, TV	M	M
Projected computer images	P	V, H	I, S, M, L*, H*	Sh, S, Demo	Y	S	¢–$$	I	D–M	M–D	S	M	$	M	E, H, F, T	Pr, Scr	M	L
Textbooks/ printed material	Y	V, A	I, S, M, L, H	Sh, R	N	S	$	I	D–W	E–M	S	E	¢	E	N, A		M	H
Self-study guides/ books	Y	V	I, S, M, L, H	Sh, R	N	S	$$	I	W–M	M	S	E	¢	E	N, A		L	H
Checklists	Y	V	I, S, M, L, H	Sh, R	N	F	¢	I	D–W	E	S	E	¢	E	N		L	H
Ques-tioning	P	H, A (V)	I, S	Tutor, D	N	F	¢	R	I–D	E	N	E	¢	E	E, F		H	L
Group discussion	P	H, A (V)	S, M	Tutor, D, PS	N	F	¢	R	I–D	M	S	E	¢	E	F, E		H	L
Case studies	P	H, A (V)	S, M	Tutor, R, D, PS	N	S	¢–$$	I/R	D–W	M	S	E	$	E–M	F, E		M	M
Instructor -learner (tutoring)	P	V, H, A	I, S	Tutor, D (Sh, Demo)	N	F	¢	R	I	E	N	E	$	E	F, E		H	L
Computer -based training	Y	V, H, A	I	Tutor, S, Sh, Demo, PS, Prac	Y	S	$–$$$	I	W–>4M	D	A	E	¢–$	E–M	N, A	C	M	H
Interac-tive video	Y	V, H, A	I	Tutor, S, Sh, Demo, PS, Prac	Y	N	$$$	I	W–>4M	D	A	E	¢	E–M	N, A	C, P	M	M

	AUDIENCE CHARACTERISTICS			CONTENT			DEVELOPMENT					USE						
Item	Delivered on Demand?	Senses Stimulated	Group Size	Category	Capable of Showing Motion	Content Stability	Cost	Cost Curve	Time Required	Ease of Development	Professional or Experienced Resources Needed	Ease of Distribution	Cost of Distribution	Setup	Role of Instructor	Special Equipment Needed	Flexibility of Use	Usability as Reference Tool
	Yes **N**o **P**ossibly	**V**ision **H**earing **T**actile **K**inesthetic **A**ffective	**I**ndiv. (1 or 2) **S**mall (3–14) **M**ed. (15–29) **L**arge (30–75) **H**uge (>75)	**T**ell (live) **S**ound **Sh**ow **D**iscuss **T**utor **Demo**nstrate **P**lay/**S**imulate **P**ractice	**Y**es **N**o	**N**ever changes **S**ometimes **F**requent changes	Low (**¢**) Med (**$**) High (**$$**) Expensive (**$$$**)	**I**nitially **R**ecurring	**I**mmediate **D**ays **W**eeks **M**onths **>4** **M**onths	**E**asy **M**edium **D**ifficult	**N**one **S**ometimes **U**sually **A**lways	**E**asy **D**ifficult	Low (**¢**) Med (**$**) High (**$$**) Expensive (**$$$**)	**E**asy **M**edium **D**ifficult	**H**ost Content **E**xpert **F**acilitator **T**echnician **A**dvisor/Admin **N**ot Needed	**P**layer **S**ource **C**omputer **S**peakers **C**hart **M**arkers **S**creen **P**rojector **TV** **M**onitor **S**imulator	**L**ow **M**edium **H**igh	**L**ow **M**edium **H**igh
Real-life demonstration	P	V, H, A, T, K	I, S	T, S, Sh, Demo, PS	Y	F	¢–$$$	I/R	I–D	E–M	S	E–D	¢–$$$	E–D	E, F		H	L
Role playing	N	V, H, A	S, M	PS	N	F	¢	R	I–D	M	S	E	¢	E	F		H	L
Games	P	V, H, A (T, K)	I, S, M	PS	N	S	¢–$	I	D–W	M	S	E–M	¢–$	E–M	F		M	M
Simulation	P	V, H, A, T, K	I,S,M	PS, P	N	S	¢–$$$	I	D–>4M	M–D	S	E–D	¢–$$$	E–D	F, T	Sim?	M	M

*special equipment needed

Includes work of Allen (1967), Reiser and Gagné (1983), Romiszowski (1988), Schramm (1977).

3) Consolidate the instructional content, events, methods, and delivery media into a chart or document and review with subject matter experts, potential users, and management for their comments and approval to proceed.

Notes on specific media

Table 26.1 provides comparisons of various media and their relative merits. Some selected types of media are discussed in more detail below. For additional information, references are provided at the end of this chapter.

Some of the information provided below touches on issues and activities covered in the development phase. They are included here, not to indicate they need to be completed at this point, but rather to guide your thinking as you select the most appropriate media.

Lecture

Lectures, or presentations, are something we all have experienced, either as speakers or as audience members. Frequently, when we think of "training," it is this format that comes to mind. It is relatively simple to do, inexpensive, flexible, frequently dull, uninvolving of the audience, and not *really* suited for many of the situations for which it is used. The skills of the speaker are extremely critical to the success of this vehicle.

Lectures are appropriate for *providing information*. They work best with people who have considerable experience in receiving information this way, such as professionals and management personnel. Lecturing should *not* be high on your list of media. If you do use it, incorporate other media (visuals, demonstrations, questioning, case studies, etc.) to supplement it.

Overhead transparencies

Sometimes called "foils" or "acetates," these devices are frequently used as visuals. They may contain

- Words or phrases,
- Diagrams,
- Graphs,
- Flowcharts, and/or
- Illustrations.

Transparencies can be made simply (with a marker pen) or by using a computer graphics package. They are best used when they *reinforce* the speaker's words, not when the speaker reads them word for word.

Live video

Live television is coming back as an instructional tool and vehicle. Many new office buildings are being wired to deliver TV signals into individual workstations, offices, and conference rooms. Many hotels and conference centers have "downlinks" that can receive satellite broadcasts. There are more than eighty private business networks in the United States that distribute programming via satellites. Large corporations (GM, Federal Express, Digital Electronic Corporation [DEC]) have their own networks. Other companies and organizations can rent time on satellites and establish their own one-time or limited-use networks. As the costs for renting satellite time come down, this tool for distance learning will expand even more, since this saves learner travelling time and expense. Programs delivered over this medium have "broadcast quality" images and sound; viewers frequently use phone lines (with toll-free "800" numbers) to ask questions and participate in discussions.

Another live video tool is video conferencing. This method connects two or more parties in different locations, with video and audio links. Graphics and other visuals can be shared by computers and facsimile machines connected into the system. Video-conferencing is typically done in special conference rooms that an organization has or ones that can be rented from a telecommunications vendor such as AT&T or Sprint.

Most video conferencing in the early 1990s uses a technique called video compression that results in "jerky TV." It looks fine when people are not moving or still visuals are being shown, but moving images have a noncontinuous or jerky appearance.

Personal experience with both forms of live television leaves these impressions and suggestions:

- Video-conferencing provides the opportunity for more interaction between small groups of people;
- Video-conferencing works if the participants can get beyond the picture-quality issues;
- Broadcast quality video is needed if you are trying to create an impact, teach fine motor skills, or change attitudes; and
- Either technique works very well in reaching many locations at the same time to simply share information; feedback mechanisms are needed if *instruction* is the goal.

Videotape

As technology improves, low cost video equipment performs as well as professional equipment did ten to fifteen years ago. Desktop video is beginning to revolutionize the video-production industry in much the same way that desktop publishing did to the typesetting, printing, and publishing industries in the late 1980s.

While this can be exciting, there is also a negative side: Users without an understanding of "video literacy" and technical know-how will produce hour upon hour of bad TV. (As an example, look at some of the community access programming available on cable television systems.) Bad TV, incorporated into training programs, wastes money and time and destroys credibility.

One of the frequent and worst uses of video is taping a presentation and then expecting others to watch it and learn something from it. (Many training professionals have experienced shudders, when intelligent, upper management recommend this approach be used.) One cure is having those suggesting this sit down and watch the material and then tell you what *they* learned and how effective it was.

As with all the other methods and vehicles for delivering instruction, there is no one magic bullet. Videotapes can be just as detrimental to a program if used incorrectly as they can be powerful when properly used.

Projected computer images

New display systems such as video projectors or LCD displays (placed on overhead projectors) allow computer-generated (or video) images to be projected for large groups to see. Visuals such as diagrams, words, animations, and the like, previously confined to transparencies, 35 mm slides, or video, can now be generated and stored on personal computers. LCD projection panels have limitations, especially when it comes to displaying bright images; video projectors are typically superior.

Using computers in this way makes presentations easier to modify since no slides or video is involved. The downside is reliability: Computers *sometimes* will not deliver exactly what you want when you want it. Experience and familiarity with the hardware and software improve reliability; however, it is a good idea to have backup materials just in case.

One other caution involves overuse of some of the capabilities of presentation software. Transitions and special effects can be used, but use them in a way that fits the content and structure of the information.

Self-study books and guides

One means of providing "training on demand" is by using self-study materials. Self-study materials are useful in helping to teach procedures and can include diagrams, pictures, and so forth. Another advantage is that they can be useful reference materials. While they *appear* simple to produce, to be meaningful and effective, self-study materials need to be developed by someone who has had experience with this medium.

Printed materials: "handouts"

For many training groups, providing handouts or "souvenir" materials is customary. Consider, however, if people really use them, either during or after the course. Alternatively, you may want to provide written materials only to those who ask for them; they may have a learning style that is supported by reading.

Instead of providing a binder for every course, you may want to initially distribute one large binder to each person that they simply add information to.

Another option is to give out job aides, such as laminated cards with an outline of steps to follow (e.g., for getting into a computer system, or questions to ask people who are calling for information).

Questioning

One of the earliest ways of instruction is the asking of questions, the "Socratic method," named after the Greek philosopher who used it extensively. Quality advocate Edward Deming is also a practitioner of this approach.

Questioning makes use of two of the principles of adult learning. First, adults have a wealth of experiences to draw on, and second, they want to be actively involved with their learning.

An example might be in teaching quality auditors how to audit. The instructor (with expertise in auditing) walks around a facility with the learners, asking questions such as the following:

- Do you see anything here that concerns you?
- Why?
- Why not?

- What about . . . ?
- What problems could it cause, now or later?
- What might happen if . . . ?
- How could this affect the safety or fitness-for-use of the final product?

Questions can also be used as a part of a presentation or in a group discussion.

Case studies

Case studies can be used to teach problem solving and other intellectual skills and attitudes. The learners apply their knowledge and skills to a particular situation. A well designed case study takes time to prepare; it usually requires refinement after the first few times it is presented.

An example of a case study is in teaching management and technical personnel how to apply the concepts of cGMPs.

The "case" would be an observation made by an FDA investigator (called a "483 observation"). The learners might be asked to form small groups and come up with answers to the following questions:

- Is the observation a violation of the cGMPs?
- What specific paragraph in the cGMP regulations might be cited?
- How might the situation affect the safety, identity, strength, purity, and quality of the final product?
- How could a consumer or patient be affected?
- What should be done to correct the problem?

Instructor-learner (tutoring and coaching)

For certain intellectual or motor skills, one-on-one tutoring may be appropriate. This might also be viewed as "coaching" a person. On-the-job training (OJT) makes use of this way of delivering instruction. The instructor or coach can provide feedback to the learner and, as needed, suggest alternative approaches or "tricks" learned by experience. It may be possible to have one instructor coaching several learners at the same time. While this can be a powerful technique, it is time and resource intensive on the part of the instructor.

Computer-Assisted Instruction (CAI)

Computers as delivery systems have been used for a number of years; however, as personal computers become more powerful, as networks electronically link people and workstations, and as authoring systems become easier to use, CAI is seeing a rebirth. The capability of adding video, high-quality graphics, and sound are additional driving forces. "Multimedia" is a technology that integrates video, graphics, sound, text, and so forth into a CAI program (see Chapter 59).

CBT, computer-based instruction, fits into the larger category of CAI. CBT usually includes frequent, meaningful learner/instruction feedback loops in order to measure the learner's progress in achieving the objectives.

Other types of computer-assisted instruction include more informational materials, such as hypertext and hypermedia systems that allow the user to "navigate" through large amounts of information. In these systems, fewer feedback mechanisms are used. This approach is appropriate for some audiences and objectives, but not for others.

CAI is a powerful instructional tool, but it can be expensive to initially design and produce. However, a well-developed program can increase the effectiveness of the instruction, give learners more opportunity to practice or simulate, and do all of this in less time than conventional methods. On the other hand, poorly developed programs, frequently called "page turners," are nothing more than expensive, electronic books that make funny sounds and use blinking lights for no real instructional purpose.

To produce an effective, efficient CAI course, you need to work with a group of professionals who have expertise in graphic design, computer programming, and instructional design, as well as content experts. Good CAI involves almost as much art as technology. There are many examples of well-intentioned, very expensive programs that do not meet the expectations of management because of poor design and development.

If you are considering CAI, invest time looking at examples of a variety of programs, not necessarily related to your particular topic. Use some courses recommended by instructional designers and programs that have some evidence of effectiveness. After analyzing various materials, you will develop a feel for good and not-so-good programs.

Interactive video (IV)

Interactive video is related to CAI. It is another type of computer-assisted instruction that usually involves a computer as well as a laser disc player and TV monitor.

IV is powerful when matched with the proper application, such as teaching intellectual skills, certain motor skills, and in shaping attitudes. IV is also very expensive; custom applications can easily be in the six figure range. If content is stable and learner performance is critical, and if there are a number of learners, IV may be the ideal platform.

IV has typically used laser discs as the storage medium for the video material; however, new videocassette players have been introduced that use videotape, reducing the costs of development and production. Other new platforms, such as CD–I (Compact Disc–Interactive) are similar in performance to IV. Also, CD-ROMs, with "compressed" video segments can perform many of the same functions that true IV can. (See Chapter 59, Using Multimedia Technology.)

If you need to show moving images and/or outcomes of decisions, IV may be a potential delivery device. As with CAI, a multidisciplinary team is critical to achieve success.

Games

Learning can be fun; games are one way of making it so. Games are usually separated from simulations in that games do not have "serious" or real-world outcomes. Games are not as closely linked to "reality" as are simulations. A game is "an *activity* among two or more independent decision makers seeking to achieve their objectives in some *limiting context*" (Abt 1987).

The objective could be to assemble a piece of equipment; the limiting context might be in the shortest amount of time. Another example could be a game modeled after the TV program "Jeopardy," where the first learner (the limiting context) to supply the question for an answer related to cGMPs or procedures (the objective) receives points.

Games that make use of simple rules or rules that are modeled after other familiar games are best, since time does not have to be spent teaching complicated rules and tactics.

While games are fun, care must be taken so that the *game relates back to the course and lesson objectives.* If the objective is for the learner to "apply cGMP concepts," a game that emphasizes memorization is not going to get you to meet the objective.

!!!	Several pharmaceutical firms use games in the training of technical personnel. Game formats like "College Quiz Bowl" or "Wheel of Fortune" are used. One firm has different divisions complete, with the semifinal and final matches conducted at Disney World in Orlando.

Simulations

Another highly interactive approach is to use simulations. These can range from very simple "make-believe" situations to complex computer-controlled simulators such as used in the nuclear and air transport industries.

Simulations involve participants who have functional roles (e.g., FDA investigator, supervisor, customer, pharmacist). In addition, the participants are provided enough information on an issue, problem, or subject to enable them to function as professionals. Simulations are done in a risk-free setting.

As with games, simulations must have a tight connection with the objectives. Other characteristics of simulations include:

- Instructors must not help the learners "succeed."
- Mistakes are both inevitable and desirable; people learn from their mistakes. "The greater the disaster, the greater the learning."
- Providing the essential information is critical.
- A simulation does not have to attempt to re-create reality; sometimes too much reality gets in the way.
- Not all simulations produce factual answers; sometimes experiencing the process is a very important outcome.
- Simulations usually have debriefings; these periods of reflective learning help the participants really understand what happened.

Ideas for simulations include the following:

- An FDA investigator makes a facility inspection or follows up on a patient's complaint.
- A pharmaceutical product that has suddenly become associated with serious side effects, prompting an internal investigation of the product's development and its manufacture.

For more information

As you decide upon what what media to use, you may want some additional details, especially if a particular medium is new to you or your organization. The following books are focused on media and their uses, as well as how to make the best use of them.

Selecting and Developing Media for Instruction, Second Edition, by R. H. Anderson. Van Nostrand Reinhold Company, 1983.

Planning and Producing Instruction Media, Fifth Edition, by J. E. Kemp and D. K. Dayton. Harper and Row, 1985.

Instructional Media and the New Technologies of Instruction, Second Edition, by R. Heinich, M. Molenda, and J. D. Russell. John Wiley & Sons, 1985.

27

Identify Potential Instructors and Monitors

Not only is there an art in knowing a thing, but there is also a certain art in teaching it.

—Cicero

Description

If instructors help deliver or facilitate the lesson or course, develop criteria for selecting them and identify those people who meet the criteria and are available to teach. Monitors help administer self-study or CBT courses.

Why do it

Having an idea of who will serve as instructor(s) (if used in your training intervention) will help as you later develop the instructional materials and the instructor's guide. If the instructors you need are not available in your organization, you may need to develop them, re-think the instructional methods and media choices, or find professionals on the outside who can assist you. Doing this early in the process gives you the chance to explore different options since nothing has yet been developed.

Who is involved

Identifying potential instructors or monitors for the course is done by the designer with input, as needed, by potential learners, subject matter experts, and management.

Output

Upon completing this task, you will have criteria for selecting an instructor or monitor and candidates who meet the criteria. You may get as far as selecting those who will teach or help with CBT courses.

Comments

An unfortunate and derogatory description (attributed to George Bernard Shaw) has been around: "Those who can't do, teach." That is especially untrue when it comes to instructing adults. Instructing demands a large set of skills and knowledge. Sometimes, it might require the teacher to demonstrate a particular motor or intellectual skill; other times, he or she will need to have skills in facilitation or developing useful materials.

Another misconception, the flip side to the one above, is, "Those who *can* do, *can* teach." Just because someone is successful in their job or task *does not* make the person a successful instructor. Instructors need to have an interest in teaching, the skills required to transmit the information, evaluate learner performance, and offer constructive feedback.

As you design and develop a course, there are some trade-offs that can be made. For instance, if a moderate level of technical expertise is needed in a program, technical information can be provided in the instructional media (slides, video, etc.) or can be detailed in the instructor's guide.

Another way is to utilize the knowledge and skills the learners themselves already have. Maybe the learners can demonstrate and serve as experts with the instructor acting as facilitator and leader.

!!!

One healthcare firm needed to expand its pool of instructors to teach GMP programs. To do so, and also to provide job enrichment, a group of professionals was required to instruct and facilitate several different courses.

Even though the courses were well developed and the trainers had extensive instructor's notes and a "train-the-trainer" workshop, the course evaluations completed by the learners showed disappointing results. The training manager sat in on all the programs and discovered several instructors did not want to teach. Their lack of interest and enthusiasm not only was obvious to all present, but poisonous to the reputation of the courses.

Despite coaching and discussions with management, several instructors showed no real improvement. In order to improve the courses' effectiveness (and the reputation of the department), the nonperforming instructors were relieved of their teaching responsibilities.

!!!	Other situations that can lead to poorly performing instructors are a lack of recognition and having training added to an already busy schedule. There should be some motivator, recognition, or reward for the instructor. Some firms give special lunches, boxes of chocolate, umbrellas, or "executive toys" to say a special "thank you" to their instructors. Another, sometimes more powerful reward, is a note or E-mail message from a senior member of management saying, "nice job!" (Those notes and messages get saved for a *long* time!) It is hard to ask a person, already working to their limit, to take on an assignment of training that will add another five or ten hours to their workweek. When you talk with management about getting people as instructors, also indicate the possible need to rearrange some priorities.

How it is done

1) Review the outline created earlier in the design phase, as well as the instructional events, methods, and media that were chosen. What skills does a person need in order to effectively use the plan that was developed? Technical expertise? Experience in the subject matter area? Group facilitation skills? Public speaking ability and skills? If the course is self-study or uses CBT, what type of expertise would a monitor need?

2) Identify the skills, knowledge, and experience the instructor must have and what can be developed. For example, if you are teaching changeover procedures for a complex piece of equipment, you might put more emphasis on experience and motor skills, realizing you can coach someone who is interested and willing in the skills of a demonstrator and an on-the-job-trainer.

3) Consider some of the other options, such as:

- Utilizing learner expertise;
- Having an expert present for brief question and answer segments;
- Using videotape, teleconferencing, or satellite links; and
- Group exercises where the learners discover information on their own.

4) If you cannot find a match between your needs and available instructors, understand the issues (no people available, no expertise, too much time required, etc.). Revisit the choices

made for instructional methods and media and see if there are other options that can be used. (You may be surprised at how a "limitation" can result in a stronger, more effective course!)

!!!	Be realistic. There are few people available as instructors who can motivate trainees, communicate effectively, apply all appropriate regulations, coach with sensitivity, and have comprehensive knowledge of pharmaceutical manufacturing and control. If you need an instructor or facilitator with special skills, how can you help people develop them? Not only will it help meet your need, but, in many cases, it will help the other person develop personally and professionally.

Example

For the course you are developing to motivate personnel to wear the required safety equipment (refer to Table 24.5 on page 163), you wanted a vice president to speak to the learners. While you believe this is still a very good idea and he is interested in doing this, the executive's time is limited. He might not be available for all the sessions, causing scheduling problems.

Instead of having a "live" presentation, you decide on using a videotaped appearance. As you develop the concept, it could have the vice president actually walking into the area and modeling the correct behavior while he explains why it is so important to do so.

Using this method and medium, you will still effectively meet your objective based on the model for the Attitude Domain (see Table 24.1 beginning on page 156). In addition, videotape will give you a consistent message at all of your sessions, provide more flexibility in showing what is actually required, and make more cost-effective use of the executive's time.

To lead/facilitate the course, you select a supervisor who is available, well liked, and has been a strong proponent of worker health and safety.

28

Refine the Curriculum

Description Complete the arrangement of lessons and other instructional units. Identify the sequence in which the units should be taken.

Why do it Instructional units are arranged so that

- Learners complete them in a logical, systematic way;
- More advanced lessons build on knowledge and skills previously learned;
- There is no unnecessary duplication of instruction; and
- All topics presented are needed for the learner to achieve the objectives and goal (or subgoal).

Who is involved The designer is primarily involved. Content experts are used to confirm the arrangement.

Output Titles and descriptions of instructional units are written. A curriculum map or learning plan is also produced during this task.

Comments While rather simple in concept, this task is difficult to explain. In arranging the instructional units, you are making sure the learner has been provided all the knowledge and skills he or she needs to succeed in the next lesson or course.

The metaphor of a map is a good one. You are planning a trip for the learners, with movement from point to point occurring in the most expeditious way possible. You do not want to waste their time by having them return to a previous point because they forgot (to learn) something. At the same time, you do not want to plan a route with unnecessary stops that waste time. There will be some points that everyone must pass through in the same sequence; other times the travelers can make stops when they want.

Since each instructional unit was derived from the preceding one, much of the sequencing has already been accomplished in earlier design-related tasks.

How it is done

1) Write the subgoal, objectives, and topics covered for each course and its lessons on a piece of paper or index card (this makes it easier to move things around).

2) Beginning with the program goal (the destination, going back to the map analogy), work backwards, identifying the course(s), from the most advanced to the most basic.

3) Check to see that the goals and objectives can be achieved (i.e., that there are not any instructional pieces missing).

4) With a content expert or supervisor, go from the most basic to the most advanced lessons, checking the completeness and arrangement of the lessons and courses.

5) Develop a name for each unit as well as a description for the course. These will be included in learning plans, announcements, course catalogs, and so forth.

6) On a separate piece of paper draw the sequence (a flowchart) of courses a learner needs to complete. This is the curriculum map (Figure 28.1).

7) A less graphic representation of the information is a simple listing, in sequence, of the courses the learner must complete. This is called the learning plan.

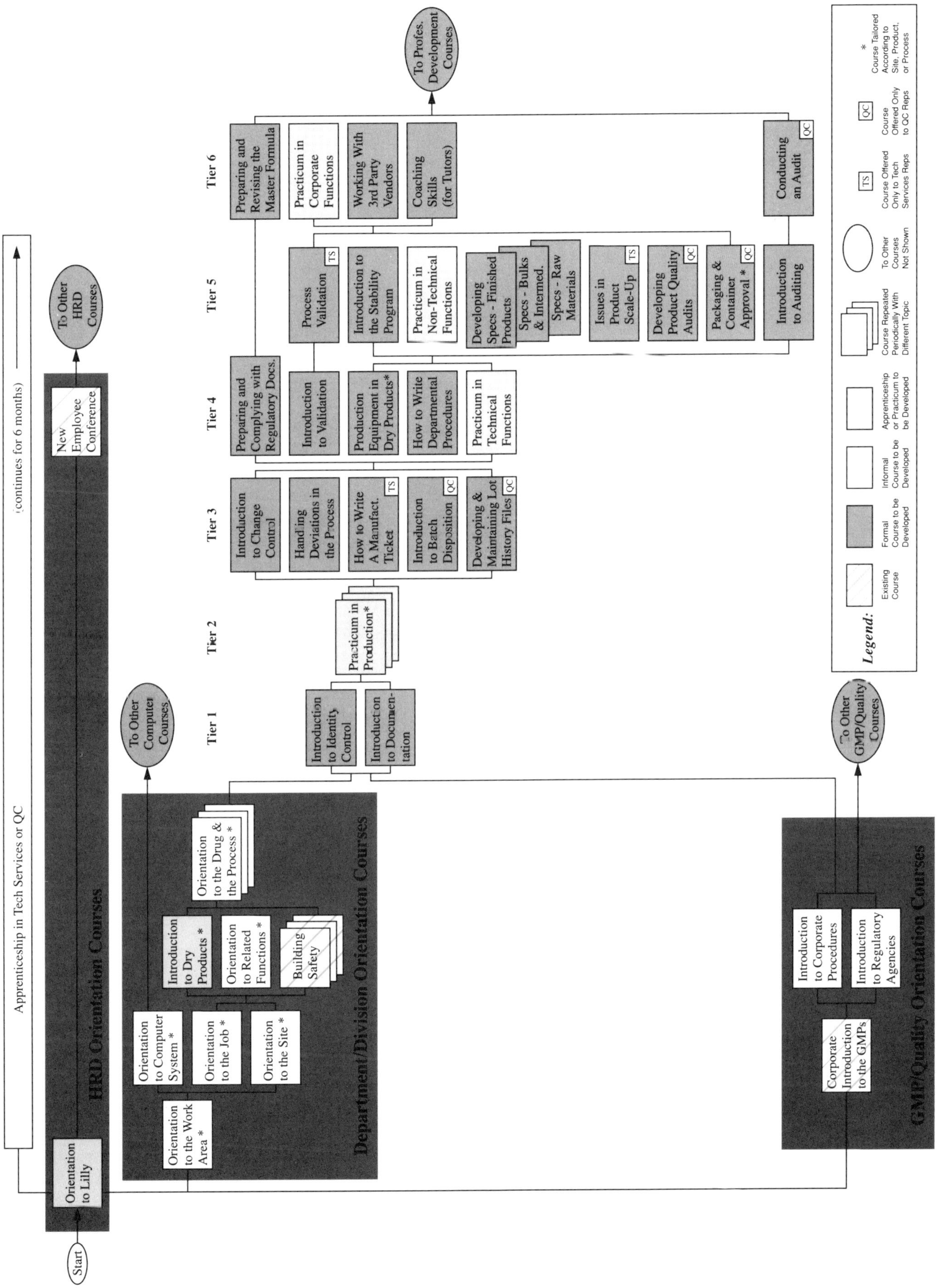
Start
Orientation to Lilly
Apprenticeship in Tech Services or QC
(continues for 6 months)
HRD Orientation Courses
New Employee Conference
To Other HRD Courses
Department/Division Orientation Courses
Orientation to the Work Area *
Orientation to Computer System *
Orientation to the Job *
Orientation to the Site *
To Other Computer Courses
Introduction to Dry Products *
Orientation to Related Functions *
Building Safety
Orientation to the Drug & the Process *
GMP/Quality Orientation Courses
Corporate Introduction to the GMPs
Introduction to Corporate Procedures
Introduction to Regulatory Agencies
To Other GMP/Quality Courses
Tier 1
Tier 2
Tier 3
Tier 4
Tier 5
Tier 6
Introduction to Identity Control
Introduction to Documentation
Practicum in Production*
Introduction to Change Control
Handling Deviations in the Process
How to Write A Manufact. Ticket
TS
Introduction to Batch Disposition
QC
Developing & Maintaining Lot History Files
QC
Preparing and Complying with Regulatory Docs.
Introduction to Validation
Production Equipment in Dry Products*
How to Write Departmental Procedures
Practicum in Technical Functions
Process Validation
TS
Introduction to the Stability Program
Practicum in Non-Technical Functions
Developing Specs - Finished Products
Specs - Bulks & Intermed.
Specs - Raw Materials
Issues in Product Scale-Up
TS
Developing Product Quality Audits
QC
Packaging & Container Approval *
QC
Introduction to Auditing
Preparing and Revising the Master Formula
Practicum in Corporate Functions
Working With 3rd Party Vendors
Coaching Skills (for Tutors)
Conducting an Audit
QC
To Profes. Development Courses
Legend:
Existing Course
Formal Course to be Developed
Informal Course to be Developed
Apprenticeship or Practicum to be Developed
Course Repeated Periodically With Different Topic
To Other Courses Not Shown
TS
Course Offered Only to Tech Services Reps
QC
Course Offered Only to QC Reps
*
Course Tailored According to Site, Product, or Process

29

Check Quality

Description

Assemble the output and decisions generated in the design phase and review for consistency, accuracy, and integrity.

Why do it

Before investing time, resources, money, and energy in actually developing the instructional content and materials, you should review the work done to this point to be sure it is correct and all of the pieces fit together. Changes and improvements can be made more easily now than when materials are in production.

Who is involved

Checking the quality involves the designer, subject matter experts, potential learners and instructors (if used), and possibly selected management. It may be very helpful to have an additional person who can provide a detached, neutral perspective.

Output

After completing the review, you will have the correct

- Program and course goals;
- Curriculum;
- Course name, description, subgoals, objectives, topics;
- Evaluation strategy;
- Section and lesson name, subgoals, objectives, topics;
- Lesson outlines with correctly sequenced instructional content and events;
- Instructional methods and media; and
- Criteria for choosing instructors.

Comments

The rationale and process used in this quality check is very much like the one done earlier in the analysis phase (Chapter 14). It gives you the opportunity to step back, look at the work done, and make any needed mid-course corrections. If you find everything is great and no changes are needed, you either have been *very* lucky or you missed something. Even experienced instructional design professionals frequently make adjustments prior to beginning the development phase.

How it is done

1) Assemble all the major pieces of output together, looking at each piece with an understanding of how it all fits together.

2) Ask questions, such as the following:

- Is there a logical flow in how the pieces move from one to another?
- Were any leaps in judgment made for which there was little data? Are the results still correct?
- Were the objectives correctly written? Are they clear?
- Are the learning domains correctly identified for each objective? Was the correct model used in developing the instructional content and events?
- Were the appropriate methods chosen? Will they support the accomplishment of the objective?
- Are the media appropriate ways to deliver the instructional content and materials? Do they fit with the restraints (budget, development time, and resources) that you must live with?
- Are instructors or monitors available? Do you know who they will be? Will any special workshops or support need to be provided? Can this be done?

3) After challenging yourself with these questions, make the appropriate changes and adjustments. Talk to others for their opinions and suggestions.

4) Review the modified design materials with a small group of other people, such as content experts and a potential learner and instructor (if used). Ask them to offer comments and suggestions. Consider all of the information provided as well as the information you have collected and analyzed. If any suggestions are incorporated into the curriculum or a course, be sure there will be no other "ripple-effects" in other parts of your design.

30

Prepare the Written Instructional Plan and Have It Approved

Description

Assemble the output and decisions generated in the design phase into one complete package and, as appropriate, have it approved by management.

Why do it

This step creates the final blueprint and specifications for what the instructional program, course, and lessons will look like. This will be the basis for the development phase that comes next.

Who is involved

The designer is primarily involved. Members of management or other sponsors of the project may be called in for their approval.

Output

You will have the approved instructional plan that includes the following:

- Program and course goals;
- Curriculum, lesson plan;
- Course name, description, subgoals, objectives, topics;
- Evaluation strategy;
- Section and lesson name, subgoals, objectives, topics;
- Lesson outlines with correctly sequenced instructional content and events;
- Instructional methods and media;
- Criteria for choosing instructors;

- A description of how it will be implemented; and
- Other relevant items or issues.

Comments

Just as engineering teams working on new facilities or equipment additions have their design manuals, so you have your instructional plan. If you have been systematic in collecting and saving data and information, preparation of this plan will neither be difficult nor time consuming.

The answer to *"how big does the plan need to be?"* depends, in part, on the size of the training intervention that has been designed. For example, if it is a relatively small program that will be delivered one time to a group, without any major expense, the written instructional plan can be very modest—a blueprint that can be used to develop the course.

On the other hand, if you have designed a major, corporate-wide training initiative with many courses, expensive media to be produced by outside vendors, and other components, the instructional plan would be significant in size.

Do what makes sense . . . write an instructional plan that will get the development phase accomplished and also meet the requirements (and expectations) of your firm's management.

Your firm may have a presentation style used for other capital-expenditure projects that you may want to model your instructional plan after.

How it is done

1) Gather the documents reviewed and modified in the previous step (Check Quality) and assemble them in one place. A three-ring binder, divided into sections is a useful, easy way to do this. (You may want two binders—one for raw data and supplemental information, and one containing design-specific information.)

2) Prepare a written plan about how the design information will be transformed, in the development phase, into a training program or course. This would include what needs to be done, who will be involved, benefits, costs, and issues.

3) If elements need to be purchased or produced (e.g., CBT, booklets, color slides, custom-made videotapes, demonstration equipment), quotes can be obtained by sending vendors the appropriate pieces of the instruction plan for use as specifications.

4) Your management (or client) may want to see a one or two page summary document describing what will be done, the benefits, costs, issues, and so forth. This could be included as an "executive summary."

Example

The analysis and design phases were completed for a firm who wanted cGMP-related training programs for their management and technical personnel (forty-five—in number). Four courses were proposed—three leader led and one CBT; the investment for the development and production is estimated to be $95,000.

Copies of the executive summary were distributed to management; an oral presentation of the business case for the course and other parts of the instructional plan's material were presented at a meeting where approval for starting the development phase was sought (and received).

An instructional plan was written. Its contents are shown in Table 30.1.

Table 30.1. Contents from a written instructional plan

I.	Executive Summary, Approval/Sign-off Sheet	page 1
II.	Introduction, Performance Need, Problem Definition, Methodology Used	3
III.	Program Goal, Benefits	6
IV.	Evaluation Strategy	8
V.	Curriculum Map	9
VI.	Course Descriptions, Goals, Objectives, Topics	10
VII.	High-Level Outlines (including instructional methods and media to be used)	13
VIII.	Estimated Production Investments, Financial Justification	17
IX.	Constraints and Issues	19
X.	Development Timeline	21
Appendices		
Appendix A.	Job Analysis Data	
Appendix B.	Task Analysis Data	
Appendix C.	Audience Characteristics Analysis	

IV

Development Phase

31

Introduction to the Development Phase

How did I get here?

In the design phase, you created an instructional plan, which is the equivalent of a blueprint and design document. This, along with some data from the analysis phase will be used in development phase.

Purposes of the development phase

You use the development phase of the instructional systems design (ISD) process to

- Produce the training intervention to specifications found in the instructional plan;
- Produce instructional materials, such as computer-based training, printed materials, videotapes, and so forth;
- Develop the methods and tools that will be used to evaluate the learner's reaction to the instruction and how well the intervention did what it was supposed to do; and
- Produce and conduct a "pilot" and collect information so the course can be improved before it is widely distributed.

What you will be doing

Figure 31.1 lists the tasks to be accomplished in the development phase.

Caution!

Depending on the size and complexity of your training intervention, this is the phase where things can get out of control very quickly. Missed deadlines can have ripple effects into other parts of the development process. This is especially true if the course being created is complex (multimedia programs, video with coordinated printed materials, etc.).

It may make sense to have someone focus on orchestrating all of the activities, for instance, naming the project administrator early on to help with the details.

Software packages are available and might be useful to help with project management tasks.

Development Phase

Task	Description	Output
1) Write detailed outline	Expand outline to include content, examples, details, methods, materials, and media.	Sequenced, detailed instructional outline
2) Sketch or storyboard visuals and other materials	Develop rough models of the final visuals and other instructional materials.	Treatments, sketches, storyboards, drawings, and the like, as needed
3) Check quality	Review the detailed outline, sketches/storyboards, and the like for completeness, accuracy, and suitability.	Reviewed and approved materials ready for further (and final) development
4) Develop lessons and activities	Obtain the detailed content to be covered and instructional activities for each lesson	Details incorporated into instructional materials
5) Develop evaluation tools	Produce tools based on the evaluation strategy selected.	Response forms, tests, questionnaires, etc.
6) Produce visuals and other instructional materials	Develop instructional materials using previously selected designs and media.	Instructional materials as earlier specified
7) Plan implementation and rollout of course	Develop the timing and logistical plan for delivering the the final course.	Course administrator selected, tentative, schedule, issues and needs
8) Prepare instructor's or monitor's manual	Produce the manual or guide that instructors use to prepare for and deliver the course.	Completed instructor's or monitor's manual
9) Conduct pilot course	Present the course to a specially selected group; obtain and utilize feedback to improve course.	Critiqued course; changes made in outline, content, materials, and the like as appropriate
10) Approve the course	Obtain approvals from designated areas.	Documented approval of course

Figure 31.1. Tasks associated with the development phase

32

Expand the Instructional Outline

Description

Expand the high-level outline (from the design phase) incorporating details of instructional content, examples, methods, materials, and media for each lesson.

Why do it

This task begins adding content depth and substance to the outlines prepared earlier. This instructional outline becomes the basis for developing materials, media, and the instructor's guide.

Who is involved

The course designer/developer performs this task, with the assistance of a subject matter expert.

Output

A detailed outline is generated listing (in sequence) the instructional event, content to be presented, the method, and materials/media used. The outline can be the basis for the an instructor's guide, with ancillary information added as necessary.

Comments

We have *finally* arrived at the point where we can start producing the lessons and the course. The investment made in the analysis and design phases starts to pay off since we have a well-founded plan on which to base development.

The amount of content the detailed outline contains depends, in part, on how much information you have available to you at this point. It may be easier to write the phrase, *History of the FDA* and then add in the appropriate dates, events, and specifics at a later time (when you develop lessons and activities). On the other hand, if you know or have access to details, it is certainly fine to include them now.

If you are preparing a CBT or multimedia-type course, the detailed outline will make the storyboarding task much easier, especially if you have established a clear goal for each instructional activity.

How it is done

1) Consult the high-level outline previously developed and the recommended models (see Table 24.1 beginning on page 156) for the learning domain of the objective.

2) Using headings as shown in the example below, go through the high-level outline, step by step and record the appropriate information under each heading. For example,

- What will the instructor (or multimedia program) do first (i.e., the instructor's activity, instruction event)?
- What is the content?
- How will this be done (tell, show, demonstrate, etc.)?
- What examples, illustrations, analogies should be used?
- What materials and media will be used?

3) Continue until the outline is complete.

Example 1

Table 32.1 shows part of the outline for an information domain objective. The high-level outline is found in Table 24.2 on page 160.

Example 2

Table 32.2 shows part of the outline for a motor skills domain objective. The-high level outline is found in Table 24.4 on page 162.

Use stories

For thousands and thousands of years, stories have been a major way of passing information between people and generations. Virtually all societies have myths that relate a person to the world in general and also to the specific group to which the person belongs. Among other things, myths have an instructional function (Campbell 1988). Myths or stories can be extremely powerful, as well as captivating to the listeners (or watchers). Consider how you can use stories to get your points across.

Stories can be used as positive examples (the way something *should* be done) or negative examples (what can happen if something is done incorrectly).

One potential source of stories are the people in your organization. You can easily find people who can tell you about "the way we used to do it" or "when Pat saved the embarrassment of a recall by questioning an odd lab result." Many firms have "legends" about their founders or key achievements. Tom Peters, the author of many books including, *In Search of Excellence*, makes use of these organizational stories.

Another source of stories, generally negative examples, are newspapers. Periodically, there is a situation in the U.S. or abroad where a product (food or pharmaceutical) is placed on the market and has a tragedy associated with it. A reference librarian can help you locate press clippings.

Teach one theme and several variations

There are times when people need to know how to respond to various situations—the situations are similar, yet different. Or, you might have a mixed group where different members of the audience need to react differently to a given stimuli or situation. A way this can be done is by teaching the basic situation and then showing the variations.

Example: theme and variations

For example, you are teaching a mixed audience of technical and management personnel the SOP describing the response to results from an environmental monitoring program. First you show the four-part basic approach:

1) Collect samples,
2) Analyze,
3) Review results, and
4) Take action.

These steps are the same in all situations. The differences come only in the *fourth* step.

First, show the learners what the differences are based on:

> *Results of the environmental monitoring can have one of three possible outcomes, as shown in Table 32.3.*

Next, take the learners through the actions associated with the most basic category (i.e., below-action range). After that is completed, go on to the next (i.e., within-action range), pointing out the differences. Continue as needed. (It may be helpful to use flowcharts as well.) Table 32.4 shows an example.

Table 32.1. Detailed lesson outline for an information domain objective

Objective: Describe the general activities of the U.S. Food and Drug Administration and how they came about.

Instructional Event and Instructor's Activity	Content	Method	Materials and Media	*Comments*
Welcome class		tell, show	Overhead transparency (OH)	*Helps to develop rapport with learners*
Describe desired outcome	course goal course objectives	tell, show	OH	*Builds motivation by showing relevance and links to job.*
Describe —agenda for session —how it will be accomplished —meeting room facilities	major topics and time instructional methods used use of participant's workbook location of coffee, restrooms	tell, show	OH	*While learners have little control over times, they can at least know what to expect and when the coffee breaks are scheduled.*
Introduce self to class	instructor's background, why he/she is involved	tell	none	*Helps establish credibility of instructor, builds rapport.*
Class members introduce themselves	include name, background, current job assignment	question, learners tell	none	*Information can help instructor choose examples, address concerns; establishes rapport within group.* *Also starts learners' involvement in session.*

Ask class, *"Why is this topic important?"*	Desired responses: — FDA regulates pharmaceutical industry — FDA protects consumers — firm must comply with regulations to remain in business	question, discussion	OH of question	*Discussion gets group involved, gives instructor a sense of group's knowledge. Establishes importance of why they are there.*
Summarize reason	(as above) basic reason: to protect *us* as consumers	tell, show	OH	*Summarizes responses; key theme is presented.*
Ask class, "*Why is this important to **me**?*"	Desired responses: — help protect our customers — protect my family who uses our products — help keep the firm in business; keep my job	question, discussion	OH of question	*Group is involved again; answers relate to* "What's in this for me?"
Summarize reasons	(as above)	tell, show	OH	*Reinforces* "What's in this for me?"
Present approach to be used	Advance organizer: What the FDA does and is now has been shaped by past problems. Looking at past events can give an understanding as to why the FDA wants to prevent similar or new tragedies from occurring.	tell, show	OH	*Advanced organizer presented; remainder of course is focused around this.*
Introduce videotape	Two sentence summary of what the videotape contains; also include tape length (time).	tell, show	OH	*Lets learners know what is coming and what to look for.*
Play videotape		tell, show	VHS videotape	*Videotape allows fast-paced, consistent view of FDA history.*

Table 32.2. Detailed lesson outline for a motor skills domain objective

Objective: Prepare clean equipment for steam autoclaving.

Instructional Event and Instructor's Activity	Content	Method	Materials and Media	*Comments*
Introduce lesson; describe desired outcome	name of lesson lesson objective demonstration of process (wrapping and identifying a valve to be autoclaved)	tell tell tell, demonstrate	use actual valve, tags, wrapping material	*Instructor is known to learner; participants all known to each other.* *Entire process is shown to learner.*
Ask, *"Why is this done?"*	Desired response: — protect product contact surfaces from particulate and microbial contaminants	ask, discuss		*Builds motivation by showing relevance and linking to job.* *Question gets learner involved; the "whys" of doing the task are explained and reinforced.*
Ask, *"What could happen if this is not done correctly?"*	Desired responses: — particulate and/or microbial contaminants could cause product to be rejected: $$$$$ lost — contaminants might affect the patient who uses the product	ask, discuss		*Question gets learner involved and also emphasizes importance of the task; starts to get at,* "What's in this for me?"
List subskills involved in the activity	List each subskill in sequence and where it is performed	tell, show	visual of flowchart	*Ties task in with entire equipment preparation process; links task with procedure (SOP)*
Show how learner starts	locations of equipment, wrapping materials, tags, log forms	tell, show	diagram of work station; examples of tags, forms	*"Starting point"; also covers when learner will do the task.*
Demonstrate subskill #1		demo		
Let learner practice, demonstrate	subskill #1	practice		

Table 32.3. Situations requiring action to be taken

Below-Action Range	Within-Action Range	Above-Action Range
Less than 10 organisms per cubic meter of air	10 to 15 organisms per cubic meter of air	More than 15 organisms per cubic meter of air

Table 32.4. Actions taken by various personnel involved in the environmental monitoring program; example of teaching a theme and variations

Below-Action Range	Within-Action Range	Above-Action Range
Less than 10 organisms per cubic meter of air	10 to 15 organisms per cubic meter of air	More than 15 organisms per cubic meter of air
QC representative:	*QC representative:*	*QC representative:*
Note on daily log: no action required (NAR). Initial and date entry.	Request immediate resampling. View data maps of results to look for time or location trends. If all data is normal, wait for next results.	Request immediate resampling. Inform QC and production management. View data maps of results to look for time and location trends. Begin immediate investigation.
QC management:	*QC management:*	*QC management:*
No actions required; review trend and historical data at end of month.	No actions required; review trend and historical data at end of month.	Review data maps. Review potential products at risk.
Production management:	*Production management:*	*Production management:*
No actions required; review trend and historical data at end of month.	No actions required; review trend and historical data at end of month.	Consider results in terms of location and potential for affecting current/ scheduled production.

33

Sketch or Storyboard Visuals and Other Materials

Description

Develop a rough model of the final visuals and other instructional materials.

Why do it

Sketching or storyboarding lets you try various ways of presenting information before spending the time and resources to actually produce them. The rough sketches can be shown to

- Subject matter experts to check for accuracy;
- Potential learners for clarity and understandability;
- Graphic artists, writers, video production personnel, and so forth for pricing and initial concepts; and
- Supervision and management for updates, funding, and the like.

Storyboarding also facilitates communication between members of the production team.

Who is involved

The course designer/developer is primarily involved. Sometimes, someone with basic graphic, drawing, or computer skills is helpful to work with.

Output

When this task is complete, you will have the following (as needed):

- Sketches of all visual materials;
- Sketches/rough layouts of instructional materials, handouts;
- Rough drawings of models, simulators;
- A "treatment" of the proposed video, multimedia solution; and
- Storyboards for the video, computer screens, and so forth.

Comments

A *treatment* is a written description of what the video (or CBT program, slide/tape, or film) will be like when developed. It is more detailed and complete than a "concept." You may start with two or three different treatments—each very different. For example, for a video on the history of the FDA, one treatment might involve a narrator giving the history while historical photos are shown. Another treatment of the same topic could have an "oral" history—interviews with people who have worked for the agency describing what they did and how it affected the public's health. A third version might take a patient's point of view as he or she considers the medication he or she is about to take and wonders "is this safe?" After having various people review the treatments, you select one for storyboarding. (You could take all three through the storyboarding process, but it will obviously take additional time and resources.)

Developing a treatment is one of the most creative aspects in a videotape or multimedia project. It helps in organizing your thoughts and provides the framework for what is to follow.

Storyboards are sketches that describe in visuals and words (as needed) what will be included in the multimedia, slide/tape, videotape, or film presentation.

As you develop the treatment and storyboard, think **visually!** Let your mind's eye describe what it sees and then sketch it using pictures or words.

Think visually first. Do not paint words, paint pictures. Use visuals to get the message across. *Then* use words to enrich or expand the meaning as necessary.

Storyboards are not *always* used. If the project is small, straightforward, simple, and involves the same production team from the start, this step might not be necessary. If the project is complex, involving a novel use of technology or creativity, or involving different people at different times, this step should be done.

There are various ways to "storyboard." For 35 mm or overhead transparencies, use a piece of paper with a box the same dimensions as your final slides. For video, a method is to use 4" by 6" cards with a box drawn to represent a TV screen.

It is important that you understand how the instructional materials will be used. If there are word-slides for an overhead projector, do you expect the instructor to use the points as an outline for his or her presentation? Are the handouts something that will be used as a reference tool? These considerations can affect how much information you will provide in these materials and how they will be produced.

If your outline calls for a discussion, case study, game, or simulation, begin to sketch it out at this point as well.

Some researchers and developers of multimedia and computer-based instruction are using the concepts and principles of game design and theater as they develop their ideas. They approach the computer as a medium and their roles as artisans rather than as software engineers (Heckel 1984).

How it is done

1) If needed, develop a treatment (for multimedia, slide/tape, video, and film projects). Use the treatment as the basis for the storyboard to follow.

2) If appropriate, create storyboards. Using a simple template, begin to sketch out the visual elements. Stick figures or rough shapes are fine. If words are to be used on the visual, add them as well. If sounds or music are involved, describe them in words as best as you can.

3) Begin to assemble the cards or individual drawings and rearrange them as needed to tell the story in a logical sequence. Keep it straightforward and simple.

4) Go back and look at the sequence. Is there something missing? Rearrange or add other cards as needed.

Other guidelines for planning and developing visuals and materials

Since the sketches and storyboards are the basis for what is to follow in the development of the instructional materials, there are some general guidelines to help the process.

Specific guidelines for the media in which you are working are found in several instructional media and technology books; three are suggested in Chapter 26 (page 189).

- *Use a variety of visuals.* If using 35 mm slides, use images of people, machines, instruments, and so forth as well as words or diagrams. (However, do not use different delivery vehicles and keep bouncing back between them [e.g., overhead slides, then 35 mm slides, then overheads, then etc.].)

- *Have a consistent look and feel.* For word slides, keep the typefaces and styles simple. If you do change typefaces on a slide, do it for a reason.
- *Do not lose people.* Show them what they are going to see (an overview or "wide-shot") before going to the specifics (a "close-up"). This is true with both written and visual information.
- *For instructor-led materials, do not duplicate on visuals the words that the person is to say.* Part of the reason in using visuals is to make use of the part of the brain that can process visual information. Use this to your advantage! If you want people to simply read, there are better ways to do this than using overheads or slides.

  (Note: In multimedia and video work where the visuals reinforce what the speaker is saying, this specific guideline is not followed. Different words may cause confusion on the part of the learner.)
- *Keep slides and visuals simple.* Do not even *try* to get everything on one screen or slide.
- *Do not place the instructor in a situation where he or she must apologize.* (For instance, "Sorry about the poor quality of this slide for you people in the back of the room, but I wanted to show this anyway . . ." [There should be a special torture for presenters who do this.])
- *Keep things interesting.*
- *Use humor and creativity, but use it correctly.* Do not try to be cute or clever with visuals, as it will frequently backfire. Be especially careful if the material will be used in another culture or country.

!!!

Use the strengths and resources you have available.

At a recent training conference, participants in a session were impressed by one pharmaceutical trainer who was gifted in cartooning. He included humorous drawings to illustrate various points in the lesson; he did so in a very effective way. The people at his site always looked forward to new programs to see what he had done.

Few of us are gifted in cartooning, but most of us have other talents and skills (some of which we discover as we get involved in training!). People in our work areas also have skills that can be used in developing materials. *Their* help can make your materials better and at the same time be personally rewarding to them.

!!!

Before asking someone to give their assistance to your venture, have a very good idea of what you are going to be getting. If not, you may be very surprised, disappointed, and be put into a delicate situation. If you are working with someone who is developing a skill, such as photography, try and find someone else who is skilled to act as a coach or mentor. In this way, the end results will be much more acceptable and satisfying to all parties involved.

For more information

- *The Visual Display of Quantitative Information* by Edward Tufte. Chesire, CT: Graphics Press, 1983.
- *Envisioning Information* by Edward Tufte. Chesire, CT: Graphics Press, 1990.

34

Check Quality

Description

Review the detailed outline and sketches/storyboards to check for completeness, accuracy, and suitability.

Why do it

Checking for completeness, accuracy, and so forth now will reduce the need for potentially time-consuming and costly changes later.

Who is involved

Checking the quality involves the developer, content experts, potential users, supervision, and possibly management.

Output

Detailed outlines, sketches, and storyboards that are approved and ready for further development.

Comments

This is the last check before "production" to be sure everything is as it should be and the way people are *expecting* it.

Expectations can be the hardest to deal with, since they are typically in one's mind. Rarely are expectations fixed or solid. It is important that the users, management, and learners talk about what they are expecting and how your sketches and storyboards meet/do not meet these expectations. Try and separate content and substantive issues from more stylistic and appearance-related ones.

Depending on the situation and organization, there can be formal sign-offs on sketches and storyboards. This is sometimes done when consultants or outside personnel are involved or if the client-group is known to make last minute changes.

How it is done

1) Identify those to be involved in the review.

2) If the materials are self-explanatory or if the people have had experience with them before (e.g., storyboards), send them out in advance for their review before the meeting.

3) At the meeting, share with the group exactly what you want to accomplish during the review session. Describe the materials and how they will be used by the learners; then go into the materials one at a time.

4) Consider the observations and comments. As hard as it may be at times, do not be defensive, but provide explanations as to why certain things were done or decisions were made.

5) Make changes as appropriate.

!!!

A pharmaceutical firm was using a consultant as they designed and developed a training course. One of the examples and analogies on the topic of probability involved playing cards.

As the material was being reviewed, several people from the firm noticed the playing card example and commented upon it. They knew a number of people at the plant had very strong religious objections to cards and gambling. Using the example might cause them to miss the point that was being made. Instead, an analogy using a box of colored beads was used.

The review unveiled a small detail that only people familiar with the organization—its culture and its people—would have seen. The change was made very simply.

35

Plan Implementation and Rollout

Description	Develop the timing and logistical plan for delivering the final course.
Why do it	Planning the details of the course delivery is the road map that will be followed. Doing it weeks before the actual implementation will simplify and smooth out the delivery process.
Who is involved	The course administrator, developer, supervision, and management.
Output	A course administrator is selected and a list of issues and needs is developed along with a tentative schedule for delivering the course.
Comments	This task can be done at almost any point concurrent with other development activities.

The administrative functions of "rolling out" a course to the learners can be simple for a relatively small course to extremely complex for a corporate-wide program.

Chances are, your organization has methods in place for employee meetings (i.e., United Way fund drives, employee benefit meetings, financial reviews, etc.). Understand how these events are accomplished and arranged. You might find a model you could copy, or even a mechanism already in place for accomplishing the rollout tasks.

!!!	Two of the biggest complaints line supervision and trainers have about "corporate" training programs are 1) they are informed about them very late in the process, and 2) corporate expectations are unrealistic. If you are a supplier of a course that is to be used by others outside of your immediate area, let the management in the affected areas know as early as possible. Be clear and realistic about your expectations (Do they supply the instructors? When is course delivery to be completed? Are they required to schedule personnel, etc.). Show the area management how you have (hopefully) built the area into the program during the analysis, design, and development stages. Any ownership of the program and benefits you can share with the area will help to reduce possible friction and stress. There should be no big surprises for anyone at this point. Management should have been informed at earlier review and approval meetings about what will soon be occurring.

How it is done

1) Identify and select a course administrator. This is the person who will be called in the event something goes wrong (e.g., a CBT program has disappeared from the computer network, an instructor gets sick, or the workbooks are missing). It might be helpful for this person to be a qualified instructor who could step in at the last minute should an emergency arise. The course administrator should also have a complete set of instructional materials available in the event a set gets misplaced or lost. One of the key criteria in identifying an administrator is his or her ability to remain calm and be flexible in stressful situations.

2) Review and confirm the validity of the decisions made in the task, "Identify Potential Instructors and Monitors" (Chapter 27).

3) Define the completion goal. When will the first program begin? When should the last person or group have completed the course?

4) Are there any "pre-events" that need to happen? Will you send out letters to participants (from an executive) requesting their attendance? Will posters or announcements be distributed? Are people comfortable enough with computers or will you need to do something in advance of implementing a CBT course?

5) Do a reality check. Can the implementation schedule really be done? Is there delivery equipment (e.g., computers, video equipment) available? Are there facilities and instructors available to meet the goal? Will all the instructional materials be ready on time? Do supervision and management understand the impact this will have on their production or operation schedules?

6) Tentatively set the dates of the course, taking into account any special production, maintenance, holiday, and vacation periods. (Also consider school holidays and breaks, as this is a prime time for families to vacation.) Share this with appropriate levels of supervision and management for their approval.

7) Based on the methods, media, and instructional materials used, go through each element and see what needs to be scheduled, arranged for, obtained, and so on. Check availability based on the tentative schedule. Items to check include the following:

- Meeting rooms and facilities;
- Room set-up;
- Instructors and backup instructors;
- Computer or multimedia equipment;
- Course monitors for CBT or self-study programs;
- Duplication of materials;
- Delivery of materials;
- Audiovisual equipment, models, and so forth; and
- Learners who will be present.

8) Develop a written plan with the schedule for how the program will be accomplished. Be sure all involved know and agree to their responsibilities.

> *!!!*
>
> One pharmaceutical firm has groups that design, develop, and deliver courses on various subjects (cGMPs, EPA, etc.) and one centralized group that schedules and administers the courses. This central group acts as a "booking agent" (setting up the dates, arranging for instructors, materials, etc.). The central group then works with local departments and assigns seats to the participants. For some programs, the central group is also in charge of documenting participation.

36

Develop Lessons and Activities

Writing comes more easily if you have something to say.
—Sholem Asch

Description	Obtain the content to be covered and the instructional activities for each lesson.
Why do it	Content information is passed on to others (instructors, writers, computer programers, etc.) who will add value to it in the way it is presented and delivered.
Who is involved	The course developer and content experts are involved in this task. Others who will be using the information may be involved to ensure that it is in the required format.
Output	The output depends on the media used to deliver the instruction. For leader-led instruction, a written document of some type is produced in this task; the instructional materials that are used will determine the specific format. It may be an expanded outline or an instructor's guide and associated handout materials. Other content information may be supplied to video script writers or computer programmers.
Comments	As mentioned earlier, the task of developing the detailed outline (Chapter 32) and this task sometimes blend together. The important thing is that the instructional content, activities, methods, and materials are complete.

The detail to which the content is expanded and written down depends, in part, on how course will be delivered. If the instructors are used who are experts in the field, less content detail needs to be provided than if a less-experienced person is presenting the content. Depending on the methods used, however, you may need to provide significant information (and training) on the activities, and so forth.

In a CBT or multimedia course, content is supplied based on the needs of the programmer, animator, and other technical personnel. Sometimes, content may be in the form of rough drawings or slides and images, or may be electronically supplied as text.

How it is done (leader-led)

1) Review the detailed course outline and, in particular, the "content" and "methods" column.

2) Understand the level of skills and knowledge current and future instructors will have and what you need to provide.

3) Consult the appropriate content expert and other resources for additional information.

4) If there are specific activities (such as discussions, games, simulations, case studies, etc.), provide the required content and instructions to the instructor and participants. Write the case and instructions for use by the participants.

How it is done (other information users)

1) Understand the requirements and needs of other information users. For example, a computer graphics animator may need to see drawings or photos of a laminar-flow hood and how it works in order to make a computer animation of it.

2) Consult the appropriate content experts or sources for the information; present it in the appropriate format.

Scripting alternative

Another approach in putting the content together is to first develop a script of what an instructor might say. You could extract key points from it or instructors could be furnished the script or a condensed version of it (such as a detailed outline, etc.). If you have taught the course in the past, this approach can be a helpful way in giving the details to others.

A drawback of the script method is that some instructors may use it entirely, reading from it, without adding any of their own experiences or perspectives. In certain situations this may be desired, but frequently it will result in a very dead, boring presentation that sounds stilted (since it was not written with the speaker's speech pattern in mind).

Example 1

Table 36.1 shows an expanded content outline for a previously-used information domain objective.

Example 2

Table 36.2 shows parts of the same example as above, with an instructor's script included.

Table 36.1. Expanded content in a detailed lesson outline (information domain objective)

Objective: Describe the general activities of the U.S. Food and Drug Administration and how they came about.

Instructional Event and Instructor's Activity	Expanded Content	Method	Materials and Media
Welcome class		tell, show	Overhead transparency (OH)
Describe desired outcome	• Course goal: *Participants will be able to describe why and how the FDA regulates the pharmaceutical industry.* • Objective: *Describe the general activities of the U.S. Food and Drug Administration and how they came about.*	tell, show	OH
Describe —agenda for session —how it will be accomplished —meeting room facilities	• Major topics and time *—Introduction: Why do we need to know this? (10 min)* *—A Historical Look at the FDA (video, 15 min)* *—Discussion of the video (10 min)* *—Individual exercise (10 min)* *—Small group exercise (15 min)* *—Large group discussion (20 min)* *—Summary/evaluation (10 min)* • Instructional methods used —presentation —video —exercises —discussion —worksheets, handouts • Use of participant's workbook *—Binder can be used to store materials from other courses.* *—Encourage learners to share this information with families as it helps explain why pharmaceutical industry is very different from other industries.* • Location of coffee, restrooms *—varies with training facility*	tell, show	OH
Introduce self to class	Instructor's background, why he/she is involved *—varies with instructor, but include points such as:* • *Years with company,* • *Current assignment, and* • *Why I believe this topic is critical to the organization.*	tell	none

Table 36.2. Detailed outline including instructor script (information domain objective)

Objective: Describe the general activities of the U.S. Food and Drug Administration and how they came about.

Instructional Event and Instructor's Activity	Expanded Content	Instructor's Script
Welcome class		Good morning (as appropriate) and welcome to a new course that has been developed entitled *FDA Basics*. It is being presented to all personnel as part of our firm's commitment to assuring that all of our products are made according to the requirements.
Describe desired outcome	Course goal *Participants will be able to describe why and how the FDA regulates the pharmaceutical industry.* Objective *Describe the general activities of the U.S. Food and Drug Administration and how they came about.*	To better understand the requirements we have, it might be good to know why they are there and who "put" them there. Therefore, the goal of this course is for you to be able to describe how the FDA regulates the pharmaceutical industry. More specifically, when you are finished with today's 90-minute lesson, you should be able to describe the general activities of the U.S. Food and Drug Administration and how they came about.
Describe — agenda for session — how it will be accomplished — meeting room facilities	• Major topics and time *—Introduction: Why do we need to know this? (10 min)* *—A Historical Look at the FDA (video, 15 min)* *—Discussion of the video (10 min)* *—Individual exercise (10 min)* *—Small group exercise (15 min)* *—Large group discussion (20 min)* *—Summary/evaluation (10 min)* • Instructional methods used —presentation —video —exercises —discussion —worksheets, handouts • Use of participant's workbook *—Binder can be used to store materials from other courses.* *—Encourage learners to share this information with families as it helps explain why the pharmaceutical industry is very different from other industries.* • Location of coffee, restrooms *—varies with training facility*	In the next hour and one-half, we are going to be covering topics such as —why do we need to know this? — a historical look at the FDA that includes a fifteen-minute videotape; Etc.

37

Develop Evaluation Methods and Tools

Description — Develop the specific techniques and tools called for by the evaluation strategy to evaluate the training intervention.

Why do it — This task produces the tools used to evaluate the training.

Who is involved — The course designer/developer is primarily involved, along with subject matter experts and supervision.

Output — Tools used to evaluate the training, such as evaluation forms, tests, performance checklists, and surveys.

Comments — In the design phase decisions were made as to the strategy for evaluating how trainees respond to the instruction, how much they learned, how they are performing on the job, and how well the training intervention accomplished specific organizational goals. In this task you will develop the tools used to answer these questions.

Books have been written on developing testing and evaluation instruments; several are referred to at the end of this chapter.

But is it validated? In training evaluation, as in drug and device manufacturing, validation has a role. Here, validation means, *"Does the evaluation tool measure what it is supposed to measure?"* This is usually applied more to "tests" than to other evaluation methods.

Caution! — It is important that the evaluation tool does what you intend it to do. This is *critical* if you are using the tool as the basis for making a personnel-related decision. If a person's status (promotion/demotion), job position, and/or salary depend on what the test results are, you must be very careful in how the test is constructed and how it links the instruction to the actual requirements of the job.

If testing is used more for coaching, so that the person can perform better, or to improve the instruction, validation is not as critical.

If testing or evaluation are new to your organization or it has job/status/money implications, discuss this with human resource people and management before implementing it.

Types of methods

While there are a variety of evaluation methods, some are better used with certain evaluation levels than others. Examples of various methods and a discussion of their use are provided for each of the four evaluation levels. (Also see Chapter 23.)

Level I (trainee reaction)

Suggested methods include

- Interviews,
- Debriefing sessions, and
- Questionnaires.

In using reaction methods, it is important to obtain the information as soon as possible—while it is still fresh in the minds of the participants. Do not ask learners to mail forms back to you—you will be disappointed with the lack of results (few forms are returned after the fact).

Keep the questions as brief as possible; interviews or questionnaires that take a long time to complete are not appreciated by those just having finished a day-long program.

Sometimes it is helpful to have several short questionnaires (i.e., specific to one lesson) for use when the lesson is completed.

Some professionals are very critical of questionnaires, calling them "smile sheets." If the proper questions are asked, they are extremely useful, especially in improving a course.

Items like

- "Were the refreshments: Good? Not good? Adequate?"
- "The room was (circle one): too hot, too cold, just right."

will give you responses like that of the fairy tale, "The Three Bears": one-third, one-third, and one-third. This might be good information about the facility you are using, but says nothing about the instructional aspects of the course.

Table 37.1 is an example of a trainee reaction evaluation form used for a one-day workshop.

Level II (trainee learning)

Suggested methods include the following:

- Written tests,
- Oral test/discussion,
- Activity integrated into computer-assisted instruction,
- Simulation, and
- Demonstration.

The larger the difference between the evaluation tool and what the learner actually does on the job, the more knowledge and the fewer skills measured. For instance, if mechanics are asked in a paper test to sequence the activities in changing over a filling machine, you are looking at the *knowledge* they have, not their skills in actually changing over the equipment. If you ask a mechanic to demonstrate a change-over, he or she will incorporate the sequence knowledge as a part of demonstrating the skills.

Knowledge tests (and examples) include the following:

- Essay or open answer *(Describe why validation is important.)*;
- Short answer *(Significantly reducing the biological burden in a room or on equipment is called ___________ .)*;
- True/false, also called "binary tests" *(When reviewing validation protocols, the first step is knowing the criteria for approval. [True or False].)*; and
- Multiple choice *(The correct speed for running the in-line vial washer/sterilizer is: a) manufacturer's recommendation; b) within the validated range; c) below the validated range; d) dependent on production requirements.)*.

Skill or competency tests that can be a part of simulations or demonstrations include the following:

- Following a procedure (An observer watches the person perform according to a written procedure; variations are noted.);

Table 37.1. Example of trainee reaction evaluation form

Workshop Evaluation

Your feedback and comments play an important role in helping the instructor meet your needs for high quality instruction. We would appreciate your taking a few minutes to evaluate the workshop, the instructor, and the materials.

For each of the statements below, use the following scale. Rate each statement according to your level of agreement by circling the appropriate response. Use the space below each statement to add any comments.

SD	**D**	**N**	**A**	**SA**
Strongly Disagree	Disagree	Neutral	Agree	Strongly Agree

Instructional Methods and Materials

SD	**D**	**N**	**A**	**SA**	1.	The workshop accurately reflects the current Good Manufacturing Practice regulations (cGMPs).
SD	**D**	**N**	**A**	**SA**	2.	This workshop was a useful way for me to learn FDA- and cGMP-related information.
SD	**D**	**N**	**A**	**SA**	3.	The sections in the workshop were well organized and presented in a logical manner.
SD	**D**	**N**	**A**	**SA**	4.	The graphic design was effective in reinforcing the subject material.
SD	**D**	**N**	**A**	**SA**	5.	The workshop made good use of a variety of ways to present information.
SD	**D**	**N**	**A**	**SA**	6.	The pace of the instruction was about right for me.
SD	**D**	**N**	**A**	**SA**	7.	The instructor added value to the information and the way it was presented.

Content

SD	**D**	**N**	**A**	**SA**	1.	As near as I can tell, the content of the workshop was technically accurate and complete.
SD	**D**	**N**	**A**	**SA**	2.	The sequence of the content was logical and well organized.
SD	**D**	**N**	**A**	**SA**	3.	The workshop covered the aspects of the subject that were most important to me.
SD	**D**	**N**	**A**	**SA**	4.	The workshop contained information I can take and apply back at my job.
SD	**D**	**N**	**A**	**SA**	5.	I felt the instructor had knowledge, expertise, and competence in the field.

General

SD	**D**	**N**	**A**	**SA**	1	The environment and interpersonal atmosphere were conducive to learning.
SD	**D**	**N**	**A**	**SA**	2.	I feel I have learned enough to begin applying the concepts covered by the material in my job.
SD	**D**	**N**	**A**	**SA**	3.	I would recommend this workshop to others.
SD	**D**	**N**	**A**	**SA**	4.	This workshop met my expectations.
SD	**D**	**N**	**A**	**SA**	5.	This workshop was a good investment for **me** as a professional.

Additional Comments

1. Overall, I would rate this workshop as ____ (please circle your response below):

excellent • good • ok • fair • poor

2. Compared to ***other*** training programs and workshops I have attended, I would rate this program as ___________ (please circle your response below):

one of the best • better • about the same • worse • bottom of the barrel

3. What I liked ***most*** in this workshop was/were:

4. What I liked ***least*** in this workshop was/were:

5. The program could be made better ***if:***

6. One last thing I want to say is:

(This example evaluation form includes questions used by Charter Performance and Cara Corporation.)

- Performance checklist (Specific actions that should occur are listed; observer notes if the person did or did not do the action. Other checklists consider if the person's action was effective, not effective, or a missed opportunity. [An example is shown in Table 37.2.]);
- Performance rating scale (Specific actions are listed, with each denoting a level of competence. Observers watch for the performance and note it on the scale.); and
- Performance frequency rating form (Specific actions are listed; the observer looks for the action and counts how many times it occurred. [An example is shown in Table 37.3.]).

Matching the test to the objective

There are some general guidelines for selecting the type of test to use based on the learning domain that is associated with the objective (Cranton 1989).

- *Information domain (facts, knowledge)*

  For evaluating basic knowledge, comprehension, and application of the information, multiple choice,

Table 37.2. Example of a performance checklist

Task: Preparation of equipment for sterilization

Procedure(s) covered:

4952.1 (Equipment preparation),
789.0 (Autoclave rack loading).

YES	NO	PERFORMANCE
		Operator wears nonparticle shedding garment, latex surgical gloves, and hair covering.
		All valves, parts, and other items are removed from the ultrasonic washer and placed directly on the HEPA filter-protected workbench.
		Operator wraps contact surfaces with bioshield paper; secures with autoclave-sensitive tape or tag.
		Operator secures appropriate barcode tag to item.
		Operator continues wrapping, identifying all items.
		Operator places items on autoclave rack according to standard loading configuration.
		Operator follows clean-room practice throughout the task.

Operational associate performing task:____________________

Reviewer (name, initials, date): ____________ ______ ________

Table 37.3. Example of performance frequency rating form

(This form is used to evaluate the "sample batch record" the learner completes at the end of the instructional course.)

Task: Proper documentation practices

Procedure(s) covered:

SOP 843.1 (Documentation techniques)

Description of Item	Frequency of Occurrence
Entry is illegible.	
Entry is unclear as to meaning.	
Entry is not complete.	
Entry is not properly signed or initialed and dated.	
Entry does not use correct date format.	
"Notes" are not correctly placed and referenced.	
Error is not corrected properly.	
Entry is not verified by supervisor.	

Operational associate performing task:______________________________

Reviewer (name, initials, date): ________ ________ ________ ________

true/false, matching, and short answer tests are appropriate.

For evaluating the learner's use of the information, oral and essay tests are appropriate.

- *Intellectual skills (applying principles or rules, identifying differences, using certain procedures)*

  Multiple choice, true/false, matching, and short answer are usually appropriate; in some cases essay or oral tests and anecdotal evaluation (i.e., "This is what I did in a certain situation . . . ") are appropriate. For intellectual skills that can be observed, simulations or demonstrations are appropriate.

- *Motor skills*

  Written tests are *not* appropriate. Oral tests and anecdotal evaluation generally are appropriate.

Whenever possible, learners should perform in a simulation or demonstration.

- Attitudes

  To test if the learner has simply received (heard) the information, multiple choice and short answer tests are most appropriate. To evaluate if the learner is using the attitudes and incorporating them into his or her work, essay tests, oral tests, and anecdotal evaluations are most appropriate.

Level III (trainee performance)

Evaluation methods for this level are more complicated, because you are seeing not only the effects of training but also if the work environment supports the use of the knowledge and skills. Performance is best evaluated three to six months after the training intervention has been completed (Robinson and Robinson 1989).

You can conduct the evaluations at this level on individuals or on groups.

Ways to make the evaluations and resulting data more useful are as follows:

- Closely linking the evaluation to the program goals;
- Involving learners, supervision, and management;
- Focusing the questions or other tools very sharply to get specific information; and
- Collecting baseline or pretraining data to help show the change.

Suggested methods (and examples) include

- Direct observation *(Are service personnel cleaning the area as instructed?);*
- Performance indicators *(How many documentation mistakes are being made on each batch record?);*
- "Customer" interviews/questionnaires *(Are you receiving information or materials with fewer errors?);* and
- Supervision interviews/questionnaires *(Are fewer deviation notifications being recorded?).*

It is very useful to be able to make comparisons (that can be attributed to training) such as

- Trained versus nontrained groups, and
- Pretraining results versus post-training results.

Checklists, questionnaires, and evaluation forms make the gathering of data faster and more consistent.

Level IV (organizational results)

Measuring for organizational and business results is very closely tied to the original need and program goal. If the goal was specific and measurable, doing the Level IV evaluation is not difficult.

The methods and tools used for this level of evaluation are very specific to the goal and the organization.

Example

You are developing methods and tools for a Level IV evaluation of the example shown in Chapter 23.

The financial analyst for the division provides you with the number of lab tests, rejections, and work-in-process inventory related to having a batch of a product exceed a certain amount of time out of the chillroom. You also calculate the amount of time (and the hourly rate charge) of technical and management personnel to discuss a given deviation.

One year after the training intervention was completed, you analyze the numbers for the two years before the program and the year after.

Figure 37.1 shows the results that you share with all the people in the area and management.

For more information

- *Planning Instruction for Adult Learners* by P. Cranton. Toronto: Wall & Thompson, 1989. (Contains a good concise section on preparing tests.)
- *Training for Impact: How to Link Training to Business Needs and Measure the Results* by D. G. Robinson and J. C. Robinson. San Francisco: Jossey-Bass Publishers, 1989.
- *Measuring Instructional Results (or Got a Match?) Second Edition* by Robert F. Mager. Belmont, CA: Lake Publishing Co., 1984.

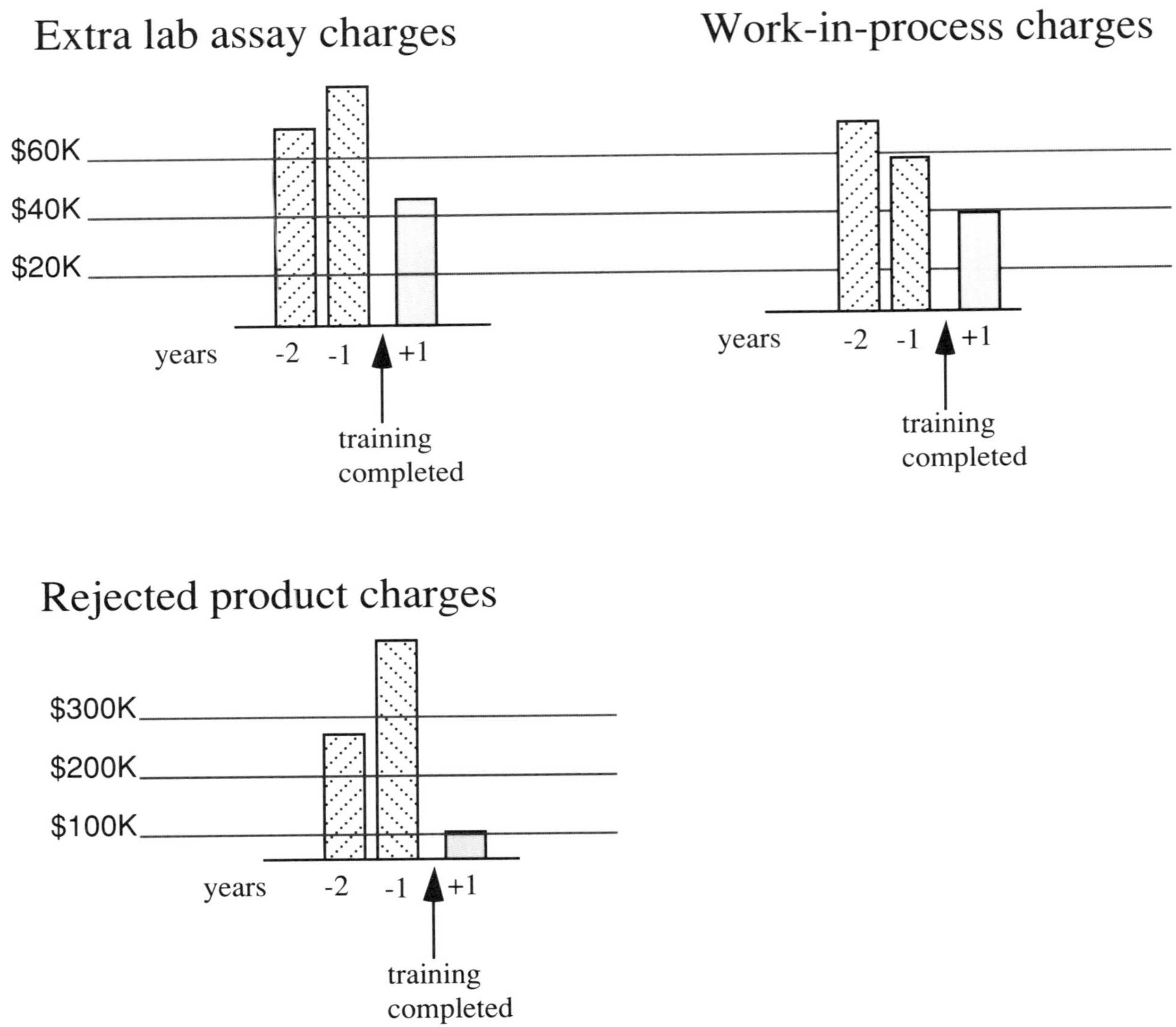

Figure 37.1. Example, results of Level IV evaluation—cost savings

38

Produce Visuals and Other Instructional Materials

Description	Develop the instructional materials using the content and the selected instructional designs and media.
Why do it	Producing the instructional materials implements the design and the methods and media selections made earlier in the process.
Who is involved	The course developer, along with specialists, are involved in the production activities. Subject matter experts and management may provide additional content and reviews/approvals as needed. Potential learners may be used in critiquing CBT screens and navigation systems.
Output	Instructional materials as specified in the design and development phases.
Comments	During this task, you see the outcomes of the investment you made in the analysis and design phases. Ideas take form and can be viewed and touched. If a detailed, careful job was done earlier, this task will not be difficult. However, if shortcuts were taken and earlier decisions were made without care and thought, this task can be frustrating—your vision will not match the reality unfolding during the production activities.

Other comments about specific media are found in Chapter 26.

Specialists and consultants can be very useful in helping produce the instructional materials you have specified. Their skills, talent, and experience can simplify and make an ordinary slide or handout something special.

For some things, such as video, self-paced workbooks, and computer-assisted training, experienced specialists are a necessity to get the most out of the media.

Instructional media must deliver content, but almost as important is the *way* it does it. If you are trying to deliver content on the topic of quality and its importance to your organization, the materials and media used need to "say" quality. If not, learners will sense a discrepancy. If an instructional program on documentation techniques contains materials that are unclear and errors, you are not modeling the performance you expect from your learners. "The message is the media."

WARNING: USE OF COPYRIGHTED MATERIALS

While most professionals have some knowledge and experience of copyright restrictions on using printed materials, such as photocopied book chapters, articles, and so forth, similar restrictions exist for other forms of intellectual property. This includes musical recordings, photos, videotaped content, and cartoons. While desktop publishing and computerized multimedia technologies give users the ability to do great and exciting things, using images, sounds, and content without the written permission of their owner puts the developer, producer, and firm at risk.

When you and your legal staff start to obtain copyright permissions, some issues to consider include the following:

- Know what rights you are buying. Be sure you have the appropriate permissions to use the material as necessary (i.e., the rights to edit, copy, display publicly, use in educational video, use in broadcast video, etc. all need to be specified.);
- Famous images may need to be licensed. Photo, video, and sound recordings of some individuals (e.g., athletes, TV/film personalities, and other public figures), either living or dead may be owned by others; and
- Things can get complicated. In order to properly use a selection of music from a current popular CD, you need to consider a variety of licenses (e.g., when cuing music to film, you need a "synch" license) and copyrights (e.g., music, lyrics, performers). Persistence, time, patience, and good counsel are required.

"Clip art," "clip photos," and "clip sounds" that are available on diskettes or on CD-ROM provide the purchaser a license to use those images or sounds in certain ways. Some sources do not allow you to incorporate the material and then resell it to someone else. Some "clip" products have broader usage licenses than others. As mentioned above, know what you are buying.

There are several "fair use" provisions in the current copyright law for educational uses. Again, talk to your legal department for their counsel.

Another source for obtaining images (such as photos, slides, drawings, etc.), is from your firm's marketing or public relations department. Many organizations have large collections of slides that not only have historical significance, but have high visual appeal and impact. Using photos of the "good old days" compared to the state-of-the-art can be a dramatic illustration of *current* good manufacturing practices.

In any case, when it concerns copyright and licensing, often the simplest and safest route is to create as many of your own images and sounds as possible.

How it is done

1) For details on how to develop materials in a specific media (i.e., overhead transparencies, handouts, or case studies), suggested references are provided at the end of this chapter. Use them as guidelines, deviating if there is a justifiable reason (and a good alternative).

2) An important aspect in developing different instructional materials is for them to be integrated and cohesive. Every instructional element you use should support the others, such as using handouts with the same definitions or drawings used in a video, or models to 35 mm slides. Some comments, suggestions, and caveats regarding material development are included below for selected items.

Visuals: Flip charts

These poster-sized pads of newsprint are cheap, easy, and handy to use for recording the results of group exercises, issues, and making fast diagrams. While good quality drawings and writings can be done on flip charts, they do not travel well or standup to repeated use when compared to other media.

If using flip charts anywhere besides a small room, lettering or drawing size and pen color are critical. Experiment and test different combinations in the room you will use. Then, based on your findings, use the best colors and sizes.

Overhead transparencies and 35 mm slides

Expensive equipment and high-level artistic skills are no longer requirements to produce good looking overheads and slides, thanks to desktop computers. Application programs, such as Microsoft's POWER POINT, Aldus' PERSUASION, and HARVARD GRAPHICS, provide examples and templates that a new user can effectively use. Overhead transparencies, when used directly by the instructor give a more "intimate" feel than 35 mm slides. On the other hand, 35 mm slides can be used for larger audiences and tend to look more professional.

The new generation of color printers can add an extra dimension to overhead transparencies. The cost, while expensive, is continuing to come down. In-house or outside service bureaus frequently have color equipment.

As with typefaces, keep colors simple and direct. Your firm may have a style guide for slides and transparencies that you need to follow. Alternatively, adopt one of the templates found in the presentation software you use.

Adding other images to slides and transparencies is much easier now with "clip-art" and desktop scanners available. Again, service bureaus can help with this.

Models

Models of facilities can be useful in showing locations and relationships between equipment, zones of cleanliness, and so on. Equipment models can be very helpful in explaining equipment, how things work, things to be careful of (e.g., safety hazards), and the like. Simple models, such as gear and belt assemblies to show "pinch points" for safety training, can be made by maintenance and crafts personnel; more complex models of equipment are sometimes available from the equipment manufacturers.

Video

If you are using either live or taped video as an instructional medium, understand the audience characteristics and the message you want learners to leave with. The quality of the video used is related to these. For instance, if you are giving a large number of people information and are shaping attitudes about quality and the importance of cGMPs, a well-made, high-quality video is congruous with this goal. Using a poorly made, rambling video is not, because it will not reinforce the message you are trying to get across to the learners.

On the other hand, if you are wanting to show a cleaning procedure or how to assemble a piece of equipment to a small number of workers, a low-budget, simply edited videotape can be justified.

Sometimes, management believes giving a video camera and recorder to someone will start the flow of many effective training videotapes. (That same logic would say that giving a concert grand piano to anyone would allow them to play like Vladimir Horowitz, Oscar Peterson, or Elton John.) Using video effectively takes experience, skill, and talent.

If you need to develop a video segment, work with someone who has done good work in the past. You may have access to an in-house video group or, video production firms. When deciding between in-house and outside vendors, check their quality as well as their price and delivery time. You may find that going outside your firm makes sense.

In choosing a video team, key people to consider are the writer, the director, and the producer. You will discover teams who frequently work together. Make sure the one you select feels "comfortable" to you and is willing to work *with* you, making use of the information you have gathered in the analysis and design phases. Find a group with experience in *instructional* videotape, not just a firm that does great commercials or "corporate image" programs. Your goal is not a "slick" finished product, but one that is a good looking, *effective* element in your instructional program. Most writers, directors, and producers will have demonstration tapes or "reels" showing examples of their work. Take a look at these to see if they have done work that matches your expectations.

A close working relationship between all parties involved is needed for the project to go smoothly and be within time and budget constraints. Work on eliminating any mistakes or changes *before* they happen. Mistakes not noticed until the final product is finished are difficult and costly to correct.

If there are sections in the videotape that might change, let the director and producer know this in advance, as he or she can edit the video and audio segments in such a way to make future changes easier.

Sometimes a "rough-cut," which is a video "draft," can be created that shows all the content but without smooth edits and transitions. This can be shown to content experts and management for their review and approval before the final version is created. There is typically an additional fee for this, but in some cases, it may be worth it. (Some of the new desktop video systems are capable of generating a "rough-cut" tape and an edit decision list used for editing the final version on high-quality equipment.)

If you require a video to show a procedure or the details of doing a task, and don't have any money in your budget, find a colleague or friend with some video experience. "How to" books are available on video production, as are workshops and continuing education courses.

If you need "stock" footage, such as video of the firm's buildings and products, contact your corporate public relations group or marketing department, as they might have such footage available.

New technology is being rapidly introduced to make desktop video editing and production as readily available as desktop publishing. Personal computers like the Macintosh or DOS machines with special software and hardware, and the Videotoaster are capable of producing moderate quality VHS tapes using VHS or 8 mm video as source material. However, someone with skill and experience is still needed to help you get the most out your investment.

Video is expensive to do. If you choose it based on a thorough needs analysis and good design criteria, it is fairly easy to justify, especially if large numbers of learners are involved. Video does not have to be long to be effective. In fact, the opposite is true. A well-made, eight to ten minute program will be received better than a twenty-five-minute rambling one.

Printed materials: Handouts, workbooks, and reference materials

Some groups of learners feel more comfortable when they have something they can write on and take away from the instructional event. Consider how the printed materials will be used during the session as well as afterwards. Strive for simplicity and consistency of look, content, and illustrations in the handouts and reference materials used.

Your organization might have a standard format that is used for printed materials. Using this format might be a requirement; however, be sure that it makes sense from *instructional* viewpoint.

A way to get people involved is through "active note taking," where handouts are given with only limited information included. It is up to the learner to add words or diagrams.

Some audiences find this helpful, others find it distracting; this could be based on the learner's past experiences and/or the culture of the organization. You may want to experiment in using active note taking in a segment of the instruction.

Reference tools or job aides can be helpful in accessing information, or in prompting intellectual or motor skill tasks; they may be called for based on the task analysis. For example, a small, laminated card with the sequence of commands for accessing computerized data can be used by learners when they go back to their jobs. Care must be taken if the job aide is linked to a cGMP-related procedure so that it is kept current and consistent with the approved procedure.

Self-study materials

In producing a self-study workbook or text (sometimes called "programmed instruction"), it is very helpful and important to work with someone who has recent experience in so doing. Effectively sequencing and gradually building on information already presented requires skill at writing such materials.

Self-study materials can be also be used in small group settings, such as staff or team meetings and in conjunction with videos or discussions.

Instructor-learner tutoring and checklists

One-on-one or one-on-several can be an effective way to coach learners on intellectual and motor skills. The instructor could be almost anyone who is an "expert" in the job and who can properly provide feedback to the learner.

Having a checklist that clearly lists performance criteria can help the learner focus on what he or she needs to do and also assist the instructor identify criteria for success.

Computer-assisted instruction

This general category includes computer-based training (CBT) and interactive video (IV) delivered on a variety of "platforms" (i.e., such as mainframe computers, microcomputers or desktop computers, learning workstations with laser disc players, etc.). Multimedia technology is also included in this category, except it is almost always delivered using personal computers or workstations capable of displaying high quality graphics, video, and sound.

Instructional courses using these tools are initially expensive and time consuming to produce, but have cost savings potential over the long-term. Experienced developers, graphic and video specialists, and programmers are essential in creating an effective program. The comments mentioned earlier in regard to choosing a video team apply for this medium as well.

Application programs such as Claris's HYPERCARD and EduQuest's LINKWAY LIVE can be used to rapidly prototype instruction and develop a product. You may want to experiment with these tools, get feedback from potential users (and management), and then develop a more refined version with a skilled team.

It is also very helpful to have potential learners critique the CBT course at an early stage. Watching a typical learner using the program and having the learner talk about what he or she is experiencing is a very valuable approach. Learner reactions on screen design, interfaces, navigation systems (used in moving from screen to screen), and the like are very important while changes can be made relatively easily. Consider doing this test-improve cycle several times while the CBT course is being produced.

Production costs are dropping as the authoring tools become more powerful. There are a variety of packages on the market for putting together a multimedia "training" program. Again, focus on the goal of effectiveness as you begin any work in this area. Just as in video and desktop publishing, people with skills and expertise are needed to get the most out of the tools. (Sec Chapter 59, Using Multimedia Technology.)

Role playing

One of the most important elements in a role playing simulation is what happens **after** the "playing" is finished. The leader needs to explore the thoughts and feelings of the actual role players **and** those watching the role play.

Role playing is a very powerful technique that can affect the participants and observers on a very deep level. If the topic is one that could trigger strong emotive feelings (e.g., ethical or moral behavior, confronting a colleague, etc.), the leader needs to have experience in handling potentially difficult and delicate situations.

For more information

- *Selecting and Developing Media for Instruction, Second Edition,* by R. H. Anderson. Van Nostrand Reinhold Company, 1983.
- *Planning and Producing Instruction Media, Fifth Edition,* by J. E. Kemp and D. K. Dayton. Harper and Row, 1985.
- *Instructional Media and the New Technologies of Instruction, Second Edition,* by R. Heinich, M. Molenda, and J. D. Russell. John Wiley & Sons, 1985.

39

Prepare the Instructor's Manual

Description

Produce the manual or guide that the instructors (or course monitors) will use preparing for and conducting the course.

Why do it

The instructor's manual contains information specific to teaching the course, along with the outline, visuals, and the like. This helps to

- Achieve consistency between instructors;
- Give added "security" and support to new instructors; and
- Provide a way of communicating expectations, suggestions, and other information to instructors.

Who is involved

The instructor's manual is prepared by the course designer/developer along with the assistance of graphics and desktop publishing people as needed.

Output

A completed instructor's manual.

Comments

The instructor's manual is the "operations manual" for the course. It tells the instructor what to do, when to do it, what can or cannot be modified, typical questions or problems, and so forth.

It also states the expectations of the instructor and support personnel, such as who duplicates the material, where it is obtained, and who to call in the event of a problem.

For a self-study or CBT course, it is helpful for those monitoring it to have some written information as well. For a CBT course the manual may include diagrams for setting up the equipment (and where to find extra cables that always seem to be needed), installation of the software, common problems and solutions, and who to call in an emergency.

How it is done (leader-led)

1) Some firms have standard formats for instructor guides and manuals. In addition, some presentation graphics software packages (such as Aldus' PERSUASION) have a "notes" feature that can be used to help create an instructor's manual.

2) Decide what is important for the instructor to know about the administrative workings of the course, as well as the way the content is to be presented.

3) Ask instructors what questions they have or think they might get asked by others.

4) Test your ideas with instructors experienced in teaching other courses, as well as novice instructors.

5) Decide what information can be transmitted in writing or what needs to be shown (live or by videotape) to the instructors during a train-the-trainer workshop.

How it is done (self-study or computer-based courses)

1) Talk to the monitors about what they need to know to supervise and monitor the activity.

2) Ask them what questions they have or think they might get asked by others.

3) Based on the materials and equipment used, identify skills and knowledge required to use/administer them.

4) Decide what information can be transmitted in writing or what needs to be shown (live or by videotape) to the monitors during a train-the-monitor session.

40

Conduct a Pilot Program and Modify Course/Lessons as Needed

It is the true nature of man to learn from mistakes, not from example.

—Fred Hoyle

Description	Present the course to a specially selected group of participants and obtain detailed feedback that can be used to immediately adjust, modify, and improve the course.
Why do it	A pilot course is run to obtain information that is then used to improve the course and make it more effective prior to delivering it on a large scale. It is done for leader-led as well as self-study and CBT courses.
Who is involved	The course designer, developer, course administrator, content experts, participants, and supervision.
Output	A detailed critique of what went well and what did not go well, along with changes made to improve the course, instructional methods, and materials.
Comments	Computer and software people call this task a "beta test." Pilot programs are equally important for leader-led workshops as for computer-based or other self-study courses.

Whether this is your first course or your twentieth, conducting a pilot and getting the results back is always terrifying. You have invested a considerable amount of time, thought, energy, creativity, and money in it. Doing a pilot is putting your neck on the line.

The first thing to remember, though, is what you are striving for. You want the finished course to meet certain goals. You want it to be effective. Incorporating feedback appropriately is extremely important for the long-term success of your course as well as improving *your* skills as a designer/developer of instructional programs.

Besides the thick skin you will gradually develop, you will also be able to discern important from trivial comments. You will find some very good ones and some that are extremely strange. Even the crazy ones need to be understood. Sometimes, comments will contradict each other. If this happens, find out more about who wrote the comments and their perspective; talking to them might be helpful. You might also want to share contradictory comments with someone else who was there and see if they can explain it. If the issue is a significant one, work to resolve it right away. If not, see if it comes up again in the early implementation sessions.

Is there a situation where a conducting a pilot is not needed? There might be such a case, but the improvements that almost always occur make a pilot a *very* good investment.

How it is done

1) Select the pilot program participants. The size group should be similar to that anticipated in the final version. Various designers and developers have different views on who should attend. You might want to have potential instructors participate, or people who have considerable experience and expertise. Other options are a cross section of those who will actually be attending the course or those who have been identified as needing "extra" instruction.

Be cautious when inviting actual learners to the program. If the content changes, they might need to repeat it. Also, if the program does not go smoothly, they will probably let their associates know, creating "bad reviews" for the final version.

Members of supervision might be good participants as they will have experience and content expertise. Also, having them involved in the early stages will build them into the process, hopefully nurturing their support.

Other participants could be content experts, other training professionals, and people whose insight and opinions you value.

2) Confirm the evaluation method and develop the appropriate tools for the pilot. The strategy you use should have been selected during the design phase. (You will probably want trainee reactions [Level I evaluation] at the very minimum. Trainee learning [Level II] are very good to have as well. Depending on the topic and objectives, you may be able to obtain information on trainee performance [Level III].)

For self-study or CBT courses, you might want to have open-ended questions that an observer asks while the learner uses the material.

As you develop the evaluation tools, keep in mind the amount of time required for the participants to complete it. Some instructional developers have been known to have an eight-page questionnaire for a two-hour course, something that can antagonize those filling it out.

An alternative or supplement to the questionnaire is a verbal discussion or debriefing session following the pilot course. Having a different leader can make the participants more comfortable, thus providing more candid responses.

Also, one-on-one interviews can be used (with someone other than the instructor asking the questions).

Things to look for include the following:

- Accuracy of content,
- Clarity,
- Understandability,
- Pace and timing,
- Use of interactivity,
- Variety,
- Opportunity for discussion,
- Opportunity for questions,
- Flow and transitions between topics,
- Sequencing, and
- Use of instructional materials.

In addition, the instructor should provide comments about how things "felt" to him or her, items to be included in the instructor's manual, potential problems, and so forth.

As you develop a questionnaire or debriefing questions, do not simply find out if there was a problem with a parameter like clarity or variety. Find out *specifically* what was wrong so you will have a better understanding of how to improve it.

3) Collect and analyze the comments. Spend time considering the information. The number of comments is usually related to significance; however, one comment might be particularly insightful and carry great influence.

You may be criticized for design decisions made early in the process. How does this new information fit with the data previously obtained?

4) Adjust the course as needed.

Example

During the pilot of an introductory course on Current Good Manufacturing Practice regulations, many participants found that a fourteen-minute videotape on the history of the FDA and the cGMPs went by too quickly. Many people suggested that it be redone. Other people felt it covered the material at a comfortable rate.

Since an understanding of the FDA and cGMPs was critical to meeting the objectives of the course, the criticism was taken as valid. However, modifying the completed videotape would have been an expensive change.

The team developing the course looked at alternatives. They decided to have the instructor prepare the learners for the video by telling them what they would be seeing. Also, the learners were asked to watch for particular things. After showing the video, the instructor had a question/answer period with the learners responding with the key points of information they were asked to look for. This activity also had the advantage of making the learners more actively involved in what was previously a passive element in the program.

Follow-up questionnaires showed the changes made a significant improvement in learner's understanding and remembering of important information. The changes had no cost associated with them, and added only ten minutes to the two-hour program.

41

Approve the Course

Description Obtain approvals from designated areas prior to implementation.

Why do it This acts as the final quality check on the content and organization of the course. In addition, some FDA investigators will want to see quality unit (QC) approval for cGMP-related courses.

Who is involved The course administrator, designer/developer, content experts, quality control, and management.

Output An approved course (as documented by a completed course approval form).

Comments The process for approving a course should be described in a procedure, including the titles of the approvers, what they are to look for, and so forth. The process used may include points mentioned in this chapter; however, the process *defined by the procedure* is what needs to be followed.

This task can be rigorous or be a "rubber stamp." The intent, though, is for people with knowledge in the content area to review and approve the material that will be presented. It may be appropriate to have several people from different perspectives review and approve the course.

A review that looks at products of the instructional design process is also important. Here the reviewer/approver would look for things such as goals, objectives, detailed outlines, and lesson plans.

There have been recent FDA observations from agency investigators citing that the firm's quality unit (typically QC) was not involved in approving courses. While not specifically stated as a requirement in the cGMP regulations, this appears to be an expectation of at least some inspectors.

How it is done

1) Prepare a standard "course approval form." (An example is shown in Table 41.1.)

2) Complete the form; pass the form and the necessary materials to the reviewers.

3) If the reviewers make any changes or comments that require changing of the materials, the reviewers should have the opportunity to check that the materials have been correctly modified prior to their approving the course.

4) Save the completed approval form and keep (a copy) with the course file (as described in Chapter 47, Documenting Instructional Materials).

Table 41.1. Example of course review and approval form

Acme Fine Pharmaceuticals	**Training Course Approval Form** Form 463.1

- Use of this form is described in SOP 378, Training Course Review and Approval.
- Course objectives are to be attached to this form for review and approval.

Course title: ______________________

Course code: __________ Unit responsible: ______________

Course goal: ______________________

Procedure(s) referenced: ______________________

Target audience(s): ______________________

Delivery method(s): ______________________

Course length: ______________________

Special instructor qualifications: ______________________

Course prepared by
- name: ______________
- title: ______________
- signature: ______________
- date: ______________

Content approval (1)
- name: ______________
- title: ______________
- signature: ______________
- date: ______________

Content approval (2)
- name: ______________
- title: ______________
- signature: ______________
- date: ______________

QC approval
- name: ______________
- title: ______________
- signature: ______________
- date: ______________

Training approval
- name: ______________
- title: ______________
- signature: ______________
- date: ______________

V

Implementation Phase

42

Introduction to the Implementation Phase

How did I get here?

In the development phase, you produced the instructional intervention according to the instructional plan. You ran a pilot of the course, took into account feedback from everyone involved, and made the needed improvements. Now you are ready for the learners!

Purposes of the implementation phase

You use the implementation phase of the instructional systems design (ISD) process to

- Prepare those involved with delivering the instruction;
- Use the instructional materials (i.e., computer based training, printed materials, videotapes, etc.);
- Produce the changes in learner performance as described by the objectives;
- Record who was present; and
- Collect evaluation data.

What you will be doing

Figure 42.1 lists all of the tasks accomplished in the implementation phase.

Comments

What is actually done for the implementation of a program or course at your facility is very specific to the course, the instructional media selected, the audience, and the time frame for completion.

An item of critical importance is having *good communication* with the people and areas affected by the course. The fewer people surprised and the fewer ruffled feathers, the more successful the course (and you and your associates working on this project) will be.

Implementation Phase

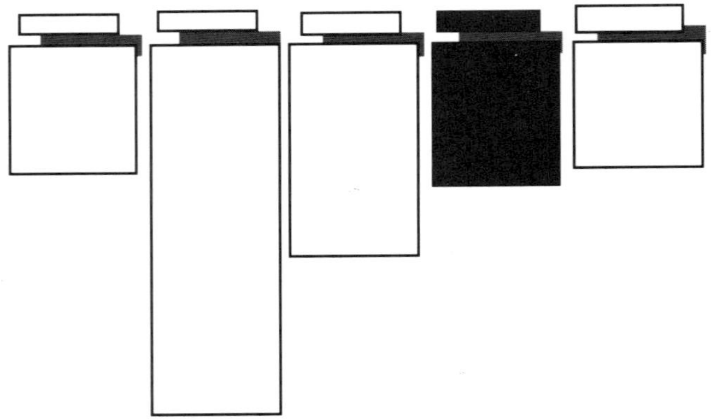

Task	Description	Output
1) Prepare instructors and monitors	Enable instructors to deliver the course or monitors to assist with self-study or CBT courses.	Qualified instructors and monitors
2) Schedule sessions	Schedule participants and instructors into sessions.	Listing of sessions, instructors, participants
3) Deliver course	Provide the lessons and course to the learners.	Learners who can accomplish course objectives
4) Document attendance	Have a record of who attended the course.	Listing of people, times, date, instructors, and other data in proper record form
5) Document instructional content and materials	Have a record of what was taught in the course.	Folder or binder of important course elements
6) Collect and assess evaluation data	Obtain data related to the course, to determine how it is meeting its goal and the learner's needs.	Completed evaluation forms or questionnaires

Figure 42.1. Tasks associated with the implementation phase

43

Prepare Instructors and Monitors

In a completely rational society, the best of us would be teachers and the rest of us would have to settle for something less.
—Lee Iacocca

Description

Enable the instructors (if involved with course delivery) to effectively present the content and instructional events, and facilitate the learning process. Enable the monitors (if used with a CBT or self-study course) to facilitate the use of the instructional materials.

Why do it

Preparing instructors/monitors is needed so that they can be effective in

- Delivering content;
- Using the features built into the course;
- Using the instructional methods, media, and materials selected;
- Making use of the instructor's/monitor's manual;
- Making and keeping the instructional situation "safe" for the learners; and
- Responding to difficulties and disruptions that could occur.

Who is involved

Experienced instructors; the course designer/developer; the course administrator; and the new, selected trainers.

Output

At the end of this step, you will have instructors qualified to teach the course or monitors prepared to supervise a CBT or self-study course.

Comments

Instructors can make or break an instructional program. Their knowledge (or lack of it), enthusiasm (or lack of it), and presentation and interpersonal skills (or lack of the same), play a major role in how well the learners react to the content, methods, and materials, and most importantly, learn.

Earlier, criteria were established for selecting instructors. If instructors have not been chosen, this must now occur.

In a train-the-trainer program, instructors-in-training typically participate as learners in a demonstration or actual session. There are two things you want to accomplish in such a program. First, you want them to experience the complete course and how you want it taught. Second, you want instructors to see the "innards" of the instructional materials, how they have been crafted and fit together.

An additional step before releasing instructors to teach on their own might be for new ones to co-teach the course with a more-experienced instructor. This takes a great deal of pressure off the new person, as well as gives the course designer/developer and administrator a better feeling of the new instructor's performance.

Some course developers conduct the instructor workshop before finalizing the instructor's manual, as this group can give valuable comments and suggestions.

One reason why qualified instructors are important is that they are required by the FDA's cGMP regulations.

> "Training in good manufacturing practice shall be conducted by qualified individuals . . . " [CFR §211.25(a)].

You or someone else may need to defend instructor qualifications during an FDA inspection.

Monitors for self-study and CBT courses

Obviously, if the course is computer-based or self-study, you will not have instructors, as such. You will, however, need monitors in the areas where the program is delivered to help answer questions, facilitate use of the materials, start-up systems, and so forth. These people need to have an understanding of the course, its materials, and how the materials are used.

Instructor certification

Some programs and firms use the concept of "certified" instructors. A person is "qualified" to teach after completing the instructor's workshop, and then team-teaches with a more-experienced, "certified" instructor. After meeting certain, specified expectations, the instructor then becomes "certified" to teach the program on his or her own.

"Certification" can involve a "master instructor," someone with expertise in adult training and considerable coaching skills. The master instructor does not need to be a content expert, but rather be someone who can observe the instructor's performance and how the learners react to it.

How it is done

1) Based on the instructional methods, materials, and media used in the course, what do the instructors or course monitors need to know and be able to do? (Yes this is another, task analysis! Some of this information may have been gathered as you developed the instructor's manual.)

2) What knowledge and skills do the instructors or monitors already possess?

3) The difference or "gap" between questions 1 and 2 is the material that needs to be conveyed to the instructors or monitors. This might be done through printed material, one-on-one coaching, or in instructor workshops. As a designer/developer, consider the best way(s) to fill the gap.

4) Generate a document describing the prerequisites for becoming a qualified instructor. This might include presentation skills, instructor workshops for the course, and/or particular technical skills. (This is not as critical for course monitors.)

5) If a train-the-trainer's workshop is needed, work together with an instructor (who has had experience in teaching other courses) and the course designer and developer. Develop objectives for the instructor's or monitor's workshop (as described in the design phase). Then, keeping in mind the other concepts and tasks of good instructional design and development, produce the workshop.

6) Schedule and conduct the workshop.

7) As appropriate, arrange for the new instructor to be observed or co-teach the course with an experienced person.

8) Develop a list of qualified instructors or monitors; include an approval by someone who has compared the qualification requirements to those of the instructor. Table 43.1 is an example of a tool used in approving instructors.

Example

For a course entitled, *An Introduction to the cGMPs*, an instructor's workshop might be conducted as follows.

Workshop goal: Prepare instructors for teaching *An Introduction to the cGMPs.*

Objectives:

- Participate as a learner in the course, *An Introduction to the cGMPs.*
- Identify key behaviors and characteristics that an effective instructor must demonstrate.
- Develop four personal examples that can be used as transitions between sections of the course.
- Using the instructor's manual and overnight preparation, teach a section of the course to a small group.

Workshop Agenda:

Day 1 (1/2 day):

1:00–1:15	Welcome and Introduction
1:15–1:30	Discuss objectives
1:30–3:45	*An Introduction to the cGMPs* (including break)
3:45–4:30	Discuss course, assignment for next day

Day 2 (1/2 day):

8:00–9:00	Features of the course (methods, materials, etc.)
9:00–11:00	Small groups/practice/critiques
11:00–12:00	Questions, administrative information, wrap-up

!!!

Who trains the trainers? What qualifies *them* to do it? This is the almost the same question raised hundreds of years ago, "Who judges the judges?" *Somebody* has to do it.

If *you* were asked this question, you might include these points in your answer:

- Technical content was collected from expert or highly knowledgeable people. Content accuracy was reviewed at several points and approved prior to delivery of the course;
- The instructional systems design process used is a well accepted methodology for producing efficient and effective instruction;
- In some situations, outside consultants or professionals with documented experience and credentials were used;
- Instructors, if used, were chosen based on rational criteria and given training, as needed, in using the instructional materials;
- Evaluation tools were developed to determine the effectiveness of the training intervention; and
- Documents are available to show that the ISD process was followed and to support decisions that were made.

Table 43.1. Example of instructor approval form

Acme Fine Pharmaceuticals	• Use of this form is described in SOP 379, Instructor Approval.	**Instructor Approval Form** Form 489.2

Course title ____________________

Couse code ____________ Unit responsible ____________

Instructor name	Meets Basic cGMP	Meets Basic Communication Qualifications	Meets Special Qualifications (On Course Approval Form)	Approved by (name)	Approved by (initials)	Date

44

Schedule Sessions, Instructors, and Participants

Description — Schedule participants and instructors (or monitors) into training sessions.

Why do it — Besides being necessary for the delivery of the instruction, scheduling in advance helps assure time for communicating course details to all parties involved. It also helps with the production and distribution of instructional materials.

Who is involved — Course administrator or scheduler, participants, instructors (or monitors), and supervision.

Output — A listing of attendees, the instructor (or monitor), and the backup instructor for each session. If a "pre-event" is used, it should be defined and implemented at this stage.

Comments — If part of the "roll-out" strategy included a pre-event, (i.e., letters of invitation, posters, etc.), once the training dates are set, this can be implemented.

An important aspect of getting people to attend the sessions has to do with the proper placement of responsibility. As a course designer or trainer, your ability to ensure that people attend is rather limited because, typically, you have no authority over the learners. If supervision knows they are responsible for their people attending a program, they can help make it happen.

Accept the responsibility for providing a well-designed and executed instructional course; defer to others who have the authority the responsibility of getting the people there.

Other approaches. If a "just-in-time," "training-on-demand," CBT, or self-study approach is used, this task is slightly different. As appropriate, you would let the monitors and area supervision know when and how the materials are available and how people sign-up or take advantage of the learning opportunities.

How it is done

As mentioned earlier, different organizations and departments have different ways of scheduling personnel. Generally, it is best to work through area supervision in scheduling personnel.

45

Deliver the Course

Men must be taught as if you taught them not.
—Alexander Pope

Description Provide the course to the learners.

Why do it To accomplish the goal(s) identified in the design phase.

Who is involved Learners, instructor(s) (or monitors), course administrator, and supervision.

Output At the end of the course, the learners should be able to meet the specified objectives and goal(s).

Comments At last! You are training people. People are actually using all of the instructional methods, materials, and media you and your associates have developed and produced!

Some unexpected things will undoubtedly occur, but the planning that was done should make the course rollout quite smooth.

How it is done (leader-led) 1) Instructors and the course administrator follow the plans that have been developed for the course.

2) Instructors use the instructor's manual for the course.

3) As an instructor, get to the room at *least* fifteen minutes early to be sure things are the way they need to be. If you are

using an unfamiliar room or any audiovisual equipment, practice with it beforehand to be sure it works and you can operate it. If you are using technology like VCRs, computers, or projection systems, it is recommended to get there even earlier.

!!!

If you are going into a new situation (e.g., giving a workshop in a hotel using a computer projection system or demonstrating a multimedia course to a senior management group) it might be better to have things tested or setup the day before. ***Do not*** listen to hotel audiovisual personnel who say, "We never have problems linking a notebook computer to this video projector." Try it in advance, convince yourself, and sleep well the night before.

How it is done (CBT, self-study)

1) Monitors and the course administrator follow the plans that have been developed for the course, with learners using the CBT or self-study instructional materials.

2) Monitors facilitate the use of the materials and equipment, frequently checking that all of the computers or workstations are working properly.

!!!

Most course designers/developers and instructors have at *least* several horror stories about teaching a course related to unforeseen acts of God or management. While surprises can be terrifying at the moment, you will survive, the participants will survive, and you will have a great story to tell in the future.

Some surprises—and how you can prepare for them—include the following:

- Projector bulbs burning out—have an extra bulb or projector available;
- The videocassette recorder eats the videotape—have access to another tape (note: This is a very rare event.);
- Extra people show up—have extra sets of printed materials;
- Guest speaker is late—have some sort of group activity available that relates to the topic or lesson;
- The computer breaks down—have overhead or paper copies of screen-prints available;
- The power goes off—have a sense of humor and know when to call the program off; and
- The airlines lost your luggage containing all the instructional materials—you *were* warned about this!

46

Document Attendance

Description Have a record of who attended the course.

Why do it To know who participated in a training course and to meet organizational and regulatory requirements. It also reinforces, to the learner, that training and the particular topic are important.

Who is involved Learners, instructor(s) (or monitors), and course administrator.

Output A listing of people who attended the session, the date of the session, the name (and number, if used) of the course, and the instructor's name and signature (for a leader-led course).

Comments Documentation of attendance is simply that. You do not take into consideration what was learned or if anyone thought about football games or wrote letters during the course. As one instructional professional described it, you are simply collecting the names of "the butts in the chairs."

Just recording the names of people is not enough to meet most regulatory and organizational needs. There must be some sort of paper or computerized record-keeping *system* to keep track of all people who have attended a particular program, as well as all the programs that a particular employee needs to take (i.e., the curriculum) and what the employee has actually completed. The system can be simple or complex; however, it is key that it be *usable* by supervision and training personnel.

Frequently, a simple sign-in sheet is used with the person printing his or her name and identification number (employee number, social security number, etc.). Some forms include space for the participant to sign, verifying that they really were there. Many forms have a line for the instructor to sign as well.

Your department or firm should have a standard operating procedure that defines the sign-in process and what happens to the sign-in form after it is completed. The procedure should include how data is entered into an electronic system and verified (if a data entry step is used), and where/how long the original document is kept.

Another method of collecting information on who attended a session is to use a data-logger or a device that puts the information directly into an electronic database. Options for this include an ID card reader, or a touch pad where someone inputs their ID number and a password.

Most computer-based training (CBT) courses incorporate some form of documentation utility into the program. This could be as simple as automatically generating a "certificate of completion" that is given to the learner, or a more sophisticated approach involving updating a data file.

Some U.S. FDA investigators expect that summaries of the training records (i.e., numbers of people trained and not trained) be reviewed and acted upon by management. (See Chapter 5, Regulatory Compliance: The Minimal Goal.)

!!!

What should you do if somebody sleeps through a session or comes late/leaves early?

Instructors should have the option to challenge someone's signing of the attendance sheet if he or she did not participate in a program, walked out early, and so forth. As an instructor, you should make a note of someone who sleeps during a program. Several times, one particular instructor has marked out signatures of people who left early or came in just to sign the attendance sheet. If this is done, a note should be made on the attendance sheet as to why the name was crossed out along with your initials and date. It is a good idea to also mention this to the area's supervision.

!!!	One nonpharmaceutical firm takes a photograph of the attendees at certain regulatory-required training classes. It is filed and used as further evidence that people really were there (at least for when the photo was taken!)

How it is done

1) Use the department's standard procedure and format for recording attendance.

2) Try and integrate it with the course (i.e., linking it to a point about documentation, into an exercise, or as part of a CBT course).

3) Before adjourning, compare the number of people who have signed with the number present to be sure all have signed. Resolve any discrepancy before the group disbands.

Example

As a lead-in to documenting attendance, an instructor shows the following slide and asks, "Would this be considered adequate training in the eyes of the FDA? Why or why not?"

> A small Texas hospital found that posting instruction bulletins inside the door of a one-seat nurses' bathroom is an effective "on-the-john" training measure, according to Physician's Weekly. [*Wall Street Journal*, December 6, 1990]

While there may be several other reasons why you might question this training method, one reason is that there is no (described) way of recording participation.

(The instructor then reiterates the need for having complete documentation that shows who was trained and makes sure all participants have signed in.) [Note: This example does not translate well into other cultures, as the word *john*, a slang term, does not have the same meaning in most other languages.]

47

Document Instructional Content and Materials

Description	Have a record of what was taught in the course and also key documents involved in the course's design and development.
Why do it	Keeping a set of instructional materials for each course provides a reference library for other training professionals and supervision. Documentation is also an expectation of regulatory agencies and most organizations.
Who is involved	The course administrator is primarily involved along with the course designer/developer.
Output	A file or binder containing the important elements of the course.
Comments	Completing this task will provide an answer to anyone who asks, *"What was this course about? What was covered? How was it done? What instructional materials were used?"*

Having copies of the materials will also help answer questions asked as part of a regulatory inspection. More likely, however, the materials will be a future reference for you and others in your firm.

Two commonly asked questions on documenting materials are:

1) How long should materials be kept? and
2) What about keeping changes made to the course?

Answers need to be reasonable and consistent with your organization's policies and procedures on document

retention and change control. Your legal counsel may recommend different time periods than indicated here.

Materials should be kept as long as the course is being offered and *at least* a year or two after that. It makes sense from a regulatory and business standpoint to have the materials available for five to seven years after they were used to provide a historical record of what was taught. Slides and video segments might also be used in the future as "historical" background.

As materials change, they should be kept in the file along with a brief explanation of why they were modified, when, and by whom. If the course is subject to a more comprehensive change-control process, then review and approval forms should be kept as well.

Retention of the key documents used in the course design and development process is valuable to others. In the future, people may need information on tasks, jobs, or audiences that your data contains. To simplify any regulatory agency examination of the training records, a suggestion would be to file the background information in a separate folder or binder.

How it is done

1) Collect the important elements of the lessons and course in a file or binder. This might include the following:

- Course goal;
- Objectives;
- Detailed outline and lesson plans;
- Instructional materials used (slides, overhead transparencies, videotape);
- Handouts, exercises, case studies;
- Requirements for becoming a qualified instructor;
- Instructor's manual; and
- Completed course approval forms;

2) In an additional binder or file, place important data collected and decision-related documents generated during the ISD process.

!!!

Having a form with a listing of all the materials required to be retained makes a good checklist to ensure that all the elements are included. This form could also serve as a table of contents for each binder.

48

Collect and Assess Evaluation Data

Description	Obtain and review data on the course and how it is meeting its goal and the needs of the learners.
Why do it	Collecting and assessing data will help you fine-tune the instruction so that it best meets the goals and the needs of those participating in the instruction.
Who is involved	Course instructors and the course administrator are involved with this task.
Output	Evaluation forms, questionnaires, tests, or checklists that have been collected and reviewed.
Comments	In the design phase, a strategy for evaluating the course was decided upon, with the methods and tools produced during the development phase. In this task, you are beginning to implement the evaluation of the course and the learners.

In practice, collection of evaluation data is done as the course is delivered. Also, if the course is leader-led, course instructors typically review the evaluation forms and make small, immediate changes the next time they teach. For example, if comments on the Level I evaluation forms indicate the pace of the course was too fast, the instructor might slow down when he or she does the course next.

In Chapter 50, a more thorough analysis of the evaluation data is discussed and how the results are used to improve the course. The current task is distinguished from that one in that the more thorough analysis would be based on more evaluation data. If early evaluation data indicates there is a significant problem, there should be an immediate modification of the course.

How it is done

1) Collect the data. In setting the course agenda, allow eight to fifteen minutes for the participants to complete the trainee reaction evaluation forms (Level I) and/or the learning evaluations (Level II). If you do not provide time, the answers will not be as complete, since most people will want to leave and, therefore, do a hurried job. Also, if you ask people to complete them on their own and mail them back to you, a considerable percentage of the participants will forget or procrastinate, and you will not get the data.

2) Position the Level I evaluations in a way so people will *want* to help you by completing them. They have expertise after completing your course. Ask them to share that expertise with you. (One instructor tells his audience when passing out the evaluation forms, "I don't mind if you give me low marks as long as you give me specifics so I can make improvements.") Also, let the learners know you will review and consider the comments made. While this introduction can be written on the forms, it should be reinforced verbally by the instructor.

If a Level II method is used (evaluating trainee learning), learners should understand its functions of assessing how much the learner has mastered **and** how the data will be used to improve the course.

3) Assess and share the results with the instructor, developer, and administrator in a timely way. Some changes can be made immediately (e.g., "repeat the questions before answering them," "position the projector so it does not block the view of people on the right side of the room," etc.). Others might take more time to correct, such as parts of the program that are unclear.

If trainee learning evaluations are used, and there is a frequently missed question, or learners have difficulty in performing a particular task, is there a reason for that? This can indicate a gap in the instruction.

4) Determine the actions required based on the feedback. This may range from no actions needed to making significant

changes. It is a good practice to write a brief memo summarizing the evaluations and actions needed/taken.

5) File the evaluation forms in an easy-to-retreive manner. This should be done in one central place, such as the course administrator's office. Generally, filing them by session and date is useful so you can later compare trends over time.

!!! Some leader-led workshops that extend over several days use daily Level I evaluation sheets. Each evening, the instructors review the comments and make their adjustments, The next morning, the results are shared with the participants. This builds a sense of openness and trust with the group and models some of the behavior discussed in the course.

VI

Evaluation and Maintenance Phase

49

Introduction to the Evaluation and Maintenance Phase

How did I get here?

In the implementation phase, the instructional intervention began. You may have been able to follow the original implementation plan exactly, or more likely, had to make minor adjustments. Integrated into your course is an evaluation strategy; you have collected some data and have methods developed to provide more data as learners begin to perform with their newly acquired knowledge and skills.

Purposes of the evaluation and maintenance phase

You use the evaluation and maintenance phase of the instructional systems design (ISD) process to

- Improve and optimize the training intervention;
- Include, as appropriate, content (written, spoken, visual, etc.) changes due to updates in technology, regulations, corporate policies, industry practice; and
- Determine the impact the training intervention has had on the learner's performance and the goals of the department and organization.

What you will be doing

Figure 49.1 lists the tasks accomplished in the evaluation and maintenance phase.

Comments

There are two main themes of this phase. First, you are preserving and optimizing the investment made in the training intervention by improving the course and its materials and including new information as needed. You are striving to keep the course as "green" as possible by watering, nurturing, and trimming it. (This might not always be true, however. You might have produced a program intended for one-time use, and then, "put in the vault.")

Once management has experienced a course, it is not uncommon for them to have the training intervention sent (with the needed adaptations) to other sites, here and abroad.

The second theme of this phase is to determine how effective the course was. This is linked to the strategic decisions made during the design phase and the Level IV evaluation methods and tools produced during the development phase.

Evaluation and Maintenance Phase

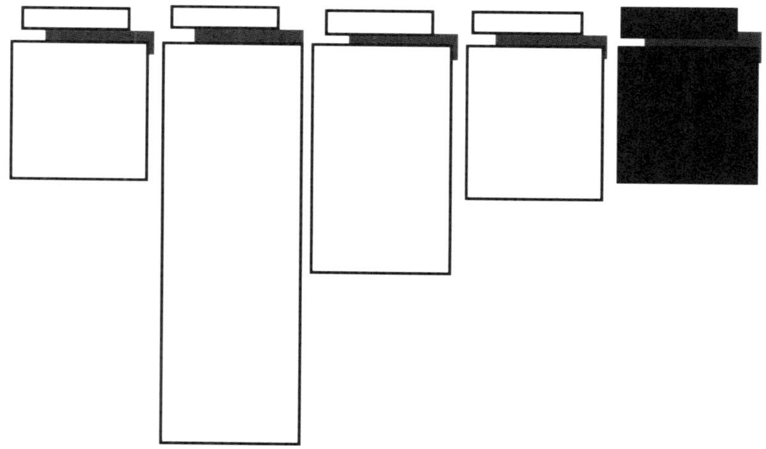

Task	Description	Output
1) Analyze evaluation data; modify course as needed	Consider evaluation data; plan and take actions to improve course, including updating content.	Summary of evaluation data, action plan, changes approved and implemented
2) Coach instructors as needed*	Observe and provide feedback to instructors.	Feedback to each instructor
3) Measure course effectiveness	Evaluate how successful course is in meeting its goals and the strategic goals of the organization.	Report describing impact of course

* only if course is instructor-led

Figure 49.1. Tasks associated with the evaluation and maintenance phase

50

Analyze Evaluation Data and Modify the Course As Needed

Description	Consider the Level I, II, III, and IV evaluations; plan and take actions to make the course more effective.
Why do it	To increase the effectiveness of the course or program.
Who is involved	Course administrator and designer/developer, with the instructors and management as appropriate.
Output	When you complete this task, you will have a summary of the evaluation data with comments and an action plan for improving the course. Also, you will implement the appropriate changes.
Comments	This task is critical in achieving the goals of the course and the unspoken goal of producing an excellent instructional course or program. In a sense, a training program is a living thing. It needs to be nurtured and cared for in order for it to stay healthy and useful.

The previous task and this one have considerable overlap. "Quick fixes" and adjustments are part of the previous task; this task looks at more significant modifications.

This task is not done just once; it is repeated periodically throughout the life of the course. Level III evaluations are best done three to six months after the training is completed. Level IV evaluations depend to a large extent on the situation, but tend to be months or even years after the training intervention occurred.

The exact process you use for evaluating the data depends, in part, on the evaluation strategy selected and the methods used (i.e., rating form or questionnaire, learner interviews, etc.).

If a course is subject to changes in regulations (e.g., courses on the topic of hazardous waste), someone should be assigned to monitor the regulations and notify the course administrator when there are significant changes.

Some firms have an SOP requiring a periodic review of all training courses. This allows for a more systematic, thorough examination of the materials.

Change control

There should be a systematic way of proposing changes, considering their potential affect, and then changing the training intervention as appropriate. This is especially true if the lesson is part of a more complex course or program, regardless of how it is delivered.

For instance, if a safety and health training program on asbestos teaches a technique that is changed due to new technology, are there other, related courses offered on the topics of hazardous waste or transporting hazardous materials that *also* need to be modified? What you are concerned about is "the ripple effect"—one small change having ramifications elsewhere.

Some organizations have a committee that reviews and approves all significant change proposals *before* they are implemented. A procedure is very useful in describing this activity.

Change review and approval forms should be maintained with the package of documented training materials.

How it is done

1) Review and summarize the individual data points from the evaluations.

2) For Level I evaluations (trainee reactions), divide the data into the following categories (as applicable):

- Training environment,
- Instructor (if used),
- Instructional materials,
- Course design,
- Topics/lessons,
- Objectives, and
- Goals

For each category, are there any trends? Are there any extreme responses?

For Level II evaluations (trainee learning), track the questions and responses or performances. Are people missing a particular question? Is there a demonstration of a skill that learners typically have difficulty with? Were these items covered in the course? What can be done to improve the performance?

For Level III evaluations (trainee performance), what comments/feedback can supervision provide about effectiveness? Are people performing better? Are fewer mistakes or deviations being made? Is there a difference in attitude or attendance? (At this level training and the performance environment are intimately connected. If performance is not occurring, look at the environment *before* making any changes to the training intervention.)

For Level IV evaluations (organizational results), is there data showing the anticipated or predicted change due to training? Is it too early to tell or is there clearly no effect? Is the effect of training less than anticipated? Are there other performance-related issues that must be addressed? (More detailed suggestions related to Level IV evaluations are found in Chapter 52.)

3) As done in the evaluation and modifications of the pilot program, what adjustments should be made? What various approaches can be used to improve the course or program?

4) Collect other proposals that would modify the course, such as those due to regulatory or organizational changes.

5) Summarize the comments and, as appropriate, discuss how they can be addressed. Also include any benefits that will occur because of the improvements.

6) Put together an action plan showing what needs to be done, who is doing it, the costs involved, and the completion times. Provide this information to supervision and management as appropriate.

7) If appropriate, use the change control procedure. Then, modify the materials and lessons as needed.

51

Coach Instructors as Needed

Description — Observe and provide feedback to the instructors delivering the course.

Why do it — To increase the effectiveness of those delivering the course.

Who is involved — A "master" instructor or coach, the course designer/developer, the course administrator, and the course instructors.

Output — Feedback to the individual instructor enabling him or her to strengthen his or her performance.

Comments — This task is not needed if self-study or CBT courses are used.

Acting as a facilitator or instructor is difficult enough; having someone else sit in a session to observe and critique it can cause more stress. Building observation and feedback into the course or program from the outset can make giving and receiving criticism much easier.

Caution! — Care needs to be taken during this task to ensure that it is done in a positive and effective way.

How it is done — 1) Review the trainee reaction comments concerning the instructor(s). (These should have already been shared with the instructor; see Chapter 48.) Are there any trends?

2) Talk with the instructor to see if he or she has had any particular problems or situations requiring help. Can these be addressed immediately?

3) Let the instructor know when you will be there observing to prevent any surprises. Let him or her know what you will be looking for. Make it as nonthreatening as possible.

4) Make observations during the program. What did the instructor do? What were the reactions of the learners? Were there any times when the instructor "lost" the audience?

(Sometimes it is helpful to make the comments on a copy of the instructor's manual.)

An observation sheet with behaviors to look for is also helpful. (An example is provided in Table 51.1.)

5) Using the appropriate coaching skills and techniques, talk with the instructor after the program, asking what he or she thought of the course. Share your observations. Focus on performance, *not* on the person.

6) During the coaching session, ask the instructor what can be done to make him or her more effective as an instructor. Can the instructor's manual be improved? Are there some presentation-skills or facilitator-skills programs that he or she could benefit from? What did the instructor do that received strongly positive ratings from the learners? What can be learned from these?

7) As appropriate, put together an action plan with the joint recommendations. Follow up at an agreed-upon date to observe changes and improvements.

!!!

Just as not all of us are artists, rocket scientists, or athletes, not all people are good as instructors or facilitators. Some people may be very effective in teaching a procedure or task to someone individually, but very poor in a large group session.

As the designer/developer, course administrator, or supervisor, know when it is time to call an end to a situation that is not working and not correctable. Do it in a way that will preserve the dignity of those involved.

"Your Big Jumbo, Roy, is your regular Jumbo with golden French fries and coleslaw. Your Super Jumbo is your Big Jumbo with slice of onion, lettuce, tomato, special dressing, and pickle wedge. I've been watching you, Roy. You're screwing up on the pickle wedge."

• •

Table 51.1. Instructor feedback observation form **(Source: Clark, G., R. Steele, R. P. Niemiec, and H. J. Walberg. 1992. Reprinted with permission from *Performance & Instruction*, April 1992, Volume (31), Number (4).)**

Observer ______________________________ Date ______________

Instructor ______________________________

Course ______________________________ Module ____________

Beginning Time _________________________ End Time ____________

Methodology(ies)

Lecture	
Lab	
Role play	
Large group discussion	
Small group discussion	
Size of group	
Facilitator's guide in visible use *(Please circle yes or no.)*	Yes No

Section One: Items Coded Once

	Observed	Not Observed	Not Applicable
1. Presents objectives.			
2. Conveys benefits of course.			
3. Clarifies expectations.			
4. Establishes behaviors/norms.			
5. Follows suggested activities.			
6. Follows time suggestions.			
7. Operates instructional media properly.			
8. Prepares legible visuals.			
9. Reviews key points.			
10. Relates key points to future activity.			

Section Two: Rated Items *(Items 11–21 should be tallied for frequency.)*

	Tallies	Comments
11. Provides clear instructions.		
12. Uses examples or analogies.		
13. Asks open questions.		
14. Paraphrases or repeats student comments.		
15. Checks for understanding.		
16. Circulates among small groups.		
17. Probes for more information.		
18. Addresses participants by name.		
19. Uses correct grammar; avoids jargon.		
20. Redirects student questions or comments back to audience.		
21. Speaks with expressiveness and varies tone of voice.		

Rate scale for items 22–24:
3 = Evident most of the time; 2 = Evident some of the time; 1 = Not present but needed;
0 = Not relevant to this module

	Rating	Comments
22. Maintains eye contact.		
23. Deals with challenging behavior.		
24. Addresses participant questions.		

!!!	Instructor support sessions or meetings are an easy way to improve communication and share information. Periodically, bring the instructors or facilitators together to share successes, "war stories," problems, breakthroughs, comments, and frustrations. These meetings can also be used to share course or program-effectiveness measurements.

For more information

- "Promoting Teacher Behaviors That Promote Student Learning" by G. Clark, R., Steel, R. Niemiec, and H. Walberg. *Performance & Instruction* April 1992, pp. 22–24.

52

Measure Course Effectiveness

Description
Evaluate how successful the course is in meeting its goals and the strategic goals of the organization.

Why do it
Measuring effectiveness is a way to show how the program has produced a return on its investment.

Who is involved
Course administrator, designer/developer, and management.

Output
A report with text and graphics describing the impact of the course.

Comments
Since you designed the course based upon specific needs, you can look to see how those needs have been met.

This is, in fact, conducting a Level IV evaluation, looking for organizational and business results. You want to show management that the training intervention really was an investment.

Some of the data may have been gathered earlier, as described in Chapter 50.

How it is done
1) Review the evaluation strategy decisions you made and follow them as appropriate.

2) Review the original goals of the course and how it was to have met specific needs.

3) Are there direct results or indicators to show change?

4) What are the changes worth to the organization or department? Has productivity increased? Are fewer deviations made, decreasing the time required for technical and management review?

5) What is was the cost of the training intervention? (See Chapter 4.) How does that compare to the savings? Calculate the return on the training investment.

6) Using graphs and other visuals, share the results of the evaluation with members of supervision and management.

What happens if you do not see any benefit?

If the problem was defined correctly at the start and there were knowledge and skill deficiencies and a well-designed training intervention was delivered, you should see good results.

If not, do not jump to the conclusion that the training was ineffective.

If there were other performance-related tools or structures that need to be put into place, or barriers that were to have been eliminated, were they? If job aides were to be a part of the solution, have they been developed? Are people using them? Are there other factors that have appeared?

Another way to analyze what is going on in this type of a situation is to look back on the Level II and Level III evaluations (trainee learning and trainee performance, respectively). Did people learn? Were they transferring what they learned back into their jobs? Are they currently performing? If not, why not? The use of Mager's process for analyzing performance problems may be useful.

For more information

- *Analyzing Performance Problems Second Edition* by Robert F. Mager and Peter Pipe. Belmont, CA: Lake Publishing Company, 1984.

VII

Related Topics

53

Deciding to Build or Buy Courses or Instructional Materials

Goals

- Discuss advantages of buying courses or instructional materials from an outside supplier.
- Identify types of providers.
- Describe options in developing a course internally.

Description

Determine if already available courses or instructional materials, that meet the instructional unit's objectives, can be obtained or purchased.

Why do it

Purchase or licensing of "off-the-shelf" courses or materials may be considerably less expensive than producing your own. Such courses or materials may be available immediately.

Who is involved

The designer is primarily involved with the locating of materials, along with librarians, purchasing agents, and others.

In evaluating materials, the designer, subject matter experts, supervision, several potential learners, and possibly management are involved.

Output

When this task is completed, you will have discovered if any materials are in-house or commercially available. You will then decide whether or not to use them.

Comments

Looking for available materials can begin as soon as the subgoals, objectives, and topics for each instructional unit are completed.

Generally, firms find it advantageous to use outside sources for content that is very general (i.e., it is less costly buying it than developing it in-house) or for content that is extremely specialized (little internal expertise is available).

Locating commercially available instructional materials specific to the pharmaceutical and medical device industries is difficult; there are few sources and limited topics are covered. Materials that are available vary tremendously as to instructional approach, content, and visual quality.

For more general skills, safety, health, and human development training, there are a number of providers. Directories, such as the *Training and Development Organizations Directory*, published by Gale Research Company or the TRAINET database, available to the members of American Society for Training & Development, can help locate providers. Providers also run ads in training and human resource trade publications.

Options to internal development

If you cannot find courses that meet your requirements, there are a few options that you might want to pursue instead of producing a program alone.

- *Professional associations.* Some professional associations have committees that focus on the training of their members or training in member firms. They may be interested in sponsoring a course or producing instructional materials for purchase by their members. Advantages of this include cost distribution over many companies as well as the establishment and solidification of industry practices.
- *Local trade schools, colleges, and universities.* With tight budgets facing many educational institutions, schools and colleges are exploring nontraditional ways of funding. They may be very willing to help develop courses or materials using a combination of academic, student, and corporate resources. Several pharmaceutical firms currently have relationships with local schools for assistance in teaching basic literacy courses (reading, arithmetic, English as a second language, etc.). Not only can instruction be developed at a relatively lower cost, but it provides students with "real-world" experience.

!!! NOTE: If a college or school is considered, be sure they have experience in the use of adult education and training techniques as discussed in Chapter 6. Some still use a pedagogical approach instead of the andralogical one geared for adult learners.

- *Agreements with course and courseware developers and producers.* Some developers and producers of materials, who usually do "custom" work, may be interested in a project where you receive what you need and they either own the material or are licensed to sell it to others. In this type of arrangement the developer/producer's price does not include their profit, but does include a base rate and out-of-pocket expenses, with the understanding that profit will be made by the producer reselling the material.

  If this type of symbiotic arrangement is used, be sure any proprietary or confidential information will not be released to other purchasers.

- *Joint projects.* Some companies have banded together, forming an alliance in which to purchase a customized videotape for use by all. Costs, equally shared by all members, are substantially lower than for each firm doing it alone.

!!! Collaborative efforts of some sort are making more and more sense as instructional needs mount and the initial development and production costs of instructional courses and materials increase. A study by the Carnegie Foundation, which has a special interest in adult learning, states,

> Much of the [worker] learning is generic in nature; it is not company-specific or proprietary to a particular organization . . .
>
> Until fairly recently, the major [corporate in-house] providers have largely chosen to go it alone. Now, however, the same competitive forces that are driving the increasing need for training are driving the formation of alliances and other new ways to provide it . . . At all levels of training for workers in many types of jobs, more cooperative programs are being put in place (Eurich 1990).

How it is done

1) Identify materials available inside and outside your organization. Locate outside providers through directories or by networking with others involved in training.

2) Screen the materials. The information you have developed, such as the course objectives, instructional content outline, events, methods, and media choices, all serve as a type of requirements document for the materials you are seeking. See how well the available materials compare to these requirements.

3) Evaluate the materials using a standardized form. This is best done using a group of the potential learners, as well as subject matter experts, the course designer, developer, potential instructors (if used), and supervision.

Suggested criteria to use in developing an evaluation form are shown in Table 53.1.

For more information

- *Training Partnerships: Linking Employers & Providers* by A. P. Carnevale, L. J. Gainer, J. Villet, and S. L. Holland. Alexandria, VA: The American Society for Training & Development and Washington, DC: U.S. Department of Labor, 1990.
- *The Learning Industry—Education for Adult Workers* by N. P. Eurich. Princeton, NJ: The Carnegie Foundation/ Princeton University Press, 1990.

Table 53.1. Suggested criteria for evaluating existing courses and materials

Design	Was an instructional systems design approach used to develop the course and materials? Is the arrangement of the instructional content and events appropriate to the type of objective? Is there an appropriate choice of methods and media?
Use of Adult Learning Concepts	Is there use of interaction between learner(s) and instructors/leaders/ facilitators? Are learners encouraged to think out solutions and apply knowledge and skills? Does the course require the learner's active participation in the learning process? Do the course materials relate to the work environment and the tasks of the learner? Can the learner proceed at his/her own pace? How much control of the learning process does the learner have?
Subject Matter	Does the subject matter have sufficient depth? Does the subject matter have sufficient breadth? Is the subject matter presented in an interesting and lively way? Is the subject matter accurate, complete, and current?
Organi-zation	Is there a unifying theme throughout the course, lessons, and materials? Can the materials be adapted for use in other ways?
Physical Makeup and Look of the Materials	Are the materials attractive? Are the visuals appropriately and sufficiently used? Are the visuals of high quality? Is the sound/narration (if used) of high quality? Can the materials/media be adapted or customized for specific needs?
Evalua-tion and Docu-mentation	Is the participant's learning evaluated? Is the evaluating method/technique used consistent with the type of objective? Is there a method provided to document learner participation?
Suit-ability	Is the course/materials appropriate to the audience? Is the course/materials appropriate to the culture of the learners and the organization? Does the course/materials send any inappropriate or mixed messages to the learners? Does the course/materials match the requirements of your analysis and design?
Costs	What is the cost of the course/materials? Are there any other costs (e.g., hardware, travel, etc.)? What are the initial costs? What are the ongoing or recurring costs? Are there any costs savings that can be shown?

54

Using Outside Professionals

Here lies a man who knew how to enlist into his service better men than himself.

—Andrew Carnegie's self-epitaph

Goals

- Discuss how current business and economic pressures are increasing the use of outside professionals.
- Describe how outside professionals are located and selected.
- List expectations a client has of its outside professional.
- List expectations the outside professional has of his/her client.

In the 1970–1980s, if you worked for a large organization and needed specialized assistance with a project, you usually found someone in your firm who could help. Graphic artists, editors, human resources professionals, and other specialists were usually available "in-house."

In the 1990s, things are different. While many firms might have limited internal corporate resources, most of these specialized functions are obtained from outside the firm. This trend not only exists in healthcare-related firms, but also across industries throughout the world. Drucker predicts this "unbundling" of support, clerical and maintenance activities will be commonplace by the end of the 1990s (Drucker 1992).

Firms are going *outside* for the expertise and talent that they need more and more. Consultants and other professionals provide an increasingly valuable, diverse, and specialized set of services to an organization.

Examples of outside professionals used by those involved with training include the following:

- Instructional designers and technologists;
- Workshop leaders;
- Facilitators/instructors;
- Graphic artists;
- Desktop publishing experts;
- Writers (for workbooks, hypertext systems, procedures, video, etc.);
- Editors;
- Video directors, producers, camera crews;
- Multimedia designers, producers;
- Content experts; and
- Training program auditors.

Why use outside professionals?

There are several reasons why you might seek outside assistance:

- You need highly specialized knowledge, skills, or processes not available internally;
- You do not have the time to do a particular project in addition to all your regular work;
- Fresh eyes, a new perspective, an outside opinion or different ideas are needed;
- You need commonly available information, assistance, or skills; or
- You want to know what current industry practice is.

Before you start looking

Before you begin the process of finding a person or group to assist you, consider the following questions.

- *Do we really know what we want to accomplish?*
- *Do we really need help from the outside?*
- *If recommendations are being sought, are we really prepared to adopt them if they are reasonable? Do we have the funds, time, and courage to make changes?*

When you can affirmatively answer these questions, then you are ready to begin.

Where the experts are

People who can provide assistance could be free-lancers, consultants in a consulting firm, production companies, or people on the faculty of a college or university.

There are several ways of locating people you need.

- *Networking.* Colleagues and peers in other (pharmaceutical as well as nonpharmaceutical) firms are good sources of names and contacts. If they have used someone, ask how satisfied they were (and still are). Would they use the person or group again?

  Also, consultants you know or those with good reputations in their own field frequently know other good people and can provide names and recommendations.

- *Publications and presentations.* Glance through pharmaceutical and training-related publications and programs to discover who is doing and communicating in the field. Not only will you get their names, but a sense of the kind of work they do.
- *Directories and data bases.* Trade publications and professional groups typically have directories of people self-identified as consultants or free-lancers in a particular field. Members of the American Society of Training and Development can use the TRAINET computerized data base that contains information on training programs and providers.
- *Mailings / contacts / advertising.* Sometimes, consultants advertise by direct mail or through journals and trade publications.

Choose the "right" one

Develop a list of several names of people or firms you can contact.

You might want to "prequalify" them over the telephone before you invite them for a visit. Also, you might ask for examples of some of their work and names of past clients you could talk with.

When you hire an outside professional, he or she is not just a walking set of knowledge, skills, and talent. You want someone you and your organization can trust. You want someone who can help *you* succeed. The professional's reputation in the industry and the specific things he/she/they have done in the past are important indicators of what you can expect in the future.

Besides trust, reputation, credibility, skills, and knowledge, another factor in selecting outside assistance is compatibility.

Will the person and the resulting training program (or analysis, etc.) be respected by those in the organization? Can you (and others in your firm) work together with the consultant? A good outside professional or consulting firm should have adaptability and flexibility.

Other criteria used in distinguishing and selecting providers include the following (Carnevale, Gainer, Villet, and Holland 1990):

- actual prduct
- background
- content
- cost
- credentials
- delivery method
- experience
- philosophy
- results
- support

For extremely large, complicated, or expensive projects, you may want to consider the "request for proposal" (RFP) approach. This is a way of formally defining your specifications, needs, and expectations and having potential providers respond with their proposals. (You also give them a list of what their proposals must include). The uniformity allows you to compare the resulting proposals more easily.

A caution: this method can take a long time to complete. The government uses RFPs when it requires services. Businesses do not commonly use them, taking a less formal (and faster) approach instead (Carnevale, Gainer, Villet, and Holland 1990).

On reputations

Consultants and others who provide professional services understand that the pharmaceutical and medical device industries (and others like it) is very well networked. If a consultant does a poor job at one or two firms, sooner-than-later, this will be known to others. Successful professionals are successful for a reason—their clients are *delighted* with what they receive.

(Consultants have an informal network of their own as well. Pharmaceutical and device firms and some of their people have reputations as to how easy [or difficult] they are to work with, get paid by, adopt recommendations, etc.)

What you should expect from an outside professional

Before engaging the professional, ask for a proposal as to what he/she/they can provide your firm. This is based upon what *you* ask for and the specifications and so forth you include. The proposal should discuss the general approach used to reach the goal and what will be delivered, when, and for what cost. (The RFP process involves much greater detail from both parties.)

Once an agreement has been reached, there are a number of things you should expect from the outside professional, including the following:

- *Integrity.* Honesty, candidness over potential conflicts of interest, and similar qualities are included in this. You *should* feel like you could buy a used car from him or her.
- *Confidentiality.* Information, stories, and suggestions should be stripped of all identifying information. Comments as to "industry practice" should not reveal confidential sources. If someone is loose-lipped about other firms, they probably will be about yours as well.
- *Competence / capabilities.* Reputation, samples of non-confidential work, and discussions will give you a good feel for this. If there is a project, however, critical to your firm or involving major dollars, you may be reluctant to try an "unknown." Instead, consider using the person or group on a pilot project or a smaller, similar one. This gives both parties an opportunity to work with one another and establish confidence and comfort levels. It also gives you an opportunity to try the solution before widely implementing it.
- *Solutions to match the particular situation.* In both medicine and consulting there is no one "magic bullet" or solution that can be applied to all situations. A consultant should have a process (that he or she uses) to discover the specific answers to your problem or project.
- *Freedom from jargon.* You should understand what the consultant is saying and doing. If a video producer starts using terms like "lower third CG" or "client supplied B-roll," be comfortable enough to ask what they mean; make sure you understand.
- *Agreed-upon scope and deliverables.* You and the professional should know specifically what you will receive. If an instructor's manual is to be developed to a certain corporate style, this style needs to be provided and agreed upon early on.
- *A different perspective.* Since the outside professional can provide a fresh set of eyes, ask for his or her opinion. An informal talk over lunch or a drink may give you a very different way of looking at a situation.

- *Timeliness.* The professional should have a written schedule of when you want the various deliverables (reports, lessons, videotapes, etc.). If there is a problem in meeting these deadlines, you should be informed of the delay. (Consultants invariably strive to meet the deadlines—missing them is bad for their reputation and can impact other jobs they have in the queue.)
- *Your maintaining control.* Some consultants experience paralysis by analysis—excessive amounts of data collected, yet no information is being acted upon. If you sense the project is "stuck" or the scope is being expanded, talk with the consultant and find out what is going on. If deadlines are being missed or the deliverables are not what you expected, talk to the consultant and come to an understanding.
- *Other issues observed.* Frequently, the professional sees other issues that need to be addressed. You should have a mechanism so that these issues can be captured (in a report or on an issues list, for example) and addressed at the appropriate time.

What the professional expects from you (the client)

A good relationship between a firm and outside professionals is just like any other important relationship—it involves each party equally committed to its success. The person or group you engage needs certain things from you and your organization as well:

- *Reporting structure.* The consultant (or other professional) will want to know who he or she reports to on a regular basis and also who is sponsoring the project. If all questions and requests for information need to go through a central point, identify that person and what should be done if the person is not available.
- *The* ***real*** *goal of the project.* If there is a "hidden agenda" in the project, inform the consultant about it. For example, "evaluate and improve operator training" might have a very different outcome than the unspoken, intended goal, "evaluate and improve operator training so that they can function with fewer supervisors."
- *Agreed upon scope and deliverables.* This is just as important to the consultant as it is to the client firm.
- *Expectations.* If you want a certain level of quality or something done in a particular way, it will *only help* the

project for the professional to know this as early as possible. For instance, if an expectation in your department is for all reports to have a one-page summary and appendices with all the raw data, tell the consultant up front. It will save time, frustration, and reputations.

- *Feedback.* Positive and negative feedback are very important to professionals and to the quality of the finished project. *They want you to be happy and excited* about what they are providing to you. If you are pleased by a particular lesson or visual, tell them; they will try and do more. Similarly, if there are comments from others suggesting the professional use a different approach, relay this as well. This can be difficult at times, but the earlier it is done, the better for all involved.
- *Open communications.* This is where trust between the client and the consultant is critical. This might involve feedback or the discussion of sensitive personnel or organizational issues.

Working together

One of the most important parts of a successful collaboration is the sharing of information between the partners involved. Table 54.1 suggests some of the roles for a firm and a provider of an instructional intervention.

For more information

- *Training Partnerships: Linking Employers & Providers* by A. P. Carnevale, L. J. Gainer, J. Villet, and S. L. Holland. Alexandria, VA: The American Society for Training & Development and Washington, DC: U.S. Department of Labor, 1990.
- *Clients and Consultants: Meeting and Exceeding Expectations, Second Edition* by C. Bell and L. Nadler. Houston, TX: Gulf Publishing Co., 1985.

Table 54.1. Information flow between a hiring firm and the provider (consultant or outside source) (Source: Carnevale, Gainer, Villet, and Holland 1990)

Role of the Provider	Role of the Firm's In-House Staff
Training needs analysis	Staff collaborates with the provider to collect data necessary to conduct the analysis.
Consultation and guidance for the development of an in-house program	Staff collaborates with the provider to learn how to develop a successful training program.
Design a company-specific program	Staff collaborates with the provider to supply information on program content and to convey desired results.
Develop a company-specific program	Staff collaborates with the provider to supply information on program content and to convey desired results.
Provide training materials	
Customized	Staff collaborates with the provider to give information on what the needs are.
Off-the-shelf	Minimal interaction between the employer and the provider—staff simply requests a program on a specific topic.
Delivery	Staff collaborates either significantly or minimally with the provider, depending on training program or subject area needs.
Train-the-trainer	Staff collaborates either significantly or minimally with the provider, depending on who conducts training and whether it is conducted on or off the employer site.
Provide an entire program from start (analysis) to finish (evaluation)	
Customized	Staff collaborates with the provider to supply data and information on what needs are and what employees should learn.
Off-the-shelf	Staff has little or no interaction with the provider—a program is selected and the provider supplies it—the staff gives very little in the way of specifications.

55

Having and Using Procedures

Knowledge has an important property. When you give it away, you don't lose it.

—Raj Reddy

Goals

- Describe six functions of procedures.
- Discuss the cGMP-requirements of procedures.
- Identify common problems found in many procedures.
- Identify ways of writing better procedures.
- Discuss, using the instructional systems design model, how procedures are related to training.

Why procedures?

More than in most industries, the pharmaceutical industry makes extensive use of procedures (sometimes called standard operating procedures or SOPs). The FDA requires that procedures be written and followed; other regulatory agencies, such as OSHA, mandate similar written programs or procedures.

Why use procedures?

We all have tried to use procedures or instructions that turn what should be a relatively simple task (setting the clock on a VCR or assembling a toy) into something difficult and incomprehensible. This can occur when producers of the equipment's instruction manuals do not consider the user.

Procedures should be a tool to *improve* performance, not to complicate or interfere with it.

Procedures have important business and human performance functions. Procedures help provide

- Increased understanding of the task,
- Standardization of the task,
- Continuity and coordination,
- An instructional tool,
- Reference information, and
- Compliance with change control.

Increased understanding of the task. The process of describing, in diagrams and words, what initiates the activity, what happens, and how materials and information enter and leave the step, can help highlight inconsistencies, missing or redundant steps, and so forth.

Standardization of the task. As discussed in the section on task analysis, there may be several different ways of accomplishing a particular goal. One way might be better, safer, or provide a higher probability of success. Correctly following a procedure that incorporates the best of all the methods can provide its users with the single "right," and hopefully, best way of doing the task.

Continuity and coordination. Some tasks involve several people and are spread out over time or location. The procedure links the performers and activities together so that the efforts fit together. Using a checklist as part of the procedure, where users can mark off what they have done, is a good way to insure that the tasks have been accomplished.

Reference information. Many tasks are done on an occasional basis. For example, passifying new stainless steel piping used for special, high quality water. A well-written procedure preserves for future users some of the "tricks" in accomplishing a task as well as the specifications, and so forth. New personnel or someone who has not done a task can read the procedure and discover the acceptable temperature range, the location of hard-to-find valves, who needs to receive copies of reports, and so on.

Compliance with change control. There are many business and compliance reasons why changes to a process or task should be documented. A procedure provides part of the baseline against which changes can be compared.

The FDA and procedures

In the FDA cGMPs for pharmaceutical products, the phrase (or something similar) *procedures shall be available and followed* appears more than twenty times. Not having and not following procedures are frequent criticisms made by the agency during inspections, as seen in FDA 483 observations.

The FDA has certain expectations when it comes to procedures; these are found in several sections of the pharmaceutical cGMPs [i.e., §211.100, §211.160, §211.22(c)]. Basically, the agency requires that

> written procedures, including any changes, shall be drafted, reviewed, and approved by the appropriate organizational units and reviewed and approved by the quality control unit . . . they shall be followed . . . and shall be documented at the time of performance. Any deviation from the written procedure shall be recorded and justified. [§211.100 (a) and (b)].

Reviewing and approving procedures

Approved procedures need to be signed and signers must understand exactly what their signature means. For example, does it mean the procedure is correct from a content standpoint? Does it follow the standard style or format? Does it meet the cGMP requirements? Reviewers and approvers of procedures need to know exactly what they are to look for and what to base their approval on.

When a procedure (draft #1) makes the rounds of review and approval, things are frequently changed. If this happens, the modified procedure (draft #2) must be circulated again so that all of the reviewers of the first draft can evaluate the change. This can go on *ad infinitum* (i.e., forever and ever), unless someone is closely managing the process.

For someone managing procedures, it is important to be current with the agency's criticisms of procedure programs of other firms through FDA 483 documents available through news services and Freedom of Information requests.

Procedures and the ISD process

During task analysis (in the analysis phase), tasks related to a particular job are defined and broken down into sequenced steps and substeps. These are the basic elements of a procedure.

A flowchart, showing the inputs, process, and outputs for a step, is extremely useful in understanding, simplifying, clarifying, and instructing others on the procedure.

!!!

Sometimes, organizations and departments fail to understand how procedures and training are related. One firm, in an effort to get procedures out as quickly as possible, wrote them in a way that made training extremely difficult and time consuming. If more attention, and a little more time, had been spent in initially writing the procedures, the whole process of writing and training would have taken less time. In addition, the procedures would have been more usable.

Other parts of a procedure

There are a number of standard features (such as title, description, definitions, effective dates, revision number, etc.) that must be included in a procedure and are part of the control and maintenance system that needs to be an integral part of a procedure program.

Problems frequently seen in procedures

Most of us generally are not exposed to well-written procedures that *help* users accomplish tasks more effectively and efficiently. Therefore as writers, we tend to perpetuate the same typical mistakes and include the same deficiencies in the procedures we prepare.

Many procedures in use today suffer from one or more of the following problems.

- *Procedures not written for those who use them.* Technical personnel sometimes write procedures that include language more appropriate to a doctoral dissertation rather than simple, clear, action-based statements.
- *Poor organization.* Sometimes procedures, in an attempt to cover every potential situation, become a collection of unconnected statements. If the process were to be flowcharted as written, a complex web of pathways would emerge. Correct sequencing of the steps and substeps is also missing.
- *Procedures not based on reality.* Procedures need to describe what *really* takes place in an operation, not the "ideal" way or the way a supervisor "thinks" it is done. It is not uncommon for a person to say, "We have a better way to do it than the method described in the SOP." Frequently, internal auditors and agency investigators will take a procedure in hand and compare it to personnel actually doing the task. Just having a procedure is not enough, it must be *followed exactly* as written.
- *Buried actions.* Frequently, procedures are not used because the user cannot find out what he or she is

supposed to do. Actions are stated passively in the middle of explanations, cautions, or specifications.

- *Use of outdated procedures.* Achieving standardization and coordination will never happen if people are using various versions of the same procedure. Unless a controlled way of issuing new procedures and destroying the old ones is followed, outdated procedures will find their way into use.
- *Procedures and training not viewed as related.* Procedure writers do not always consider the implications of a poorly written document on the training that follows. Training personnel have been known to rewrite a procedure so that it can be used in training. Sometimes, users prefer the instructional material so much that they use the training material *instead* of the official procedure—a practice that does not find favor with either the firm's quality assurance personnel or the regulatory agency.

Suggestions for having better procedures

For procedures to be effective, they need to be clear statements of what is to be done and how to do it. They need to be developed for the *users*. To write better procedures, keep in mind the common problems mentioned above, as well as the following suggestions.

- *Involve the real experts at the job in preparing the procedure.* Typically, these are the people doing the task. (If you correctly do the task analysis, these people will be included.) Not only will they provide a reality check on how the job is performed, they may also give suggestions on how it can be simplified and improved.

  (NOTE: Caution must be used when considering a change. Even a small change can have a significant impact later in the process or to the final user. Your firm should have a formal change control system for evaluating potential changes.)
- *Flowchart the process and include this in the procedure.* Showing the inputs, processing, and outputs is extremely helpful in writing and following a procedure, especially where material or information crosses organizational or physical boundaries.
- *Use strong, clear, action verbs.* Begin each point with what is to be done so that the user does not need to hunt

for them. You will not win a book award prize for literature, but that should not be your goal.

- *Consider alternate procedure formats.* There is nothing written in the FDA's regulations requiring a certain format for your procedures. Think about how they are used. New personnel will need more information (such as switch locations, safety cautions, etc.). Experienced workers who have performed the task repeatedly need a checklist that reinforces the proper sequence and specifications. Does that mean two different procedures? No, try two columns, one with the action, the other with additional details. Table 55.1 provides a comparison of different styles. Zimmerman and Campbell (1988) show other formats as well.
- *Do not set yourself up for failure.* If a step has certain time, temperature, pH, or other limits, provide a range if possible. For example,

  instead of saying "mix for 8 minutes"

  consider, "mix for 7–9 minutes."

This flexibility gives the user a better chance of conforming to the procedure. Of course, if something must be exact, it should be written that way. (Note: validation needs to support whatever value or range is provided.)

Other things to include in a procedure

If you are in a city that is new to you and following someone's directions to get from one point to another, you sometimes wonder if you are still on the correct path or if you are lost. Good directions, and procedures, should include some information that can be used as guidance or feedback (Wurman 1989).

The user (and his or her performance) will benefit if the procedure includes the following:

- *Time.* This is the estimated time the steps and substeps take to perform. For example, if the procedure calls for a laboratory technician to inject a sample into an HPLC instrument and then compare the peak to the standard, it is useful for the technician to know the typical sample retention time is seven to eight minutes. The same is true with changing over a labeling machine; you can include the statement, "typical changeover time by experienced mechanics takes two hours." If it takes a significantly

Table 55.1. Comparison of three procedure formats

NARRATIVE FORMAT

1. Pressure to Input Calibration

After removing the transmitter from the loop by disconnecting the input and outputs, connect the pressure source to the transmitter input fitting. When a multimeter is connected to the output terminals, adjust the transmitter for the appropriate pressure to read 0% on the output and then record input pressure, current equivalent, initial output current, and the tolerance code.

OUTLINE FORMAT

1. Pressure to Input Calibration
   - 1.1 After removing the transmitter from the loop by disconnecting the input and outputs, connect the pressure source to the transmitter input fitting.
   - 1.2 When a multimeter is connected to the output terminals, adjust the transmitter for the appropriate pressure to read 0% on the output.
   - 1.3 Record input pressure, current equivalent, initial output current, and the tolerance code.

ACTION/EXPLANATION FORMAT

Step	Action	Explanation
1.1	Remove transmitter from loop by disconnecting the input and outputs.	Input leads are white, output leads are black. No need to cover lead ends.
1.2	Connect pressure source to the transmitter input fitting.	Use pressure source AGR-100.
1.3	Connect digital multimeter to transmitter output terminals.	Use multimeter Craftsman #21 or equivalent. Meter must have valid APPROVED FOR USE tag.
1.4	Adjust transmitter input to the appropriate pressure that results in 0% current output.	Current output is displayed on meter's digital readout. This step sets the "zero" reading.
1.5	Record on calibration sheet: • input pressure • current equivalent • initial output current • tolerance code	"Current equivalent" is what the initial output current indication is compared to.

shorter or longer period, the user can then evaluate if something has gone wrong.

- *Anticipation.* What should the user expect to see or experience while following the procedure? What signs or signals confirm the user is on the right track? For example, if a chemical reaction must be manually stopped at a certain temperature, it helps the operator to know the typical temperature profile of the reaction. In this case it might be useful to tell (or show in a graphic) that right before reaching the final temperature, the reaction reaches a steady temperature for a while, then slowly ramps up to the end point.
- *Failure.* When has the user let a process go too far? What signs or indications does the user have that something was incorrectly done? What corrections should be made? For example:

  > If more than one cycle in the cabinet washer is required to remove all visible material, the stainless steel components were not precleaned properly. Repeat precleaning and then rewash in the cabinet washer.
  >
  > **or**
  >
  > *Expected yield:* 24,000 vials.
  > *Acceptable range:* 23,900 to 24,100 vials.
  > *If actual number of vials produced is not within the acceptable range, contact quality control immediately.*

  (Note: calculation of yield at various points in a manufacturing process is a requirement of the pharmaceutical cGMPs.)

A procedure system

A drug or device manufacturer will commonly have hundreds, if not thousands, of procedures describing all aspects of its manufacturing and control operations. Therefore, a systematic approach to the organization, writing, distribution, maintenance, and control of procedures must be in place. Turnbull and Higby (1985) and Zimmerman and Campbell (1988) discuss some of the broader issues and features of a procedure system.

Teaching a procedure

A procedure is a description of selected skills and knowledge arranged in the proper sequence required to perform a task. If an instructional design approach is used in delivering training on the knowledge and skills, training on the procedure *per se* is very simple. The organization of instructional events would be that of teaching intellectual skills and motor skills. (See Table 24.1 beginning on page 156.)

A useful approach

One technique that may be useful when teaching a procedure that involves information or materials passing between different groups is to have at least one large-group session involving all the users. (The details of what each group does are best covered individually or in small groups, prior to the large-group session.) In the large-group session, each group can describe what information or materials they receive, who they get it from, what they do, and to whom they pass their product. This approach, using visuals of the procedure flowchart, not only helps the participants to understand how all the pieces fit together, but also clarifies expectations of internal suppliers and customers.

Document and evaluate procedure training

There are various ways to show that a person has participated in a training program for a procedure (such as signoffs, attendance lists, etc.). However, if the goal is correct *performance* of the task, there must be some indication that the person can actually perform the procedure. For example, someone could recite from memory the correct sequence of steps in putting on a sterile gown; however, it is more important that the person can actually do it. Skill and movement coordination are critical. Opening sterile packages and putting on the pieces of the gown must be done properly to prevent contaminating the suit (and potentially, the aseptic manufacturing area).

Fortunately, evaluating whether or not a person correctly performs a task as described by a procedure is relatively easy, particularly if the procedure is well written. One caution, however: *You cannot simply look at the outcome* (such as, is the person wearing the sterile gown or not) to determine correct performance since the *process* used (as described in the procedure) to accomplish the task is just as important as the outcome.

Ways for evaluating performance of a procedure include the following:

- A supervisor watching the user, comparing observed performance to that required by the procedure.
- A supervisor observing the performance, using a checklist of critical items that must be completed. (The checklist might include items from several, related procedures.)
- Designated "experts" observing performance using the procedure or checklist.

(If the observation is made at the end of a training program, it would be considered Level II evaluation. If it is done several weeks after the training program, as the person works, it would be Level III evaluation. Both types of evaluation are discussed in Chapters 23 and 37.)

In all cases, the observer must sign or initial a training documentation form indicating the person can perform the task as defined by the procedure. Some firms also have the performer sign the form.

What about "refresher" training for procedures?

A frequently asked question is, "How often should training on a procedure occur?" An easy answer such as "once a year" or "once every two years" does not make sense if *performance* is what is important.

Once a person can do a task, additional training adds no value. *Retraining someone on a procedure he or she is correctly performing is a waste of time and effort.*

Periodic, documented performance audits to determine if a person is following a particular written procedure (and then appropriate follow-up if he or she is not) is of far more value than indiscriminate "refresher" training.

If a person who was able to perform a task or procedure no longer is performing as desired, there are usually other reasons that need to be explored. If the procedure is not frequently performed, maybe practice with feedback is needed before doing it "for real." Performance analysis (Chapter 2) is used to investigate and correct these types of performance problems.

!!!

Do not confuse procedure training with cGMP regulations and some other types of compliance training. *They are different* and have different requirements as to how often they are given.

56

Auditing Human Performance and Training Programs

Goals

- Describe the purposes of an audit.
- List the four phases of the audit process.
- List the five levels of information examined during an audit and questions that correspond to each level.

What is auditing?

Auditing is a process where records, programs, information, and systems are reviewed for accuracy, reliability, integrity, completeness, and control. An organization's financial transactions are reviewed in a financial audit by internal and external auditors. The auditors examine not only if the numbers are correct, but that the firm's accounting methods and controls are consistent with widely accepted, standard practices. External (outside) auditors then examine and certify the results.

In addition to financial auditing, there are operational audits that look at the economical and efficient use of resources and the accomplishment of goals and objectives related to the particular programs (Stettler 1982). Operational audits can be focused on quality, cGMP compliance, worker safety and health, and environmental (EPA) controls; each of these take a particular point of view of what is occurring (or not occurring) in an organization.

The U.S. General Accounting Office has a broader definition:

> *Audit:* A term used to describe not only work done by accountants and auditors in examining financial statements, but also work done in reviewing (1) compliance with laws and regulations, (2) economy and efficiency of operations, and (3) effectiveness in achieving program results (U.S. GAO 1981).

In the pharmaceutical, diagnostics, and device industries, audits focused on quality and cGMP compliance are standard practice, just like financial audits, and typically involve a corporate group visiting an operational unit. The auditors review records, facilities, and personnel; then reports are presented to management of the unit and corporation as to how well the unit is complying with corporate and regulatory requirements and expectations. In some cases firms hire consultants to add objectivity and new perspectives to auditing a site.

Quality audits (as well as all other types) require a significant investment of time, personnel, and money. It is not unusual for a team of two or more auditors to spend two weeks preparing for an audit, three weeks conducting the audit, and three to five weeks writing the reports and following up on the findings.

Auditing is becoming increasingly sophisticated. Some firms equip their quality auditors with laptop computers that have copies of all applicable regulations, procedures, reference materials, and a defined, systematic set of questions that must be covered during the audit.

Benefits of an audit

Conducting a quality audit can be an exhausting and sometimes difficult event for everyone involved. However, audits provide the unit and the larger organization significant benefits, such as

- An objective view of the area for local and corporate management;
- A review using standardized criteria or generally accepted practice;
- Additional support for justifying capital expenditures and/or personnel additions;
- A learning experience for all parties involved; and
- An avenue for communicating concerns, goals, and successes.

Auditing versus program evaluation

There is some overlap between auditing and program evaluation. In this discussion, we will look at auditing as being different from program evaluation.

Auditing is concerned with compliance to corporate and regulatory standards and expectations. It has more "yes" and "no" responses. Auditing would look at the evaluation levels (Chapter 23) used by an organization or department to see if they are satisfactory or not.

Evaluation looks more at meeting the specific program or organizational outcomes: How much are people learning? Are they learning the right things? How well are people performing? How much organizational benefit is being obtained from the investment of training dollars? Evaluations can be semiquantitative.

Auditing your own work

Since the purpose of auditing is to get a different view or outside perspective on an organization's operation, you should *not* be involved as an auditor of your own program. It would raise questions about the audit's objectivity.

One way of using your expertise as a training professional would be for you to be involved in a training audit of another site, division, or facility where you have no vested interest.

The audit process

There are four basic phases of the audit process.

1) *Preparation*—planning what will be covered based upon previous audits and current concerns or interests.
2) *Auditing*—conducting the audit according to the plan.
3) *Reporting*—developing the report, having it approved, and circulating it to management.
4) *Follow-up*—reviewing the responses and commitments from the audited area and periodically checking commitments.

Phase 1—preparation

Focusing on a training program could be done as part of a broader quality audit in a particular area, such as the quality control laboratory, or it might be the single focus of a review in one or more areas across an organization.

Preparing for the audit involves reviewing previous audit reports, talking to management about their concerns, and having an understanding for regulatory issues affecting the area. You and your coauditors should define the scope and the specific systems, areas, or topics that each person will focus on; this is typically a written plan that will be followed.

The audit team will seek answers to several basic questions:

- Is there a system for human performance/training? Is this system integrated with other systems?
- Does the area have a written plan (or procedure) for training?
- Does the plan contain the correct and appropriate elements?
- Is there evidence to prove that the plan is being followed?
- Are the goals and objectives of the program being achieved?

What to look for when auditing a training program

As mentioned above, there are several basic questions you as an auditor would ask when examining a training program. You would also look for specific elements based upon the requirements of the area's particular program or procedure.

What you look for can be divided into five levels. The firm may or may not have structures or elements in place at each level. The levels are as follows:

I—Systems
II—Procedure (or plan) availability
III—Contents of the procedure
IV—Operation according to the procedure
V—Learner performance

Table 56.1 describes each level in more detail.

Phase 2—auditing

Many auditors (and FDA investigators) will conduct an audit from a conference room. They will ask for all types of records, spend hours and days examining them, and, oftentimes, never visit the areas where the tasks are actually performed. One can answer many questions this way; however, it is difficult to obtain a real understanding of *performance* without observing it. A comprehensive audit of a training program includes both reviewing records **and** observing performance.

Systems level

Business systems theory, as described by Deming, Juran, and others, says everything in an organization is connected. Everyone is a vendor of goods, services, or information. Everyone is a customer. Each step in the process has the potential to either add value or decrease the value of the product.

At the systems level, you are looking for the degree of integration of human performance and training into the very fabric of

Table 56.1. Hierarchy of information used during an audit

Level	Examples of Specific Questions	Criteria Used for Making Evaluations
I—Systems	Is there a human performance or training system in place? Is this system integrated with other systems? Is the system dynamic and optimized?	Evidence of systems Use of systematic approaches
II—Procedure (or plan) availability	Does a written procedure or plan exist describing the human performance or training system? Is the procedure properly written, reviewed, approved?	Regulatory requirements and expectations for procedures Corporate procedure, policy for procedures
III—Contents of the procedure	Does the procedure contain the correct and appropriate elements of a training program?	Regulatory requirements and expectations for training Corporate policies, requirements, expectations
IV—Operation according to the procedure	Are all requirements, tasks of procedure being met? Is there documentation and other evidence as required by the procedure? Are resources, people, and funds available? Is documentation organized, systematic, and readily available?	Procedure (or program)
V—Learner performance	Are learners performing as required? Are there deviations or problems that are training-related?	Program and course goals and objectives

the organization. An organization with little integration will have training isolated and minimally effective.

(FDA investigators are moving more and more towards evaluation of systems during the course of their inspections.)

Procedure availability and contents

Examining the second and third levels is straightforward: You ask management and supervision for the training procedure and then you evaluate it according to the appropriate criteria.

Operation according to the procedure

There are different ways to determine if the area is operating according to the procedure; two examples are given below. Your choice depends on a number of factors, such as available time, past experience with the area, and detail required. You might want to use a combination of these suggested methods.

- *"Cohort" review.* With this approach, you would look at all the members of the department or area, comparing training requirements to training experiences completed. You look for "holes" in the data or inconsistencies. Specifically, make sure all people currently working in the area show up in the training records, including supervisory, maintenance, technical, engineering, and management. Comparing listings of training records with the names of people listed in signature logs, "reserve" and temporary employee lists, and batch or lab records will test how comprehensive and complete the training records are.

- *The "Lucky Louie" review.* Using this method, you choose at random one to three people [the "lucky Louie(s)"] and trace back all the training information, requirements, documented experiences, and so forth on these people. It is almost like pulling a thread in a piece of fabric and seeing what happens. In a well controlled/developed training organization you should be able to start with a name, obtain all of the courses that person is required to finish, all courses actually taken, test scores (if used), course outlines, course modifications, and any other documentation related to the course. Observe how accessible and organized the records are. At the end of the audit, you will have a very complete and detailed understanding of the training of these people.

Learner performance

- *Observation of performance.* Here, you compare what the person does against what they are supposed to do. If the person does not perform correctly, you do not know if there is a training deficiency or not; you need to have evidence that the person was able, at least once, to perform the task.

  If the firm uses a Level III (performance) evaluation (see Chapters 23 and 37), you may be able to audit those results instead of, or in addition to, doing it as part of the audit.

- *Interviews.* Informal conversations with the learners can provide information as to whether or not the person has the required knowledge for the job. For example, if the person has completed a course with the objective of "describe two reasons why proper documentation is important," the person should be able to do that. You should not be looking for the "textbook" answer, but rather that the person has an *understanding* of the topic. Asking the person for examples is also useful.

- *Training/performance-related problems.* According to the pharmaceutical cGMPs, firms must investigate and document deviations that occur in drug manufacturing and control operations. Some firms classify the deviations as to cause; "inadequate training" is a frequently used category. Deviation reports are a source of information related to training and performance.

Sometimes, the "inadequate training" category is used as a catchall. This can be a problem both for an auditor trying to examine performance as well as the firm. There have been several recent FDA 483 citations where a firm was criticized for not implementing corrective training measures after saying a deviation was "training related."

Use of a performance analysis [as described in Chapter 2 or by Mager (1984)] can help isolate those problems that are truly training related.

If deviation reports are examined during an audit focused on training, follow up on how the "inadequate training problems" are handled.

Phase 3—writing the report

Before writing the final report, it can save considerable embarrassment, credibility, and your relationship with the audited group to double check your facts, *especially* if they are critical or negative. Some firms use verbal report-out sessions between the auditors and auditees so there are no mistakes and surprises.

Many firms have their own traditional style or standard format for audit reports. Generally, audits contain observations of fact without the auditor drawing any conclusions about compliance, noncompliance, or improper behavior. It is "just the facts." This method is used to minimize the impact of someone taking a passage out of context and using the information inappropriately.

Recommendations

You may be asked to present your recommendations orally to a management group or in a separate section of the audit report. A concern of giving a specific recommendation, for instance, what you have done, is that it might not be a correct match for the audited facility. (This is especially true if the facility has a different culture or is in a different country.)

If you provide recommendations, focus on the principle involved and try to give several suggestions that the site can consider.

Phase 4—follow-up

Most firms have their own requirements for when and how the audit report is responded to by the area audited.

Appropriate actions need to be taken in a timely way to correct the problems and improve the operation. Follow-ups by the audit team can help assure improvements are occurring.

57

Transferring Programs and Courses Abroad

Goals

- Discuss the importance of considering culture when preparing or adapting a program for international audiences.
- List cultural and technology differences that need to be considered.
- Describe ways to improve the transfer of instructional courses between cultures.

The world continues to become smaller and smaller because of changing technology, politics, and economics. Connections are made and strengthened as communications and information transfer becomes faster, less expensive, and more reliable. Organizations are becoming more geographically distributed as research, development, manufacturing, and support activities span the globe. It is not uncommon for a given vial of a drug product to begin its life in one country and then pass through several countries, each stop adding value to the product, before it is finally delivered to the patient.

In the interest of reducing costs and increasing consistency, many firms try to share training programs and instructional materials between sites, both within a country and internationally. For organizations to benefit the most from this sharing, the courses need to be designed (or least adapted for) different cultures, always thinking of the needs of the target audience(s). While this chapter looks primarily at some of the issues in transferring programs from one nation to another, most of the principles are also valid when going from one *culture* to another.

What can happen if not done properly

If an instructional program and materials are not transferred thoughtfully and carefully from one country or culture to another, the consequences could range from minimal to significant, including:

- Learners will not understand an example or analogy;
- Learners will not understand written or spoken words;
- Unfamiliar images, words, situations will cause distraction;
- Program or material will be rejected as "not relevant here";
- Learners will not learn, resulting in wasted time and expense; and
- Learners will sense themselves being viewed as "one of them," not "one of us" (especially if the program is coming from corporate headquarters!).

Using a training program in different cultures has significant benefits as well as some risks. Your goal, as a training professional, is to maximize the benefits while reducing the risks.

Differences to consider

Sending a program to the nation closest to your border or to the other side of the world requires some thought of the differences that might be encountered, including:

- *Language.* While one of the most obvious differences between many nations, it can also be a problem between countries that use the same one. For example, British and American English are very similar, but many words and expressions have very different meanings. Similarly, there are differences in the Spanish language used in Spain, Mexico, and Puerto Rico.

- *Culture.* Cultural differences is the broadest category and can include everything from greetings (handshaking and kissing) to dinner conversations to punctuality to the use of "Ms.," "Mr.," and "Dr." Books have been written examining and contrasting cultural differences (Axtell 1990; Copeland and Griggs 1985).

- *Learning styles and expectations.* People in some cultures, possibly because of tradition and instructional material availability, learn differently than others. Some are very reluctant to volunteer or participate in discussions (having experienced corporal punishment as a child for speaking openly in class). Latin Americans prefer demonstrations and oral explanations over written instructions (Copeland and Griggs 1985). Many cultures have certain expectations for their teachers and instructors. Instructors from the U.S. who, in their teaching, tend to be more informal than others, risk not being taken seriously or viewed as not having credibility in the subject.

- *Relationship of the individual to the group.* In some countries, "face," or respect in the eyes of others, is easy to lose and difficult to reclaim. Another consideration is "teamwork"—some cultures value it, while others are much more individual-based. Working in groups composed of diverse persons is made even more difficult in some countries where religious, educational, class, or ethnic differences cause conflict or suspicion.
- *Centrisms.* All of us have a certain pride of the communities and heritage with which we are connected. We develop a perspective based on these connections. However, when our perspective becomes the standard by which all others are judged and other cultures, traditions, technologies are thought of as less, a person is ethnocentric. To a person from a different culture, the ethnocentric person is very quickly discounted and loses respect and effectiveness. To those traveling with one who is ethnocentric, that person is annoying and extremely embarrassing.

!!!

> Disregarding a cultural difference, even out of total ignorance, can cause difficulties in relationships. While working in India in a pharmaceutical facility, I was changing from my "outside" shoes to a dedicated, "inside" pair. An Indian colleague waved "hello" to me; I waved in return, holding the shoe that was in my hand. Immediately, I sensed a problem. For two days she avoided me and refused conversation. Finally, when we talked, she told me I had shown her great disrespect by waving a shoe at her, and even worse, the sole of the shoe—the dirtiest part. After apologizing for my ignorance and lack of thought, I filed away in my mind one *more* thing of which to be careful.

Audience factors

In deciding how much customization needs to be provided in a program, consider the educational level and cross-cultural exposure audience members have experienced. Personal experience has shown that language issues and cultural differences and problems are more easily accepted (or tolerated) in people with a broader experience base. As long as people are open to new ideas and minimally ethnocentric, and there is a sense of respect to all individuals, mistakes, differences, and other problems encountered can be laughed at or discussed.

Suggestions for programs being transferred abroad

Adapting an existing program, course, or materials can be done; however, it is much easier if a course is designed with the thought of transfer and adaptation from the outset.

Some design decisions that will allow for easier transfer are relatively simple, painless, and add little extra time or cost.

- *Work with others.* Try and develop a working relationship with a person at the site(s) that will be using the course. A collaboration will not only help to make the materials more meaningful, but can help with the acceptance of the course. (*You* will learn a great deal about the culture, too.) Electronic mail, facsimiles, and the telephone make long-distance work much easier. Even better is getting together and working on a program side-by-side. (One firm had an instructor in the U.S. and in England each working on a different course, with the plan that they would get together and collaborate for a week in adapting each course for the other audience.)

- *Conduct an audience analysis.* Having potential learners in all locations complete questionnaires can help define *their* learning styles, knowledge, and so forth. Alternatively, talk with people who have lived and worked in the culture. It may also be helpful to know any potential barriers that an instructor may experience, such as multiple primary languages, people with limited experience working in groups, previous experience using computer-based training, availability of computers, video players and other audiovisual equipment.

- *Design the course using modules.* Think of the instructional methods and media you use as pieces that can be plugged in or taken out and replaced with something similar. For example, a demonstration with an equipment model may not be possible in all situations; labeled drawings and a series of photos (or a video) of the device in operation may be a good substitute. If an element is a live "call to action" by an executive, think of how that could be replaced by either a local member of management, or a video of some sort (Morical and Tsai 1992).

- *Create a detailed instructor's manual.* Include more details as to what the goal or purpose of an exercise is, explanations about what must be included and can be modified, and what can be replaced with other things. If case studies are used, identify the important elements that a local case study should have (Morical and Tsai 1992).

- *Focus on the goal of the lesson and the concepts and principles involved.* For example, if you are teaching gowning practices for aseptic operators, think of the lesson as "dressing appropriately for the aseptic area," rather than "putting on the Acme X19 Sterile Gown." This provides a more inclusive frame of reference (for those who might use a different type of gown). It also takes into account that there might be other issues other sites may need to address (e.g., based on *our* local situation, what else do *we* need to do before entering the area?) (Morical and Tsai 1992).

- *Suggest examples.* If examples, illustrations, and analogies are used, there should be a way for the local instructor or contact to help select meaningful local ones. Make sure you put any specifications required of the example or the goal of using it. (This is similar to entertainers, comedians, and politicians who customize their standard jokes and stories with locally recognizable people, locations, and traditions. The joke does not differ in essence, only in the names used.)

- *Be sensitive of the words used.* "Alien," "foreigner," and "international guest" might mean similar things, but what they connote is very different. What would you prefer being called when traveling abroad? Many languages have formal and informal forms; be respectful in social and business interactions with people.

- *Time differences.* The work day in another country might have different starting and ending times and also different periods of time that people are accustomed to sitting down, listening, and so forth. Modularization of lesson material helps accommodate breaks.

!!!	If you have a case study or something based upon an FDA 483 observation, there may not be anything similarly available in other countries. The U.S. is unique in making that type of information available through the Freedom of Information Act. (Sometimes international audiences question the purpose of the act and how it works.) Before using an FDA 483 case abroad, be sure it is relevant in the local situation.

Technical considerations

Production of instructional materials for shipment abroad can cause some unexpected problems unless you are wise to some of the differences.

- *Paper, binders. . . .* Different countries have their own standard paper sizes (and, therefore, their own standard binder sizes). This can affect everything (original page layout, hole punches, drawings, etc.). It is much simpler (and easier to carry) to take a properly designed master set of materials to the other country (or send them ahead) and have them duplicated and assembled there.

  (The U.S. paper standard is 8.5 inches by 11 inches; in Europe the comparable standard is called "A4" and is 8.27 inches by 11.69 inches.)

- *Video and videotapes.* There are three different television standards in the world: NTSC, PAL, and SECAM. Equipment, TVs, videotapes, or laserdiscs of one system do not work on another. Table 57.1 shows the standards for some countries.

  There are several ways to get around this problem. The first is a "hardware" solution. There are some VHS videocassette recorders and TV monitors capable of multistandard use (e.g., Panasonic makes such equipment.) NOTE: You need to have both a VCR *and* a TV that are of the same format.

  The "software" solution involves converting a videotape from one format to another. Video postproduction companies can do this or refer you to one (perhaps in a larger city). If you are converting a VHS videotape, you will probably notice a small amount of degradation in the resulting picture quality.

A way of avoiding the television standards issue is by using a technology like CD–I (Compact Disc–Interactive), developed by Philips. One of main features of this delivery platform (and the specially developed software or programs that are used with it) is compatibility with all video and electrical standards worldwide. At least one pharmaceutical firm is studying the delivery of all of their international training programs by this technology.

- *Videotape language issues.* When producing a videotape, you may want to provide for the (future) capability of adding another language on one of the audio tracks. Multiple languages will also have other affects on the production, such as the amount of words ("character generation") shown on the screen and the rate at which people speak. This is because some languages are not as "compact" as others; it usually takes longer saying something in Chinese than in English; English and most European and Latin languages take *roughly* the same amount of time to deliver.
- *Electrical differences—voltage and plug/socket.* You will solve the problems by bringing your own equipment to show slides or play tapes, right? Know the electrical system of the countries you will visit as well as the type of plug required. Small transformers and interchangeable plugs are available at many luggage or electronic stores (e.g., Radio Shack in the U.S.). Some of the newer notebook computers that use transformers can be used in other countries with only the addition of an adapter plug.

When working with a second or third language

When giving a training course to a diverse international management or technical group where multiple languages are spoken, there is typically one language used; English is frequently the choice because of its wide use in business and commerce. Your audience may have other primary languages and varying levels of comprehension in the common language used. Some guidelines (Copeland and Griggs 1985) are provided below to help aid the transfer of information, no matter what language you are using.

- Speak more slowly than usual;
- Enunciate clearly;
- Use overhead transparencies or slides for visual reinforcement;
- Use short, simple sentences;
- Use active, not passive verbs;

Table 57.1. Color Television Systems in Use or Planned (Source: TV & Cable Factbook No. 60, 1992)

Country	Color System	Country	Color System
Afghanistan	PAL	Denmark	PAL
Albania	SECAM	Djibouti	SECAM & PAL
Algeria	PAL	Dominican Republic	NTSC
Angola	PAL	Ecuador	NTSC
Antigua	NTSC	El Salvador	NTSC
Arab Republic of Egypt	SECAM	Equatorial Guinea	N.A.
Argentina	PAL	Ethiopia	PAL
Australia	PAL	Finland	PAL
Austria	PAL	France	SECAM
Bahamas	NTSC	French Guiana	SECAM
Bahrain	PAL	French Polynesia	SECAM
Bangladesh	PAL	Gabon	SECAM
Barbados	NTSC	Germany	PAL & SECAM III
Belgium	PAL	Ghana	PAL
Belize	N.A.	Gibraltar	PAL
Benin	SECAM	Greece	SECAM
Bermuda	NTSC	Guadeloupe	SECAM
Bolivia	NTSC	Guatemala	NTSC
Bophuthatswana	PAL	Guinea	PAL
Brazil	PAL	Haiti	SECAM
British Virgin Islands	NTSC	Honduras	NTSC
Brunei Darussalam	PAL	Hong Kong	PAL
Bulgaria	SECAM	Hungary	SECAM
Burkina Faso	SECAM	Iceland	PAL
Burundi	SECAM	India	PAL
Cameroon	PAL	Indonesia	PAL
Canada	NTSC	Iran	SECAM
Central African Republic	SECAM	Iraq	SECAM
Chad	SECAM	Ireland	PAL
Chile	NTSC	Israel	PAL
China	PAL	Italy	PAL
Taiwan Province	NTSC	Ivory Coast	SECAM
Colombia	NTSC	Jamaica	NTSC
Republic of the Congo	SECAM	Japan	NTSC
Costa Rica	NTSC	Jordan	PAL
Cuba	NTSC	Kampuchea	SECAM III
Cyprus	SECAM	Kenya	PAL
Czechoslovakia	SECAM III	Korea	NTSC

- Do not use slang, idioms, unnecessary jargon;
- Check for understanding by asking the group questions; and
- Repeat important ideas in several different ways.

Be *very careful* when telling stories and using humor. Humor is one of the more sophisticated uses of any language. Some jokes will not be understood because of cultural differences.

Country	Color System	Country	Color System
People's Democratic Republic of Korea	PAL	St. Vincent & The Grenadines	NTSC
Kuwait	PAL	Samoa (American)	NTSC
Lebanon	SECAM	Saudi Arabia	SECAM & PAL
Liberia	PAL	Senegal	SECAM
Libyan Arab Republic	SECAM	Seychelles	PAL
Luxembourg	SECAM & PAL	Sierra Leone	PAL
Macau	PAL	Singapore	PAL
Madagascar	SECAM	Somali Democratic Republic	PAL
Malaysia	PAL	South Africa	PAL
Maldives	PAL	South West Africa	PAL
Malta	PAL	Spain	PAL
Martinique	SECAM	Sri Lanka	PAL
Mauritius	SECAM	Sudan	PAL
Mexico	NTSC	Surinam	NTSC
Monaco	SECAM & PAL	Swaziland	PAL
Mongolia	SECAM	Sweden	PAL
Morocco	SECAM	Switzerland	PAL
Mozambique	PAL	Syria	SECAM
Nepal	PAL	Tanzania	PAL
Netherlands	PAL	Thailand	PAL
Netherlands Antilles	NTSC	Togo	SECAM
New Caledonia	SECAM	Trinidad & Tobago	NTSC
New Zealand	PAL	Tunisia	SECAM & PAL
Nicaragua	NTSC	Turkey	PAL
Niger	SECAM	Uganda	PAL
Nigeria	PAL	Union of Myanmar	NTSC
Norway	PAL	United Arab Emirates	PAL
Oman	PAL	United Kingdom	PAL
Pakistan	PAL	United States	NTSC
Panama	NTSC	Uruguay	PAL
Paraguay	PAL	USSR	SECAM
Peru	NTSC	Venezuela	NTSC
Philippines	NTSC	Vietnam	N.A.
Poland	SECAM	Yemen Arab Republic	PAL
Portugal	PAL	Yemen (People's Democratic Republic)	N.A.
Qatar	PAL	Yugoslavia	PAL
Reunion	SECAM	Zaire Republic	SECAM
Romania	PAL	Zambia	PAL
St. Kitts	NTSC	Zimbabwe	PAL
St. Pierre & Miquelon	SECAM		

(A Puerto Rican associate, despite much time spent in the northern U.S. did not understand a joke about Groundhog Day—it is not celebrated in Puerto Rico.) Jokes that use national or gender stereotypes should be avoided.

!!! Constantly check for understanding. A colleague from Puerto Rico was presenting a program in English to an affiliate in

Italy. One of the participants kept nodding in affirmation and saying yes to what was said. The instructor tried something different: she asked a question that required a "no" answer to be correct. The learner responded with a "yes," indicating that he really did not comprehend.

Periodically ask questions that require more than a "yes" or "no" answer or for the participants to summarize what they have learned so far. This could be done orally or in writing.

Translation and interpretation

If you are invited to give a program where you and the audience do not have a common language, you will need to use a translator and/or interpreter.

Whenever possible, instructional materials should be translated and customized for the local audience. This should be done by a local person and reviewed by someone (including a subject matter expert) to insure correct connotation. (See below for some examples.)

For spoken presentations, an interpreter is involved. Interpretation could be simultaneous (such as done at the United Nations when the second language version is provided within several seconds) or consecutive. In this latter case, the speaker gives a short passage in language *A*, then pauses while the interpreter changes it into language *B*. Consecutive interpreting is the more common occurrence in meetings.

If there are technical words that may be unfamiliar to the audience or interpreter, it helps the interpreter be more effective and accurate if you talk with him or her about the words and ideas beforehand.

Visual or sign languages

You may have the opportunity to work with people whose primary language is a sign language, either in your own country or abroad. Interpreters are used; simultaneous interpreting is typically done although consecutive interpretation is sometimes requested since it is generally more accurate.

Sign languages, like spoken languages, vary from country to country. American Sign Language (ASL), used primarily by deaf people in the U.S. and Canada, is one of many sign languages used in the world. The various languages differ from each other in terms of grammatical structure and the signs themselves. For example, what is a rude street gesture in the U.S. is (by coincidence) the sign for brother in Japan.

(ASL also has some regional variation, similar to dialects of a spoken language).

!!!

Bryan (1989) tells of signs he has seen while traveling; international visitors to the U.S. probably have their own examples of fractured translations.

- "All customers promptly executed" (a barber in Tokyo).
- "The provision of a large French widow in every apartment adds to the visitor's amenities" (hotel in Spain).
- "Visitors are expected to complain at the office from 9 to 11 A.M. daily" (hotel in Athens).
- "A sports jacket may be worn to dinner, but no pants" (hotel in Paris).
- "Competitors will defile themselves on the promenade at 11 A.M., and each car will have two drivers who will relieve themselves at each other's conveniences" (regulations for an international motoring event, of unknown origin).

Other considerations

Whether you are delivering a program abroad or working with international visitors in your own country, there are some other things to keep in mind.

- *Consider the effects of jet lag.* If the traveler crosses a number of time zones, be aware of what that can do for performance and comprehension. It is better to have the person arrive several days before the course so they can be mentally and physically in synch with the local time. (As a colleague who frequently travels abroad told me, "Don't make any really big decisions on your first day.")

- *Carry on training materials.* Do not entrust your instructional materials, videotapes, and other essential tools to even the most reliable airline checked baggage systems.

- *Stay flexible.* Look for opportunities where you can use the diversity to the group's advantage.

- *Be prepared to learn.* One of the best parts about working in a cross-cultural situation is how much you can learn about other parts of the world. Your ideas may be challenged and you will come away with a broader perspective.

- *Be prepared for an adventure.* When working abroad, be ready and open for some very different experiences. Even if they are uncomfortable at the time, smile, because you will at least have a great story to take home with you.

VIII

Looking into the Future

58

The Changing Audience

The most important educational institution in the country is not Harvard or Yale or Caltech—it's television.

—Newton Minow (1979)

Goals

- Describe the demographic, educational, and organizational changes occurring in the workplace.
- Discuss the changing expectations of audiences.
- Discuss what can be developed with future audiences in mind.

Workplace demographics are changing. The typical workforce of fifteen years ago is not common today and will be completely different 10 years from now. This means that the learners and users of instructional materials will be different as well. Learner/user differences may include:

- Ethnic and cultural backgrounds;
- Entry skills, knowledge, and abilities;
- Preferred (and effective) styles of learning; and
- Expectations.

The changing characteristics of learners present a challenge for the training professional who must design and develop programs that last or that can be adapted to meet the dynamics of the workplace.

Changing demographics

The Hudson Institute published a study (Johnston and Packer 1987) examining trends in the workforce and in the workplace, and found that

- The average age of the population and the workforce will rise, and the pool of young workers entering the labor market will shrink.
- More women will enter the workforce.
- Nonwhites will constitute a larger share of the new entrants into the labor force.
- Immigrants will represent the largest share of the increase in the population and the workforce since the World War I.
- Another study predicts a 22 percent decline in the college-age population in the next decade (Molnar 1990).

Entry skills, knowledge, and educational levels

Not only are the people that make up the workforce changing, but the skills and knowledge they bring to their jobs are changing as well.

- The rate of college students choosing science and engineering majors may continue its 38 percent decline of the past decade.
- By the year 2000, the cumulative shortfall in bachelor's degrees will be 430,000 (Molnar 1990).

Changes in the job market

A complicating factor is that the "fastest-growing jobs will be in professional, technical, and sales fields requiring the highest education and skill levels" (Johnston and Packer 1987).

Another analysis shows that only people who can identify problems, solve problems, and broker (or link) problem solvers and identifiers to problems will find their income growing in the next decade (Reich 1991).

Changes in the organization

Organizations are changing as well, as they focus on their core business; things not directly related to that core are being "unbundled" with contractors, temporary agencies, and consultants hired to fill in the gaps. Total "head count" goes down. In this way productivity in maintenance, clerical, and support operations increase. "In another ten or fifteen years, it may well be the rule, especially in large organizations, to farm out all activities that do not offer the people working in them opportunities for advancement into senior management" (Drucker 1992).

Preferred ways of learning information

For the next generation of workers, reading may not be the preferred way of learning. Studies of people ages fifteen to twenty-five years point to a phenomenon of "aliteracy"—the rejection of books by those who know how to read, but choose not to. Indicators of aliteracy include the amount of reading done for school and for pleasure, and the number of hours spent in libraries compared to watching television.

Reasons for this growing trend include electronics, such as video games and portable CD players that give users "immediate, sensory gratification" and television.

Learners might prefer video because of their exposure to it: Nielsen Media Research surveys in 1991 showed American teenagers watched television an average of 23 hours per week.

Expectations

All of us are subtly molded by our culture, society, and the media. As a result, we have certain expectations as to how information is presented to us.

For example, speeches and sermons of 100 years ago were significantly longer than they are today. Another indicator is the "shrinking sound bite" or the amount of material used in TV network newscasts. In the 1968 presidential campaign the average uninterrupted block of speech shown on television news was 42 seconds. By 1988, it shrank to 9.8 seconds (Adatto 1990). In other words, people want information that is quick and to the point.

Advertising and the television and film industries have also shaped our expectations. Special effects are now a major part of the budgets of many television shows and films. A TV executive said special effects are being used to help "hold people's attention while they are holding the remote control."

There are also some positive changes seen in children who spend time watching television and playing with computer games. Researchers have seen better hand/eye coordination in players of video and computer games. Also, there is an indication that young people watching television are better at "parallel processing" or doing/tracking several things that are occurring at once (Greenfield 1984). (To understand this, look at a typical TV show from the 1960s, such as "I Love Lucy"—only one main story or plot was going on at once. In the 1990s, with a program like "LA Law," there are four or five stories going on simultaneously, sometimes extending over several weeks.)

What it means

As a designer, developer, or deliverer of instructional programs, you are in a situation similar to that of a TV network executive. Both of you are battling for the attention of the audience. A person at home can use a remote control to change stations; learners have the same capability using their minds. (Glazed-over eyes, fidgeting people, and looks of boredom are indicators that they have mentally shut you, or the particular instructional method, off.) You need to anticipate the changes in the audience and their expectations and how these changes will affect your firm.

- *Basics may not simply be assumed.* You may need to consider preparatory or adjunct courses in basic reading and arithmetic skills for people to effectively learn more advanced and special skills required by the job.

- *Use the "show" instructional method as much as possible.* As the workforce becomes more diverse (and the global sharing of information more prevalent), the use of *images* reduces the number of written and spoken words that need to be used. This can help overcome potential literacy problems.

- *Think of many short chunks.* Look at how commercial television does it. The content of a program is interrupted every eight to twelve minutes with commercials. We can focus intently, but then we need some type of break or change. A friend who is a television producer, when asked about the optimal length of instructional tapes, replied, "the mind can absorb only what one's behind can endure."

- *Broaden your focus to include nonemployees.* If you use third party personnel or outside maintenance crews to clean your manufacturing facility, do they need to know about cGMPs, your company's safety programs, and so forth? Indeed they do. These people may be missed if you limit your focus to those who are on your firm's payroll. (You may not be the one to provide this type of training, but if outside personnel have an impact on the safety, purity, and/or quality of your products, *someone* needs to make sure they are properly trained.)

- *Have fun.* Like it or not, the new population of learners expect to have their education presented with some degree of entertainment; the word *edutainment* has been coined; it is one of the fastest growing areas in computer software. (Watch public TV shows like "Sesame Street" and "Where in the World is Carmen SanDiego" and see how they make learning a fun adventure.) Increasing learner involvement in the development of a course can help add elements that are fun and meaningful to the participants.

- *Think of how you can add some type of spark in every instructional chunk.* You are battling the learner's mental remote control. Each instructional method and media you use has some unique ways to keep the person involved with the learning process. Creatively build on them. For instance, if you are having a long informational seminar, or a CBT course, why not have simple, employee-made commercials (live or on video) about the principles of the cGMPs? ("Product Identity: Don't leave the area without it.")

- *As the pool of new, trained people decreases, firms will find it more and more important to retain the people they have and in whom they have invested training.* People work for more than just money. Intellectual challenges, feeling useful, being a part of a forward-moving organization, and satisfaction from a job well done are other reasons. Training can be useful in equipping a person to do a task, as well as providing stimulation to a worker. Instruction can be a tool in keeping people at all levels interested, stimulated, and performing to the best of their abilities.

For more information

- "Training and Motivating the New Labor Force: The Impact of Ethnicity" by K. Hentges, J. Yaney, and C. Shields. *Performance Improvement Quarterly* 3(3), 1990, pp 36–44.

59

Using Multimedia Technology

If I could tell the story in words, I wouldn't need to lug around a camera.

—Lewis Hine

Goals

- Define multimedia technology.
- Discuss the relationship between computer-based training and multimedia programs.
- Discuss benefits and drawbacks of using multimedia technology as an instructional tool.
- Discuss considerations that must be kept in mind when using multimedia technology.

Multimedia technology is a powerful tool for presenting information and instruction, but to be an *effective* tool, it must be used appropriately. When looking at a project or instructional program that could involve "multimedia," you must separate the hype and glitter of the technology from what you are *really* trying to accomplish.

What is multimedia?

Multimedia technology is the integrated use of sound, text, high quality images (such as high quality graphics, animation, and moving video) produced on, controlled by, and delivered using a computer. Multimedia is a *technology*, not a solution in and of itself. A well-designed multimedia program produces a synergy in the way the various elements are used—the impact of a graphic is enhanced because of the integration of audio and text. Usually a multimedia program is shown using a personal computer to one person at a time, although with projection and speaker systems, large groups can share the experience.

Some people's perceptions of computerized multimedia courses may be based on the products, development process, equipment, technology, and prices of the mid 1970s when multimedia programs first appeared. Since then, almost everyone in the field has learned from the many successes, failures, and disappointments that have occurred.

Recent advances in computers, storage media (e.g., CD-ROMs, optical disks), and software have contributed to the explosion of interest in multimedia technology. Not too long ago, computer graphics and video could not be displayed simultaneously on the same screen. Not only is that now possible, it is generally the rule.

Benefits of incorporating multimedia technology into an instructional program

Like any other instructional method and media, multimedia technology can be used and abused. When used properly, instructional programs using multimedia have been shown (Adams 1992) to have a number of benefits, including:

- *Learning gains.* Studies have found that interactive, multimedia versions of a course are as much as 56 percent more effective in increasing the learner's understanding and retention, compared to classroom versions of the course.
- *Delivery variance.* Even though learners using multimedia programs could choose different pathways through the material, studies have shown 20–40 percent less variation in what learners understood using interactive material, as compared to classroom students.
- *Reduced training time.* Learners using computerized interactive materials take 38–70 percent less time to learn the information.
- *Content retention.* When compared to traditional classroom instruction, users of interactive materials retained 25–50 percent more information (after 30 days or less).
- *Consistency and standardization of message.* Multimedia technology can give all learners the same content, thereby reducing variability. The message can be visual, aural, or textual.

- *Just-in-time training.* Firms using multimedia programs benefit from having lessons and courses available whenever the learners have time.

Other types of benefits in using multimedia technology

Alan Kay, one of the leading thinkers on computers, society, and education, has described other potential benefits from using computers in education (Kay 1991):

- Increased interactivity between the user and the application as input and output devices become more sophisticated;
- Information can be presented from many perspectives;
- Dynamic models of an idea can be simulated; and
- Widely networked computers can become a universal library.

Other benefits include user control of the program, the appeal of the content's "look and feel" to the user, the opportunity of doing something new and different, evidence of performance, one-on-one training support, and so forth.

Multimedia technology can be used in teaching people individually, in pairs, in small groups, or in large groups, giving the instructional designer the opportunity to use group interactions as well.

Multimedia technology can provide broad access to information. Information can be presented in a very linear way (e.g., A, B, C, etc.) or in a nonlinear way (e.g., L, A, Q, C, B, etc.), based upon what the *user* wants to cover at a particular moment. User control or interactivity may or may not be an advantage in multimedia-type instructional programs. In some situations, there might be a very strict sequence that must be adhered to in a lesson outline; one piece builds on another. In other situations, it makes no difference how the information is arranged for the user—a determination made in the design phase.

Why the improvements?

One reason for the improved efficiency and effectiveness of learning is that multimedia programs can provide *learning experiences* to the user (Adams 1992). Well-designed and executed programs provide users opportunities to "put the pieces together" and demonstrate that they can perform.

There is not an "official" or standardized definition of what is included in "multimedia" technology. This results in a spectrum of software. Some have very limited graphics and sound while others incorporate a great deal of rich visuals and audio.

Multimedia "titles" are being produced for business, school, and home use. Some are strictly informational and reference (encyclopedias and almanacs, for example), while others are sophisticated games. "Edutainment" is a hybrid of educational and entertainment for children and adults and has a very high potential for growth with titles such as THE MAGIC FLUTE, DESERT STORM, and TALKING JUNGLE SAFARI.

What can it do?

One of the principle things multimedia courses can do is *involve the user* at a variety of levels by affecting the visual and hearing senses at the same time. Involvement also occurs because the user can usually control where the program takes him or her. Some programs keep the users involved by the compelling use of stories.

Who does it?

Producing a multimedia program involves a developer (usually a team of content, graphic, audio, video, and programing specialists) who produces software generally written with an "authoring system." The completed program is sent to the user (via diskettes, CD-ROMs, or a network), who has a computer capable of using the particular program.

CBT versus multimedia

CBT (computer-based training), a subset of computer-assisted instruction (CAI), may or may not be delivered using multimedia techniques. Programs stored in huge corporate mainframe computers using "dumb" terminals would not be considered as multimedia, since such terminals can display only text and very limited graphics.

Conversely, simply because a program is "multimedia" does not make it instructional just as not everything on videotape is instructional. The principles of instructional design apply to multimedia products in the same way as any other instructional media.

Issues in using multimedia technology

There are costs, drawbacks, and issues in using multimedia, including:

- *Development costs.* While costs are coming down, producing a quality program is still expensive. (On the other side of the coin, however, costs might be lower over the life of a multimedia course as compared to more traditional forms of instruction.)

- *Need for talented, experienced people.* A successful multimedia project requires a broad set of skills and talents, even when compared to other media, such as video. People with these abilities might be available in an organization, but more typically, outside professionals need to be used for at least part of the project.
- *Platform issues.* There are many, many ways of delivering a multimedia program to users, such as using Macintosh, DOS/Windows, Ultimedia, MPC, CD–I, as well as other platforms (i.e., types of computers and operating systems). They are *not* necessarily compatible with each other. (It is very similar to the different formats available for video cassette players: VHS, 8 mm, Beta, etc.). There is a great deal of interest among developers and equipment providers to increase the compatibility, but it will take time. Using certain authoring (programming) languages and planning ahead helps to resolve these issues.
- *User acceptance.* Some people remain resistant and even fearful of using computers. Using a technology like CD-I which involves a television and a special CD player might make the users more comfortable, since the technology is so similar to that which people currently use in their homes.

To use or not to use

The choice of using multimedia technology to deliver instructional material to learners must be a reasoned, rational one. You must carefully examine the objectives of the lesson and course, the method of evaluation, the audience, the money and resources available in order to determine if a multimedia solution is appropriate.

As mentioned in the sections on selecting the instructional methods and media, there are often several different ways of accomplishing a particular objective. Audience characteristics (e.g., many people at various plant sites) or lack of instructors might be factors in deciding to go with multimedia tools.

When considering a multimedia solution, one particular question to ask is, *"What benefits will this provide the user?"* If your answers include things like, "opportunities to simulate and practice," "coaching," "explore relationships between. . .," and "demonstrate and document performance," you are on the right track.

Other uses for multimedia technology

In addition to instruction, multimedia technology has a host of other applications, such as the following:

- Presentation tools;
- Marketing new products to physicians;
- Product information kiosks;
- Informational directories for offices, manufacturing facilities; and
- Integration of information used in bringing a new product to the market, for clinical trial information, and so forth.

"Repurposing" information

Since the raw materials used in multimedia programs (i.e., video, graphics, text, audio, etc.) can be easily manipulated, those developed for one purpose can be used or "repurposed" for a different audience.

For example, a pharmaceutical firm developed a laserdisc program about its manufacturing facility for use by tour groups. It was very easy to write a new program and incorporate the video into a lesson for newly hired personnel on the manufacturing process and have it delivered using multimedia technology.

The public relations or marketing arms of your firm might have material that can be readily incorporated into multimedia instructional programs.

Future trends and the training professional

Multimedia technology is still a very dynamic, exploding area. There are, however, some trends appearing.

- *Multimedia programs will not go away.* Too many large firms (IBM, Microsoft, Apple, Intel, Sony) have invested huge sums of money into the development of multimedia hardware and software. It is looked at as a major growth industry.

- *Publishing, computers, and film/video will converge into a new technology.* Signs of this are appearing with electronic books and interactive broadcast TV that are now available.

- *Compatibility between platforms (computers) will increase.* This will reduce the risk for content developers and "publishers." Industry standards, alliances (such as between major computer companies), and authoring languages that can be more easily "translated" between platforms will be very helpful. A trade group, the Interactive Multimedia Association, is currently working toward cross-platform compatibility and portability.

- *Certain types of platforms will serve certain niches.* Since some technologies are better suited for some applications than others, users will be able to take advantage of these capabilities. For instance, if it is important for a firm to make one program and distribute it worldwide, CD–I technology (at least in 1993) seems to be well suited for that, since a player can be used with any TV and any electrical system in the world.

- *The differences between "presentation software" and "interactive training software" will blur.* Until recently, some application software was designed strictly for making overhead transparencies and slides. Other programs focused on stand-alone training applications. Now, however, the distinctions are becoming fewer and fewer.

- *A new breed of electronic newspapers and magazines will serve an informational and training function.* Users will be able to ask their own background or historical questions and receive the answers in a variety of ways (text, audio, graphics, etc.).

- *Increased "just-in-time" training.* Learners will be able to get their training when they need it, making training more effective since it will be more closely related to a particular user need or problem.

- *Appearance of the virtual classroom.* Users will be able to link up electronically with other learners across the hall or at a facility across the ocean. People will be able to *share* drawings, photos, experiences, and the like, resulting in instruction that is more learner centered, collaborative, and consistent. Experts will be able to facilitate understanding and provide coaching to learners via desktop/workplace computers and workstations.

"I think I will pass on this round."

One way of responding to multimedia technology is to sit back and wait for the dust to settle. If it settles at all, it will be only briefly and then a potentially brand new technology will appear. In the meantime you and your organization will have not been taking advantage of the benefits available today.

Think of multimedia technology like a car. If you buy a car that meets your needs and budget, you will have useful transportation that will continue to provide good service, even as faster, trendier models come out.

Final thoughts

- If you have a program or design that would benefit using multimedia technology, do not be afraid of it. Make sure you see through the glitz and the glitter.

- Glitz and glitter do have their place in certain situations. Multimedia-produced effects can give you the "wow" you might need in a motivational program or grab the attention of a learner or audience.

- Define and manage expectations. Because well-designed and executed materials *look* so simple and elegant, some people do not realize what it takes to produce such a product. Focusing on what you want to *accomplish* and getting all parties concerned to agree on that will help.

- Understand what you are trying to accomplish now and how multimedia courses fit into a long-term (three to five year) vision.

- If you are selecting an authoring system, do it carefully, with an understanding of who will be using it, your content/delivery requirements, the platforms on which the material will be delivered, the "power" and complexity of the language, and so forth.

- Try using multimedia technology on a small project first and plan on learning a lot. Your second one will be a major improvement over the first.

- Think of what the user will focus on. Since so much can be occurring simultaneously in a multimedia program, make sure what is important is not lost amid the bells and whistles.

- To greatly increase your probability of success, use people who do multimedia courses professionally. Look at their past work and talk with some of their clients. (A good sign is when a vendor or producer has repeat business from a client.)

For more information

- *The Media Lab* by Stewart Brand. New York: Penguin Books, 1988. (While a little dated, Brand discusses how the MIT Media Lab is helping to define the new technology that results from the convergence of publishing, computers, and film/video.)
- *Managing Interactive Video / Multimedia Projects* by Robert E. Bergman. Englewood Cliffs, New Jersey: Education Technology, 1990. (An excellent overview of multimedia projects; very complete checklist at the end.)
- *Computers as Theatre* by Brenda Laurel. Reading, Massachusetts: Addison-Wesley Publishing Company: 1991.
- *NewMedia*. A magazine published by Hypermedia Communications, Inc., San Mateo, California.
- *Multimedia Review*. A magazine published by the Meckler Corporation, Westport, Connecticut. (Covers topics of multimedia, virtual reality, and some instructional aspects of the technologies.)

60

Electronic Performance Support Systems

"What is it?" asked Arthur.
"The Hitchhikers Guide to the Galaxy. *It's a sort of electronic book. It tells you everything you need to know about anything. That's its job."*
Arthur turned it over nervously in his hands.
"I like the cover," he said. " 'Don't panic.' " It's the first helpful or intelligible thing anybody's said to me all day."

—Douglas Adams, *The Hitchhikers Guide to the Galaxy*

Goals

- Define an electronic performance support (EPS) system and its parts.
- Distinguish between EPS systems and other types of job aides and training interventions.
- Describe what an EPS system can do.
- Identify situations where an EPS system can be of value.
- Discuss considerations when thinking of an EPS system.

During the design phase we paused to ask the question, *"what else is needed besides training for people to perform the task safely and effectively?"* One of the things frequently identified are "job aides" that can provide the trained worker a fast way to access certain information. For instance, a job aide might include the basic steps and sequence to follow in setting up a filling machine or the proper sequence for putting on a sterile gown.

The convergence of computer, information storage and display, networking, and human performance technologies are turning the job aide into something very different, called electronic performance support (EPS) systems. The resulting powerful resource might change the way we all do our jobs and the way skills training is delivered.

What is electronic performance support (EPS)?

Electronic performance support (EPS) is a concept for integrating and delivering, on demand, the information, tools, and methodologies a worker can use in order to perform the task more safely, efficiently, effectively, and consistently.

Well-designed and developed EPS enables the user by providing whatever is necessary to generate performance and learning at the moment of need. It takes advantage of whatever technologies are appropriate in delivering support, when and where its needed, and in the most useful form (Gery 1991).

What can EPS systems do?

While no current EPS system can perform like (or have the charm) of *The Hitchhikers Guide to the Galaxy* or the computer HAL in the book and film *2001: A Space Odyssey*, there are systems in place today that provide

- Integrated reference material, training, and coaching for users of *Word for Windows;*
- Customer service representatives with consistent, complete, and current information as well as guidance through recommended models for solving customer problems and inquiries;
- Reference materials (high quality graphic and video images) so operators can quickly and accurately eliminate defects in the manufacture of computer chips; and
- Support to teams involved with total quality management (TQM) problem identification and solving. The EPS includes tools, support, and coaching for using the firm's standardized methodology, from data collection and display to statistical tools and report generation.

!!!

Currently, one pharmaceutical manufacturer uses a relatively simple EPS as an "electronic procedure" describing the tasks and responsibilities different groups have regarding stability testing and placing samples on long-term stability tests. The EPS flowcharts the process and then breaks each task into more explicit tasks and subtasks. Glossaries, sample forms, lists of staff resources and phone numbers, plus much more is contained in this networked Hypercard stack.

Benefits of using EPS systems

Firms that have implemented EPS systems have found a number of benefits (Gery 1991), including

- Consistent, high-level performance;
- Accelerated performance and improved learned;
- Decreased training costs;
- Improved information and communication flow; and
- Reduced waste of materials and time.

Why the improvements?

Firms have received these benefits from their investment in EPS because the systems *enable and support* the worker. Training is provided when it is needed (i.e., "just-in-time") and when it can be linked to a specific problem the user has.

EPS systems anticipate the types of questions a user of any level has, and respond immediately with video, graphical, text, and/or audio information (Figure 60.1.). They are flexible enough to account for an individual's own learning style and preferences, allowing faster learning and performance. Advanced EPS systems can monitor how the task is being performed and automatically provide reference information or coaching as appropriate.

The parts of an EPS system

An EPS system consists of several parts, some of which are hardware-related, others of which are information-related.

- *Hardware.* Users must have retrieval and display devices so they can access the information. Storage and communication equipment, such as hard (magnetic) or optical (CD–ROM) disks and networks are also used.
- *Information ("infobase").* This is all the information, in various forms and arrangements, the user will inquire against, access, or have presented to him or her to do the job. This could be training material in the form of a video ("clean the tubing like this"), animation ("load the autoclave rack in the sequence as shown"), text (procedures, GMP requirements), and so forth.
- *The support system.* The support system is the set of connections that appropriately link the user to the resources

Figure 60.1. Diagram of a complex Electronic Performance Support System (From: *Electronic Performance Support Systems* by Gloria J. Gery. Weingarten Publications. Used by permission.)

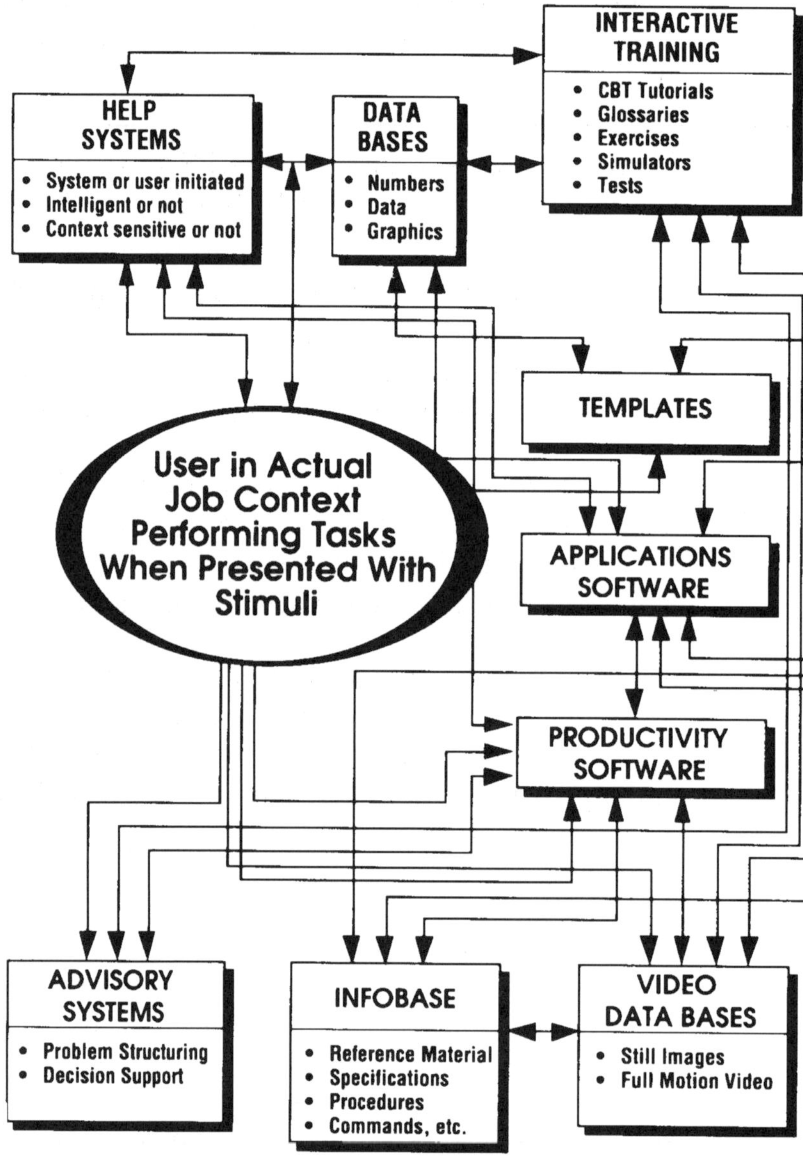

available. It can also include utilities, such as help systems; expert systems; and monitoring, assessment, and feedback systems. Some support systems require the user to select certain resources. Other, more sophisticated programs automatically call in the electronic resource when it senses a need.

- *User interface.* This is the user's connection with the system. It must be understandable, easy to use, and consistent. It should also permit the user to take a variety of paths and navigate easily through large amounts of diverse types of information.

How EPS systems fit with training

An EPS system is not the answer to all of the instructional needs a worker and an organization have. Based on the FDA's expectations (of the early 1990s), for example, it would be difficult to deliver cGMP regulation training in a "just-in-time" environment. Also, EPS systems do not lend themselves to providing users a needed overview or orientation to an entire process (Clark 1992).

On the other hand, including procedure and skill training in an EPS system would be very useful. Beyond training, however, an EPS system must make learning (and performance) as easy as possible at every step (Carr 1992). Much of the detailed information that comes from a performance, job, task, and audience analysis is used in the design and development of the EPS system.

For example, if the task were hand-cleaning a mixing tank, EPS might provide

- The cleaning procedure,
- Locations of approved cleaning materials,
- A video of how to do it,
- "Experts" who could provide audio/video advice and coaching on the "tricks" of cleaning the equipment,
- How to be sure the tank is really clean,
- What to do if something goes wrong,
- Labeled graphics showing the parts of the tank,
- Built-in documentation and logs to support the fact the tank was cleaned,
- Links to instruction on why cleaning is critical,
- Links to the GMP requirements of cleaning, and
- Links to the validation of the cleaning process.

All of this information would be available to the user in an easy-to-access way. If the user had not done this specific procedure recently, the system would recognize that and show the video first, and, perhaps, ask questions about the process that the user must correctly answer before continuing. This training would be documented and added to the computerized list of completed training courses the worker had taken.

EPS compared to other tools

EPS systems are similar yet different when compared to other tools and technologies (like traditional job aides and computer-based training). The main feature is that it has some "intelligence" that can work with the user to solve a problem or complete a task (Raybould 1990). Tables 60.1 and 60.2 show comparisons between several of these tools and EPS systems.

When considering an EPS system

Developing an EPS system for an existing task or process forces you to take a very different view of it. If you simply add computer support to what is currently being done, you might complicate the situation, or at the very least, not take advantage of simplifications that could be made (within the requirements of the cGMPs and the product's registration) from re-engineering. Wasted duties need to be eliminated with the EPS system focusing on value-adding duties (Carr 1992).

Table 60.1. Comparison of performance support systems with job aides
(From: *Electronic Performance Support Systems* by Gloria J. Gery. Weingarten Publications. Used by permission.)

Performance Support	Job Aides
Can support simple or complex task performance; can address multipathed, conditionally branched integrated processes via expert systems.	Typically support simple, linear sequential procedural tasks.
Can accept user input or data as a basis for situationally specific branching, advice, information presentation, etc.	Do not accept user input or data. Structuring occurs in advance of need and addresses limited situations.
Provide task structuring, advice, and related information.	Provide task structuring but not related information.
Can present customized views of the system to individual users.	Structured in advance and do not accommodate individual user requirements.
Can incorporate multiple modes of information presentation (e.g., text, audio, images, animated sequences).	Typically paper-based with possibility of passive multiple modes (i.e., text and still images). When electronic, could incorporate multiple modes, but is mostly text and still images.
Can provide alternate access to the information (e.g., menus, alphabetical listings, context-sensitive to software or condition, hierarchical access through outlines, or relational access through hypermedia).	Typically provide predetermined and structured access. Because the infobase is not integrated, the path is usually linear.

Table 60.2. Comparison of performance support systems with conventional computer-based training. **(From: *Electronic Performance Support Systems* by Gloria J. Gery. Weingarten Publications. Used by permission.)**

Performance Support	Computer-Based Training
Contains an organized, interactive, hyper-reference inforbase that can be accessed in multiple ways or prelinked to other components of the system.	Contains an infobase that is typically structured within predetermined presentation sequences. When inforbase in CBT is organized with hypermedia and linked to interactions or applications software, it is more similar to EPSS than traditional training.
Contains a broad range of support mechanisms, including interactive advisory or other problem structuring and decision support mechanisms to assist users with specific problems or situations.	May outline procedures or processes as part of information presentation, but rarely includes other interactive support mechanisms.
Can accept and manipulate user input or data.	Typically uses pre-established examples for task practice. Does not accept specific user input to address a given user problem, situation, or need.
Permits very flexible navigation and information access by users in nonlinear structure.	Typically structured in advanced by developer to present optimal sequence and approach to communicating information and task practice. Can permit some learner flexibility in access and navigation, but most often control is limited to sequencing prestructured modules.
Available on demand, in context, on the job to provide information and support.	Most often organized as an event with the goal of teaching to be experienced prior to job performance. When available on-demand at the job site, CBT is typically designed to be experienced as a sequential training event, rather than as a reference or support environment.
Emphasis is on user construction of an individualized learning sequence.	Structured to present information and experiences as organized by the developer.
Multimedia possible.	Multimedia possible.
Can include monitoring of user performance in a task or system and provide context-sensitive advice, information, control, or various types of support.	Monitors and tracks user activity either to record user paths or performance on questions or exercises. When CBT is concurrent with applications softwarte, it can "know" where users are and provide pre-linked instructional sequences or content.
Granular.	Modular.

Another consideration when thinking about EPS systems is if your organization is ready for it. "No matter what technologies you are using or what activity you are trying to support, the main issues in system development are always more organizational than technical" (Gery 1991).

For example, if workers have more access to more information, they might spend less time locating and talking to supervisors. People would be enabled by better and faster access to information. In other situations, individuals who kept information to themselves and used it as a tool (or weapon) would find their power eroded.

During the development process the team might discover other informational, equipment, facility, and organizational issues that need to be addressed.

In other words, since the primary benefit of performance support systems is improved performance, and many factors affect performance, installing an EPS system would have ripple effects throughout the organization.

Another consideration is implementation of the technology involved and ramifications related to it. (For example, if "electronic" procedures are used, where do they reside? How will they be controlled, networked or distributed, etc.?).

Working through these issues takes time, resources, funds, and frequently the expertise of an outside consultant. However, when the proper application is chosen, the benefits mentioned earlier can occur.

When an EPS system might be a solution

When should an EPS system be considered? When is the investment likely to have its largest payback?

- *When the cost of failure is high.* This could be measured in terms of waste (of materials, product, time), loss (unsatisfied customers, patients, hospitals), or safety (worker, community, facility).
- *When many people do a particular task / when consistency is required.* The uniformity imposed by an EPS system helps to produce more consistent outcomes.
- *When the task is critical.* If a certain activity in a process is not done correctly, there might be serious consequences.

For example, "identify the proper number of samples to be placed in a stability testing program." If not enough samples are tested at the required humidity, temperature, and lighting conditions during product development, a new drug product could be delayed for months or even years.

- *When the task does not need to be instantaneously performed.* If the user has the time to look up information, an EPS system makes sense; on the other hand, if the task is an immediate reaction to an event, such as in an emergency, using an EPS might take too long.
- *When the task is complex.* If there are many potential pathways that can be taken, it may be critical that a certain sequence be followed, or at the very least, all checkpoints cleared properly.
- *When the task is done infrequently.* If someone has not done a task in a while, he or she might need a quick "refresher" that could be accomplished by simply watching how it is done or by coaching provided by an EPS.
- *When supervisory and resource personnel are not readily available.* As most organizations are trying to reduce support and overhead costs, more people now report to a supervisor. People with a depth of experience are not as available. An EPS system can be a repository and delivery device for an organization's knowledge and wisdom.

Final thoughts

"An EPS system should be designed first and foremost to support the value-adding duties of a position. It should do so by developing and enhancing the skills of the human performer. It should never, under any conditions, substitute for or diminish these skills" (Carr 1992).

One of the most important raw materials and products any pharmaceutical firm uses and produces is information. Procedures and specifications and the knowledge and skills of the employees are all involved in making a high-quality pharmaceutical product. Besides the finished drug product, information also comes out—batch records, deviation reports, logs, numbers, test results, and the like.

As organizations discuss and design their "factories of the future," information flow must be given as much thought and consideration by experts as is given to HVAC, utilities, and filling equipment.

Utilizing the concepts behind EPS systems is a significant advantage to a firm so that people are provided easy access to the information and tools that will enable them to perform to the maximum of their abilities.

Additional information

- *Electronic Performance Support Systems* by G. J. Gery. Boston: Weingarten Publications, 1991.
- "Solving Human Performance Problems With Computers" by B. Raybould. *Performance and Instruction 30(10),* Nov/Dec 1990, pp 4–14.

61

Virtual Reality as a Training Tool

Any sufficiently advanced technology is undistinguishable from magic.

—Arthur C. Clark

Goals

- Define virtual reality and virtual environment.
- Describe the spectrum of virtual reality by giving three examples.
- Discuss the current state of virtual reality technology.
- Identify when virtual reality may be an effective instructional tool.
- Provide examples of existing and potential learning applications involving virtual reality.

One cutting-edge technology with tremendous instructional potential is virtual reality. Virtual reality is related to "simulators" in the same way that the Concorde is related to a DC 3 airplane. And, like the Concorde, which gets its passengers from Paris to New York in half the "normal" flying time, virtual reality is expensive and glamorous, but useful in well-defined situations. One can expect, however, as the computer and the infant virtual reality industry continue to develop, costs will go down and capabilities and applications will increase.

What is virtual reality?

Virtual reality is a way of enabling users to participate directly in real-time, three-dimensional environments generated by computers (Hensel 1992).

Virtual reality (VR) puts the user into a virtual environment (VE), sometimes also called "cyberspace." (Not only is VR a convergence of technologies and disciplines, it is sometimes a merger of words and examples from real life and science fiction.) In other words, *VR creates a computer-generated world with which the user can interact.*

Levels of virtual reality

As with many emerging technologies, VR has some fuzzy definitions and distinctions. It may help to view VR as a spectrum from highly complex to less complex, all of which provide the opportunity for multiple users to interact with each other.

- *Full immersion systems.* The user wears goggles or headgear with stereoscopic, three-dimensional visual displays and binaural sound equipment. Some combination of eye-tracking devices, microphones, body suits, or "data gloves" may be used for transmitting motions, commands, and responses to the computer. High-end systems incorporate tactile (touch or force) feedback to the user. Movement and manipulation of objects and sounds in the virtual environment can be subject to the physical laws of gravity, inertia, and friction, making the experience more life-like (Lantz 1992).

- *Through-the-window systems.* A three-dimensional world appears through a computer screen that the user can steer through, using a "flying mouse." The user only receives visual and audio feedback during the experience.

- *Video-projected systems.* Video-projected worlds provide a second-person experience in which the viewer stands outside the imaginary world and looks in via a TV monitor, but manipulates virtual objects through the use of a video camera input device. Tactile feedback is not possible using this method.

- *Enhanced interactive multimedia.* This approach uses more traditional input devices (a keyboard or mouse), but the multimedia environment "provides users a sense of participating in realities different from their own" (Henderson 1990). Here the content and the way it is presented pulls the user into the virtual environment. (This model is considered by some to be "borderline" between true VR and high-powered multimedia technology.)

Virtual reality as an emerging technology

VR has been nurtured in university and high-tech company labs, as well as by NASA and the military. It is an exciting technology with incredible potential, but it has gathered "more public interest and press speculation than customers who have actually used it" (Teixeira 1992).

A recent survey showed that entertainment, education, and medical applications will be the largest markets. But what can it actually do in regard to training?

Virtual reality and training

Virtual reality can provide a highly realistic environment where a person can learn by encountering activities and situations (McLellan 1991).

As with simulations, VR as a training media has its greatest potential impact in situations when

- Information to be mastered is complex,
- Equipment to be operated is complex and expensive,
- Costs of inadequate training and practice are high,
- The activity itself is dangerous to those doing the task, and
- Mistakes have serious consequences (Geber 1990).

Because VR is an emerging technology, few training-related applications have been described in the literature. The examples that follow are operational or in advanced research and are categorized according to training situations (as shown above). Also given are some speculative examples of possible pharmaceutical applications.

Complex information.

> "Traumabase." Using 200,000 sheets of paper, 50,000 35 mm slides, hours of audio and video tape, laserdiscs, and other information from the Vietnam War, developers put together a "cyberspace database" to help plan and teach about medical casualties of war and similar disasters (Henderson 1992).

Other ideas for using this type of technology where there is complex information include

- Models for better understanding and teaching techniques for monitoring the environment in aseptic manufacturing areas for bacteria and particulates, and
- Teaching relationships of stability testing.

Complex and expensive equipment.

> "See-through reality." Researchers at Boeing are studying a system where workers would wear special see-through goggles that would impose or overlay a virtual image of a fuselage, for example, showing cables, hydraulic equipment, and so forth that is normally hidden by the metal skin of the aircraft (Bylinsky 1991).

For other situations involving complex and expensive equipment, similar ideas include

- Giving users and maintenance personnel an "inside" look at how lyophilization or autoclaves work, and
- Teaching proper design and construction of high-purity water systems (e.g., water for injection) by providing learners with a virtual "journey" through the system.

High costs of inadequate training and practice.

> "Virtual Leg." Surgeons and computer scientists from Stanford, Northwestern, and MIT have "constructed a model of the leg that surgeons can view from any angle, even peering inside joints" (Bylinsky 1991).

Potential pharmaceutical industry applications of when there are high costs of inadequate training and practice include

- Teaching proper aseptic techniques to personnel who produce sterile products and certifying their performance, and
- Teaching operators sorting techniques and validating their performance.

The activity is dangerous in itself; when mistakes have serious consequences.

> LOFT (Line Oriented Flight Training). This training program utilizing VR was developed based on research that showed most airplane accidents and incidents occur due to pilot error. Pilots using LOFT encounter a cascade of small difficulties that cause distraction from their "normal" activities. "By having pilots practice those kinds of situations in sophisticated VR simulators, they will be prepared for real-world emergencies" (McLellan 1991).

Potential examples where the activity is dangerous in itself include

- The sampling of hazardous raw materials, and
- Responding to toxic spills and emissions.

Using virtual reality

If your needs analysis indicates that practice or simulations are important, VR might be something to consider, especially as developers get more experience and the technology continues to develop.

There are some firms (e.g., AutoDesk and Virtis 3-D) currently producing "desktop" applications software where computer-savy trainers might do some of their own experimenting and developing.

For more information

- *Virtual Reality* by Howard Rheingold. New York: Summit Books, 1991.
- "The World of Virtual Reality" by Mark Fritz. *Training*, February 1991, pp. 45–50.

Appendices

A

European Community Training Requirements for Pharmaceutical Personnel

(From the Rules Governing Medicinal Products in the European Community, Volume IV—Good Manufacturing Practice for Medicinal Products, January 1992. Directorate–General Internal Market and Industrial Affairs; Commission of the European Communities. Luxembourg: Office for Official Publications of the European Communities.)

(From the Introduction to Volume IV)

Two directives laying down principles and guidelines of good manufacturing practice (GMP) for medicinal products were adopted by the Commission in 1991, the first for medicinal products for human use (Directive 91/356/EEC), the second one for veterinary use (Directive 91/412/EEC). Detailed guidelines in accordance with those principles are published in the Guide to Good Manufacturing Practice which will be used in assessing application for Manufacturing Authorizations and as a basis for inspection of manufacturers of medicinal products.

(Training-related sections from the)
Commission Directive
of 13 June 1991

laying down the principles and guidelines of
good manufacturing practice for
medicinal products for human use

Article 7
Personnel

1. At each manufacturing site, the manufacturer shall have competent and appropriately qualified personnel at his disposal in sufficient number to achieve the pharmaceutical quality assurance objective.

4. Personnel shall receive initial and continuing training including the theory and application of the concept of quality assurance and good manufacturing practice.

(Note: the above cited sections for medicinal products are identical to those found in the "Directive of 23 July 1991 laying down the principles and guidelines of good manufacturing practice for veterinary medicinal products.")

(Training-related sections from the Guidelines)

Chapter 2
Personnel:
Principle

The establishment and maintenance of a satisfactory system of quality assurance and the correct manufacture of medicinal products relies upon people. For this reason there must be sufficient qualified personnel to carry out all the tasks which are the responsibility of the manufacturer. Individual responsibilities should be clearly understood by the individuals and recorded. All personnel should be aware of the principles of Good Manufacturing Practice that affect them and receive initial and continuing training, including hygiene instructions, relevant to their needs.

General

2.1. The manufacturer should have an adequate number of personnel with the necessary qualifications and practical experience. The responsibilities placed on any one individual should not be so extensive as to present any risk to quality.

Training

2.8. The manufacturer should provide training for all the personnel whose duties take them into production areas or into control laboratories (including the technical, maintenance, and cleaning personnel), and for other personnel whose activities could affect the quality of the product.

2.9. Besides the basic training on the theory and practice of Good Manufacturing Practice, newly recruited personnel should receive training appropriate to the duties assigned to them. Continuing training should also be given, and its practical effectiveness should be periodically assessed. Training programs should be available, approved by either the head of Production or the head of Quality Control, as appropriate. Training records should be kept.

2.10. Personnel working in areas where where contamination is a hazard, e.g., clean areas or areas where highly active, toxic, infectious, or sensitizing materials are handled, should be given specific training.

2.11. Visitors or untrained personnel should, preferably, not be taken into the production and quality control areas. If this is unavoidable, they should be given information in advance, particularly about personal hygiene and the prescribed protective clothing. They should be closely supervised.

2.12. The concept of Quality Assurance and all the measures capable of improving its understanding and implementation should be fully discussed during the training sessions.

B

Resources

There are a number of professional organizations and publications geared for people involved in human performance and training. Some selected ones are included below. Other periodicals and resource materials may be found at the end of various chapters.

Organizations

ASTD—American Society for Training and Development. [Box 1443, Alexandria, VA 22313, (703) 683-8171]

> A national organization with local chapters and a special industry group for people interested in chemicals and pharmaceuticals. ASTD is the leading organization in the field and has a strong link with human resource development. It publishes *Training and Development Journal* each month. Memberships in ASTD are also available internationally. An annual national meeting is held, along with periodic regional conferences.

NETA—National Environmental Training Association. [2930 E. Camelback Road, Scottsdale, AZ 85016, (602) 956-6099]

> A professional society for environmental training professionals. NETA publishes a newsletter and manuals; it has an annual conference and offers a certification program for environmental trainers.

NSPI—National Society for Performance and Instruction. [1300 L Street, NW, Suite 1250, Washington, DC 20005, (202) 408-7969]

An international organization "dedicated to increasing productivity in the workplace." NSPI publishes the *Performance and Instruction Journal* and the *Performance Improvement Quarterly*. It has an annual conference.

SALT—Society for Applied Learning Technology. [50 Culpepper Street, Warrenton, VA 22186, (703) 347-0055]

SALT is a society for professionals in instructional technology; topics and exhibits at meetings are more "techie" than other groups. SALT sponsors two major conferences each year with special sessions related to the use of instructional technology in the medicine and health-care. They publish *Instructional Delivery Systems, Journal of Medical Education Technologies,* and *Journal of Interactive Instruction Development.*

Other organizations that focus on issues related to pharmaceutical manufacturing and quality control and that sometimes include training and performance-related topics in their meetings:

- *ISPE*—International Society for Pharmaceutical Engineers [3816 W. Linebaugh Ave, Suite 412, Tampa, FL 33624, (813) 960-2105]
- *PDA*—Parenteral Drug Association [1617 JFK Boulevard, Suite 640, Philadelphia, PA 19103, (215) 564-6466]

Publications

Instructional Delivery Systems. Published by the Society of Applied Learning Technology. (See SALT listing under "Organizations" for address.)

The Instructor's Survival Kit: A Handbook for Teachers of Adults, Second Edition by P. F. Renner. Vancouver: Training Associates Ltd, 1989. A collection of various activities, techniques, examples, and forms that can be incorporated and adapted into lead-led courses.

Performance and Instruction Journal Published by National Society for Performance and Instruction. (See NSPI listing under "Organizations" for address.)

Training and Development Alert. Published by Advanced Personnel Systems [P. O. Box 1438, Roseville, CA 95661,

(916) 781-2900] A bimonthly series of abstracts from articles published in a variety of training, development, and human performance publications. Abstracts all have detailed source information.

Training and Development Journal. Published by the American Society for Training and Development. (See ASTD listing under "Organizations" for address.)

Training. Published by Lakewood Publications, Inc. [Lakewood Building, 50 S. Ninth Street, Minneapolis, MN 55402, (612) 333-0471]

Training and Development Yearbook. Published annually by Prentice Hall, Englewood Cliffs, NJ 07632. A compendium of articles that have been published in the past year in training-related journals. Also includes brief summaries and references on topics of interest to training and performance professionals.

References and Sources

References and Sources

Abt, C. C. 1987. *Serious Games.* Lanham, MD: University of America Press.

Adams, G. L. 1992. "Why Interactive?" *Multimedia & Videodisc Monitor* (March): 20–25.

Adatto, K. 1990. "The Incredible Shrinking Sound Bite." *The New Republic* (May 28):20–23.

Allen, W. H. 1967. cited in *The Selection and Use of Instructional Media.* A. J. Romiszowski, 1988. New York: Nichols Publishing; p. 78.

Axtell, R. E. 1990. *Do's and Taboos of Hosting International Visitors.* New York: John Wiley & Sons, Inc.

Bowsher, J. E. 1989. *Educating America: Lessons Learned in the Nation's Corporations* New York: John Wiley & Sons, Inc.

Brethower, D. M., and K. A. Smalley. 1992a. Performance Based Instruction: Definition and Examples. *Performance & Instruction* (March):36–40.

Brethower, D. M., and K. A. Smalley. 1992b. Performance Based Instruction: Assuring That Learning Occurs and Transfers to the Job. *Performance & Instruction* (July):38–42.

Bryan, III, J. 1989, *Gallimaufry to Go.* New York: Dell Publishing; pp. 129–133.

Bylinsky, G. 1991. "The Marvels of 'Virtual Reality'." *Fortune* (June 3):138–150.

Campbell, J. 1988. *The Power of Myth.* New York: Doubleday.

Carnevale, A. P., L. J. Gaier, J. Villet, and S. L. Holland. 1990. *Training Partnerships—Linking Employers and Providers.* Alexandria, VA/Washington DC: American Society for Training and Development/U.S. Department of Labor.

Carnevale, A. P., and E. R. Schulz. 1990. "Return on Investment: Accounting for Training." *Training & Development Journal* (July, Supplement):S1–S32.

Carr, C. 1992. "Performance Support Systems—The Next Step?" *Performance & Instruction* (February):23–26.

Clark, R.C. 1992. "EPSS—Look Before You Leap: Some Cautions About Applications of Electronic Performance Support Systems." *Performance & Instruction* (May/June):22–25.

Copeland, L., and L. Griggs. 1985. *Going International.* New York: Random House.

Cranton, P. 1989. *Planning Instruction for Adult Learners.* Toronto: Wall & Thompson.

Cross, P. 1981. *Adults as Learners.* San Francisco: Jossey-Bass Publishers.

Davidson, G. V. 1990. "Matching Learning Styles with Teaching Styles: Is it a Useful Concept in Instruction?" *Performance & Instruction* (April):36–38.

Drucker, P. F. 1992. *Managing for the Future: The 1990's and Beyond.* New York: Truman Talley Books/Dutton; pp. 275–279.

Dunn, R., and K. Dunn. 1977. "How to Diagnose Learning Styles." *Instructor* 87: 123–144.

Eurich, N. 1990. *The Learning Industry: Education for Adult Workers.* Princeton, NJ: Carnegie Foundation/Princeton University Press.

FDA 483. 1989. Issued to pharmaceutical manufacturer, C.F. 1819470. (August 25): 27–28.

Gagné, R. M. 1985. *Principles of Instructional Design.* New York: Holt, Rinehart, and Winston.

Geber, B. 1990. "Simulating Reality." *Training* (April):41–46.

Gery, G. J. 1991. *Electronic Performance Support Systems.* Boston: Weingarten Publications.

Gilbert, T. F. 1978. *Human Competence Engineering: Worthy Performance.* New York: McGraw Hill.

GMP Trends. 1991a. (April 1) Issue #341.

GMP Trends. 1991b. (May 15) Issue #344.

GMP Trends. 1991c. (June 15) Issue #346.

Gordon, J. 1991. "Measuring the 'Goodness' of Training." *Training* (August):19–25.

Greenfield, P. M. 1984. *Mind and Media: The Effects of Television, Videogames, and Computers.* Cambridge, MA: Harvard University Press.

Hannum, W., and C. Hansen. 1989. *Instructional Systems Development in Large Organizations.* Englewood Cliffs, NJ: Educational Technology Publications.

Heckel, P. 1984. *The Elements of Friendly Software Design.* New York: Warner Books; p. 54.

Henderson, J. 1990. "Designing Realities: Interactive Media, Virtual Realities, and Cyberspace." *Multimedia Review* (Summer):47–51.

Henderson, J. 1992. "Cyberspace Representation of Vietnam War Trauma." *Multimedia Review* (Winter/Spring):12–22.

Hensel, S. K. 1992. "Virtual Reality as a Learning Medium." *Instructional Delivery Systems* (July/August):4–5.

Jackson, S. L. 1992. "What You Should Know About ISO 9000." *Training* (May):48–52.

Johnson, K. A. 1989. "The Foundations of Instructional Design." In *Instructional Design: New Alternatives for Effective Education.* ed. K. A. Johnson, 3–15. New York: Macmillan.

Johnston, W. B., and A. E. Packer. 1987. *Workforce 2000: Work and Workers for the Twenty-first Century.* Indianapolis: Hudson Institute.

Kaplan, R. S. 1984. "Yesterday's Accounting Undermines Production." *Harvard Business Review* (July–August):95–101.

Kay, A. C. 1991. "Computers, Networks, and Education." *Scientific American* (September):138–148.

Kirkpatrick, D. L. 1975. "Techniques for Evaluating Training Programs." In *Evaluating Training Programs.* ed. D. L. Kirkpatrick. Alexandria, VA: American Society for Training and Development.

Kirrane, D. E. 1986. "Cost Accounting Today." *Training and Development Journal* (September):24–27.

Knowles, M. S. 1989. *The Making of an Adult Educator: An Autobiographical Journey.* San Francisco: Jossey-Bass Publishers.

Kolb, D. 1984. *Experiential Learning: Experience as the Source of Learning and Development.* Englewood Cliffs, NJ: Prentice-Hall, Inc.

Lantz, E. 1992. "Virtual Reality in Science Museums." *Instructional Delivery Systems* (July/August):10–12.

Macromedia, 1992. *Interactive Multimedia: Return on Investment Analysis for Learning and Communication.* San Francisco: Macromedia.

Mager, R. F., and P. Pipe. 1984. *Analyzing Performance Problems,* 2nd Ed. Belmont, CA: Lake Publishing Co.

Mager, R. F. 1984a. *Goal Analysis,* 2nd Ed. Belmont, CA: Lake Publishing Co.

Mager, R. F. 1984b. *Preparing Instructional Objectives,* Rev. 2nd Ed. Belmont, CA: David S. Lake Publishers.

McLellan, H. 1991. "Virtual Environments and Situated Learner." *Multimedia Review* (Fall):30–37.

Molnar, A. R. 1990. "Intellectual Tools of the Future." In *The Power of Multimedia: A Guide to Interactive Technology in Education and Business.* ed. J. C. Cash, 27–34. Washington, DC: Interactive Video Industry Association.

Morical, K., and B. Tsai. 1992. "Adapting Training for Other Cultures." *Training & Development* (April):65–68.

Moskal, J. 1992. "Experts: Forget Job Security." *Rochester Democrat and Chronicle* (January 12).

New York *Times.* 1990. Educational Supplement, October 3.

Placek, C. 1989. "Educational, Training or Both?" *Quality* (September):20.

Raybould, B. 1990. "Solving Human Performance Problems With Computers." *Performance & Instruction* (November/December):4–14.

Reich, R. B. 1991. *The Work of Nations.* New York: Vintage Books.

Reiser, R. A. 1987. "Instructional Technology: A History." In *Instructional Technology: Foundation.* ed. R. M. Gagné, 11–16. Hillsdale, NY: Lawrence Erlbaum Associates.

Reiser, R. A., and R. M. Gagné. 1983. "Media Selection Flowchart." In *Selecting Media for Instruction.* ed. R. A. Reiser, 1–9. Englewood Cliffs, NJ: Educational Technology Publications.

Robinson, D. G. and J. Robinson. 1989. *Training for Impact.* San Francisco: Jossey-Bass Publishers.

Rogers, C. 1969. *Freedom to Learn.* Columbus, OH: Merrill Publishers.

Romiszowski, A. J. 1988. *The Selection and Use of Instructional Media.* New York: Nichols Publishing.

Schramm, W. L. 1977. *Big Media, Little Media.* Beverly Hills, CA: Sage Publications, Inc.

Spitzer, D. R. 1990. "Confessions of a Performance Technologist." *Educational Technology* (May):12–15.

Stalk, Jr., G. 1988. "Time—The Next Source of Competitive Advantage." *Harvard Business Review* (July–August):41–51.

Stettler, H. F. 1982. *Auditing Principles: A Systems-based Approach,* 5th Ed. Englewood Cliffs, NJ: Prentice-Hall, Inc.; p. 84.

Teixeira, K. 1992. "A Review of the FTS Survey of Virtual Reality." *Virtual Reality Report* (June):14–15.

Tetzlaff, R. 1991. "FDA Inspection of GMP Training Programs." Presentation to GMP Training and Education Association Biannual Meeting, October 4 at Chateau Resort and Conference Center at Camelback, Tannersville, PA.

Turnbull, D. M., and C. W. Higby. 1985. "Writing Quality Procedures." *Quality Progress (February):18–23.*

U.S. General Accounting Office. 1981. *Standards for Audit of Governmental Organizations, Programs, Activities, and Functions,* Rev. Ed. Washington, DC: U.S. Government Printing Office; p. 63.

Van Patten, J. 1989. "What is Instructional Design?" In *Instructional Design: New Alternatives for Effective Education.* ed. K. A. Johnson, 16–32. New York: Macmillan.

Wurman, R. S. 1989. *Information Anxiety: What to Do When Information Doesn't Tell You What You Need to Know.* New York: Bantam Books/Doubleday; p. 327.

Zimmerman, C. M, and J. J. Campbell. 1988. *Fundamentals of Procedure Writing,* 2nd Ed. Columbia, MD: GP Publishing, Inc.; pp. 63–166.

Index

WATERS

COLUMN SELECTION GUIDE

For USP Specification

Current USP monographs specify analytical HPLC columns to be used for bulk drug substance and dosage form preparations. Waters selection of HPLC columns conforms to the specifications listed in USP Vol. XXII, Physical Tests and Determinations, Section 621 Chromatography, Chromatographic Reagents subsection.

This guide lists the Waters column equivalents to the USP generic chemical descriptions. In some categories, Waters offers several families of high quality packing materials from which to choose. Packing families differ in hydrophobicity, surface functionality, surface area, pore size, particle size, efficiency, and container (stainless steel columns and cartridge columns) to provide a wide selection to meet your specific separation needs. In choosing one family over another, it is important to consider the chemical properties of the solutes included in the sample, the individual characteristics of the packing materials and the configuration of the container in which the material is packed.

For assistance in selecting columns, Waters worldwide staff of chromatography experts is available to answer your questions and help you determine the best column or cartridge for your application.

Waters
Division of MILLIPORE

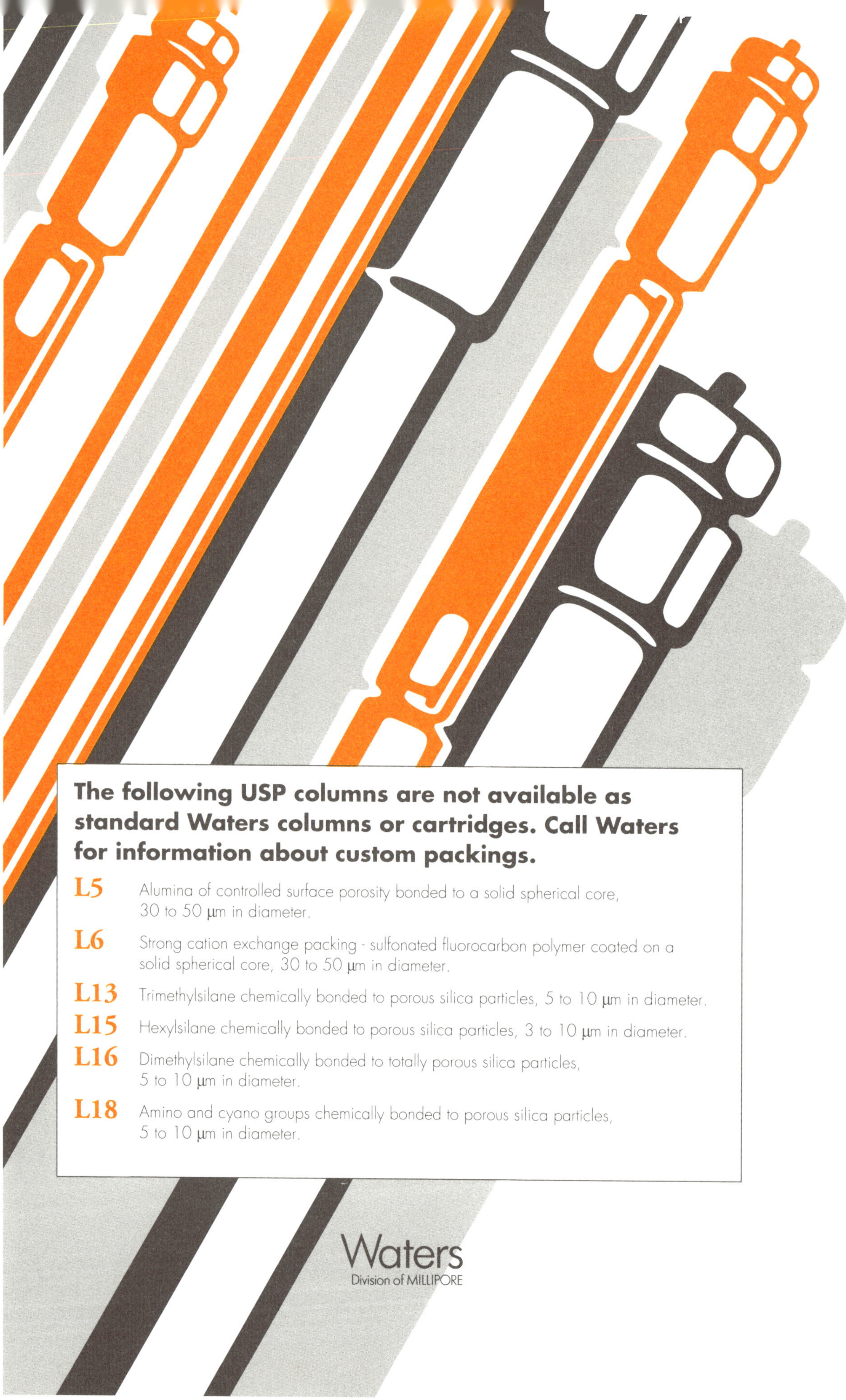

The following USP columns are not available as standard Waters columns or cartridges. Call Waters for information about custom packings.

L5 Alumina of controlled surface porosity bonded to a solid spherical core, 30 to 50 µm in diameter.

L6 Strong cation exchange packing - sulfonated fluorocarbon polymer coated on a solid spherical core, 30 to 50 µm in diameter.

L13 Trimethylsilane chemically bonded to porous silica particles, 5 to 10 µm in diameter.

L15 Hexylsilane chemically bonded to porous silica particles, 3 to 10 µm in diameter.

L16 Dimethylsilane chemically bonded to totally porous silica particles, 5 to 10 µm in diameter.

L18 Amino and cyano groups chemically bonded to porous silica particles, 5 to 10 µm in diameter.

Waters
Division of MILLIPORE

WATERS

COLUMN SELECTION GUIDE

For USP Specification

L1

Octadecyl micro-par

Nova-Pak™
Nova-Pak C
Nova-Pak C
Nova-Pak C
µBondapak™
µBondapak
µBondapak
Resolve™ C
Resolve C_{18}
Delta-Pak™
Delta-Pak C
Delta-Pak C
~~ODSpak C~~
~~ODSpak C~~
~~ODSpak C~~
~~ODSpak C~~
~~ODSpak C~~

Delta-Pak H

Nova-Pak C
Nova-Pak C
µBondapak
Resolve C_{18}
Resolve C_{18}
Resolve C_{18}

L2

Octadecy surface p 30 to 50

Bondapak®

L3

Porous si

Nova-Pak S
Nova-Pak S
µPorasil™
µPorasil
Resolve Sil

Waters Offers a Choice of Stainless Steel Columns or Economical Radial-Pak™ Cartridge Columns.

Waters stainless steel columns are the highest quality HPLC columns available. Waters offers high performance stainless steel columns for a variety of HPLC analyses. We have been manufacturing packed columns since 1964 and have continually improved packing reproducibility and advanced packing technology. Our high quality columns offer superior performance and advanced designs:

- 30% reduced solvent consumption. The inner diameter of most Waters analytical steel columns is 3.9mm vs. 4.6mm for other typical analytical columns providing 30% less dilution and thus 30% greater sensitivity for equal injection volumes. Since dilution in the columns is related to the square of the diameter, solvent consumption is also reduced approximately 30% for peaks having equivalent k's.
- Uniformity of the bed for consistent density and superior reliability ensured by a unique, proprietary column packing method.
- Minimal band spreading and sharp, precise chromatographic peaks with Waters unique true zero dead volume column end fittings.
- All Waters packing materials and columns must pass more than 30 quality control checks in the manufacturing process to ensure consistency.

Radial compression for high efficiency and long cartridge life. Several of Waters HPLC column packing families are available in Waters Radial-Pak radial compression cartridge column form. Radial-Pak cartridges have flexible, high-density polyethylene walls that are subjected to dynamic radial compression from the RCM™ cartridge holder.

Waters patented radial compression technology is the most effective way to optimize and maintain a high efficiency packed chromatographic bed in cartridge form. Applying constant pressure along the entire length and radius of a flexible cartridge, molds the cartridge wall around the packing media. Radial compression decreases void spaces within the bed and eliminates wall effects which cause channeling and loss of efficiency. Longer column life, higher resolving power, and greater reproducibility are the three key benefits not achieved from any other cartridge column.

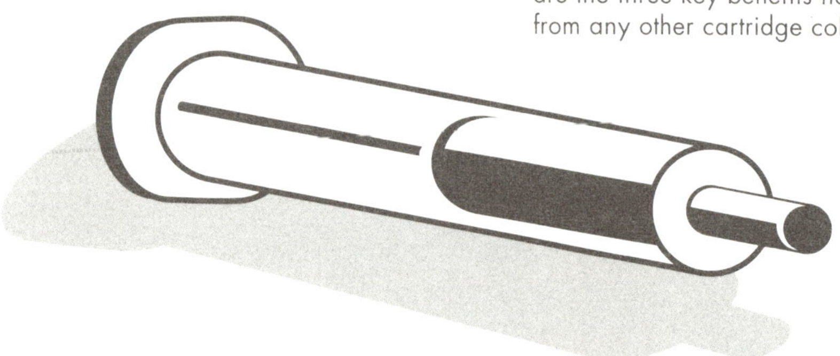

Radial-Pak cartridge columns offer other advantages compared to stainless steel columns:

- Reduced equilibration time with high flow rates during the rapid gradient step return to initial conditions without the risk of cartridge damage.
- Ease of cartridge changing requires only seconds and no special tools.
- Increased laboratory productivity by reducing cost and increasing throughput. Each Radial-Pak cartridge column costs less and can deliver 2 to 3 times as many analyses as stainless steel columns.

Choice of internal cartridge diameters. Waters offers 10cm long Radial-Pak cartridges in two different internal diameters. The 8mm ID Radial-Pak cartridge is a standard high capacity cartridge while the 5mm ID cartridges offer similar performance at lower flow rates. The smaller internal diameter increases the sensitivity and reduces solvent consumption.

Preparative capabilities. Waters offers many of these packings in larger diameter steel and radial compression cartridges which are stackable for larger scale separations.

Custom cartridges. Because Waters radial compression technology increases laboratory productivity, Waters will custom pack any spherical silica base material in Radial-Pak cartridges. Contact Waters Customer Sales for more information.

The Most Complete Line of Solid Phase Extraction Cartridges for Sample Preparation.

Sep-Pak™ Cartridges

Choose from the complete line of Waters solid phase extraction cartridges for rapid, efficient sample preparation prior to analysis. Sep-Pak Cartridges provide:

- Increased accuracy and reproducibility of analysis
- Trace enrichment of low level compounds
- Faster analysis times
- No cross-contamination
- Longer column life

Sep-Pak Cartridges are available in a variety of configurations to suit your laboratories specific needs. These cartridges are disposable "mini columns" that perform high recovery solid phase extraction (SPE). Sep-Pak cartridges contain chromatographic sorbents with different chemical selectivities allowing components of interest to separate from matrix interferences.

Sep-Pak Cartridges

- The original Sep-Pak Cartridges - easy to use with syringes
- Over 1900 published references to sample preparation procedures
- High quality, reproducible packings

Sep-Pak Plus Cartridges

- Injection molded cartridges are compatible with robotic devices such as Waters MilliLab™ Workstation, for automated sample prep
- Color coded rings easily identify the packing chemistry
- Radial compression packing procedure gives a consistent packed bed density for high recovery and reproducibility

Sep-Pak Light Cartridges

- Same design as Sep-Pak Plus cartridges
- Two-thirds less packing material for sample limited applications
- Same high quality sorbents as the original Sep-Pak cartridges

Sep-Pak Vac Cartridges

- Standard syringe barrel configuration for vacuum elution
- Easily transfer methods from existing syringe techniques
- 3 cc/500 mg of high quality Sep-Pak packing material

Sep-Pak Cartridge Chemistries and Suggested Applications

For easy identification of different chemistries all Sep-Pak Plus, Light and Vac Cartridges are color-coded.

C_{18}, C_8 and tC_{18}™ (red)

- Drugs and drug metabolites in serum, plasma, urine
- Peptides in serum, plasma
- Flavors, food coloring
- Trace organics in water

Silica (black)

- Natural products, synthetic organic compounds
- Lipids
- Fat soluble vitamins
- Alternative to silica gel open column and TLC cleanup

Florisil® (orange)

- Samples with large amounts of fats or lipids
- Official AOAC and EPA Methods (Lauric Acid Value = 90 mg/cartridge)

Alumina A (aqua green)

- Vitamins in feeds, foods
- Antibiotics, additives in feed
- Low capacity cation exchange
- Alternative to official AOAC and EPA Methods
- Alternative to acidic alumina open column and TLC cleanup

Alumina N (lime green)

- Food additives
- Synthetic organic compounds
- Alternative to Official AOAC and EPA Methods
- Alternative to neutral alumina open column and TLC cleanup

Alumina B (green)

- Sugars, caffeine
- Low capacity anion exchange
- Alternative to Official AOAC and EPA Methods
- Alternative to basic alumina open column and TLC cleanup

Amino Propyl/NH_2 (yellow)

- Low capacity anion exchange
- Drugs and metabolites
- Saccharides

Cyano Propyl/CN (Purple)

- Normal or reverse phase isolations in aqueous and organic solvents
- Drugs in physiological fluids
- Metabolites from mold and fermentation products

Diol (tan)

- Trace elements from water
- Antibiotics from cosmetics
- Hydrophobic interaction chromatography isolations

Accell™ Plus QMA (light blue)

- Alternative to DEAE cellulose and other anion exchangers
- Extraction of acidic and weakly acidic proteins, enzymes
- Isolation of immunoglobulins
- Peptide pool extractions

Accell Plus CM (blue)

- Alternative to CM cellulose and weak cations exchanger
- Fractionation of weakly basic proteins, enzymes, immunoglobulins
- Synthetic organic compounds

emically bonded to porous silica or ceramic
10 µm in diameter.

STAINLESS STEEL

	4 µm	3.9mm x 75mm column	PN 11670
	4 µm	2.0mm x 150mm column	PN 23655
	4 µm	3.9mm x 150mm column	PN 86344
	4 µm	3.9mm x 300mm column	PN 11695
	10 µm	3.9mm x 150mm column	PN 86684
	10 µm	3.9mm x 300mm column	PN 27324
	10 µm	2.0mm x 300mm column	PN 86609
	5 µm	3.9mm x 150mm column	PN 85711
	5 µm	3.9mm x 300mm column	PN 11740
)Å	5 µm	2.0mm x 150mm column	PN 23650
)Å	5 µm	3.9mm x 150mm column	PN 11795
)Å	5 µm	3.9mm x 150mm column	PN 11793
~~1A~~	~~5 µm~~	~~6.0mm x 100mm column~~	~~PN 34202~~
~~1A~~	~~5 µm~~	~~4.6mm x 150mm column~~	~~PN 34203~~
~~1/S~~	~~5 µm~~	~~4.6mm x 100mm column~~	~~PN 34206~~
~~1A~~	~~5 µm~~	~~4.6mm x 250mm column~~	~~PN 34204~~
~~1B~~	~~10 µm~~	~~4.6mm x 250mm column~~	~~PN 34205~~

NON-METALLIC

)Å	5 µm	3.9mm x 150mm column	PN 35571

RADIAL COMPRESSION

4 µm	8mm x 100mm cartridge	PN 86342
4 µm	5mm x 100mm cartridge	PN 80100
10 µm	8mm x 100mm cartridge	PN 85721
5 µm	8mm x 100mm cartridge	PN 84624
10 µm	8mm x 100mm cartridge	PN 84720
10 µm	5mm x 100mm cartridge	PN 84620

micaly bonded to silica gel of a controlled
has been bonded to a solid spherical core,
eter.

BULK PACKING MATERIAL

37-55 µm	PN 27248

s 5 to 10 µm in diameter.

STAINLESS STEEL

4 µm	3.9mm x 75mm column	PN 11680
4 µm	3.9mm x 150mm column	PN 10025
10 µm	3.9mm x 150mm column	PN 86692
10 µm	3.9mm x 300mm column	PN 27477
5 µm	3.9mm x 150mm column	PN 86016

L17

Strong cation-exchange resin consisting of sulfonated cross-linked styrene-divinylbenzene copolymer in the hydrogen form, 7 to 11 µm in diameter.

STAINLESS STEEL

IC-Pak™ Ion Exclusion	7 µm	7.8mm x 150mm column	PN 10295
IC-Pak Ion Exclusion	7 µm	7.8mm x 300mm column	PN 10290
RSpak DC-613	6 µm	6.0mm x 150mm column	PN 34223

L19

Strong cation-exchange resin consisting of sulfonated cross-linked styrene-divinylbenzene copolymer in the calcium form, about 9 µm in diameter.

STAINLESS STEEL

Sugar-Pak™	9 µm	6.5mm x 300mm column	PN 85188
SC-10011 (1 x 10³ exclusion)	7 µm	8mm x 300mm column	PN 34238
SC-1821 (1 x 10⁴ exclusion)	7 µm	8mm x 300mm column	PN 34239
~~SC-1211~~	~~7 µm~~	~~6mm x 250mm column~~	~~PN 34241~~

L20

Dihydroxypropane groups chemically bonded to porous silica particles, 5 µm to 10 µm in diameter.

STAINLESS STEEL

Protein-Pak™ 60 (1000-20,000 MW)	10 µm	7.8mm x 300mm column	PN 85250
Protein-Pak 125 (2000-80,000 MW)	10 µm	7.8mm x 300mm column	PN 84601
Protein-Pak 300SW (10,000-300,000 MW)	10 µm	7.8mm x 300mm column	PN 80013
Protein WS-802.5 (100-50,000 MW)	10 µm	8mm x 500mm column	PN 35510
Protein-Pak WS-802.5F ~~(100-50,000 MW)~~	~~10 µm~~	~~8mm x 300mm column~~	~~PN 35512~~
Protein-Pak WS-803 (100-150,000 MW)	10 µm	8mm x 500mm column	PN 35511
Protein-Pak WS-803F ~~(100-150,000 MW)~~	~~10 µm~~	~~8mm x 300mm column~~	~~PN 35513~~
Protein-Pak WS-804F ~~(500-600,000 MW)~~	~~10 µm~~	~~8mm x 300mm column~~	~~PN 35514~~
Protein-Pak KW-802.5 (100-50,000 MW)	7 µm	8mm x 300mm column	PN 35943
Protein-Pak KW-803 (100-50,000 MW)	7 µm	8mm x 300mm column	PN 35946
Protein-Pak KW-804 (500-600,000 MW)	7 µm	8mm x 300mm column	PN 36613

L21

A rigid, spherical stryene-divinylbenzene copolymer, 5 to 10 µm in diameter.

RADIAL COMPRESSION

4 µm	8mm x 100mm cartridge	PN 10987
4 µm	5mm x 100mm cartridge	PN 10986
10 µm	8mm x 100mm cartridge	PN 85720
5 µm	8mm x 100mm cartridge	PN 84634
10 µm	8mm x 100mm cartridge	PN 84730
10 µm	5mm x 100mm cartridge	PN 84630

…d surface porosity bonded to a solid spherical … diameter.

…ULK PACKING MATERIAL

37-55 µm	PN 27245

…y bonded to totally porous silica particles, …er.

STAINLESS STEEL

4 µm	3.9mm x 75mm column	PN 35877
4 µm	3.9mm x 150mm column	PN 35876

RADIAL COMPRESSION

4 µm	8mm x 100mm column	PN 35884
4 µm	5mm x 100mm column	PN 35890
10 µm	8mm x 100mm column	PN 85670
10 µm	5mm x 100mm column	PN 85672

…lly porous silica gel having a chemically …dic cation exchange coating.

RADIAL COMPRESSION

10 µm	8mm x 100mm cartridge	PN 85753

…ange packing made by chemically bonding a … a solid silica spherical core, 30 to 50 µm in

…ULK PACKING MATERIAL

~~37-55 µm~~	~~PN 27440~~

…meter having a chemically bonded, strongly basic …n anion-exchange coating.

RADIAL COMPRESSION

10 µm	8mm x 100mm cartridge	PN 85752

STAINLESS STEEL

RSpak DS-613	6 µm	6mm x 150mm column	PN 34220

L22

A cation exchange resin made of porous polystyrene gel with sulfonic acid groups, about 10 µm in size.

STAINLESS STEEL

IC Pak Ion Exclusion	10 µm	7.8mm x 150mm column	PN 10295
IC Pak Ion Exclusion	10 µm	7.8mm x 300mm column	PN 10290
RSpak DC-613	6 µm	6mm x 150mm column	PN 34223
SH-1011 (1 x 10^3 exclusion)	7 µm	8mm x 300mm column	PN 34236
~~SH-1821 (1 x 10^4 exclusion)~~	~~7 µm~~	~~8mm x 300mm column~~	~~PN 34237~~
SC-1011 (1 x 10^3 exclusion)	7 µm	8mm x 300mm column	PN 34238
SC-1821 (1 x 10^4 exclusion)	7 µm	8mm x 300mm column	PN 34239
~~SC-1211~~	~~7 µm~~	~~6mm x 250mm column~~	~~PN 34241~~
SP-0810 (1 x 10^3 exclusion)	8 µm	8mm x 300mm column	PN 36954
SZ-5532	6 µm	6mm x 150mm column	PN 34242

L23

An anion exchange resin made of porous polymethacrylate or polyacrylate gel with quarternary ammonium groups, about 10 µm in size.

STAINLESS STEEL

~~Protein IEC QA-824~~	~~10 µm~~	~~8mm x 75mm column~~	~~PN 30660~~

L24

A semi-rigid hydrophilic gel consisting of vinyl polymers with numerous hydroxyl groups on the matrix surface, 32 to 63 µm in diameter.

STAINLESS STEEL

OHpak Q-801 (1.8 x 10^3 exclusion)	12 µm	8mm x 500mm column	PN 34248
OHpak Q-801/S (1.8 x 10^3 exclusion)	12 µm	8mm x 250mm column	PN 34251
OHpak Q-802 (5 x 10^3 exclusion)	12 µm	8mm x 500mm column	PN 34249
OHpak Q-802/S (5 x 10^3 exclusion)	12 µm	8mm x 250mm column	PN 34252

L25

Packing having the capacity to separate compounds with a molecular weight range from 100 to 5000 (as determined by polyethylene oxide), applied to neutral, anionic, and cationic water-soluble polymers. A polymethacrylate resin base, cross-linked with polyhydroxylated ether (surface contained some residual carboxyl functional groups) was found suitable.

STAINLESS STEEL

OHpak KB-802.5 (1 x 10^4 exclusion)	10 µm	8mm x 300mm column	PN 36569

U.S. Headquarters

New England Waters Chromatography Division Millipore Corporation / 34 Maple Street / Milford, MA 01757 / Tel. 508-478-2000 / FAX 508-872-1990

International Offices

Australia Millipore Australia Pty. Ltd. / Waters Chromatography Division / Locked Bag 18 87-89 Mars Road / Lane Cove, NWS 2066 Sydney / (61) 2-428-7311 / FAX (61) 2- 427-0611

Austria Millipore Ges.m.b.h. / Hietzinger Haupstrasse 145 / A-1130 Vienna Tel. (43) 222-8778926 / FAX (43) 222-8771654

Belgium and Luxembourg Millipore-N.V. Waters Chromatography Division / Raketstraat 60 / Rue de la Fusée 60 / 1130 Brussels Tel. 32-2 2421740 / FAX 32-2 2422785

Brazil Millipore Industria e Comercio Ltda. Waters Chromatography Division / Rua Prof. Campos de Oliveira, 430 / CEP 04675-Caixa Postal 19065 / Sao Paulo / Tel. (55) (11) 548-7011 FAX (55) (11) 548-7923 Telex 391-1157751 MILY BR.

Canada Waters Chromatography Division 3688 Nashua Drive / Mississauga / Ontario L4V-1M5 / Tel. 416-678-2161 Toll-free 1-800-268-4881 / FAX 416-678-0882

Denmark Millipore A/S/ Waters Chromatography Division / Roskildevej 342 / 2630 Tåstrup Tel. (45) 42-528811 / FAX (45) 42-520102

Finland Millipore Oy / Waters Chromatography Division / Ruukinkuja 1 / 02320 Espoo Tel. (358) 08019077 / FAX (358) 08014640

France Millipore S.A. / Rue Jacques Monod Rond-Point des Sangliers / F-78280 Guyancourt Tel. (33) 1-30127000 / FAX (33) 1-30127182

Germany Millipore GmbH / Waters Chromatography Division / Hauptstrasse 87 6236 Eschborn Tel. (49) 6196-4940 / FAX (49) 6196-43901

Germany Biosyntech / Biochemische Synthesetechknik GmbH / Stresemann Strassee 268-280 / D-2000 Hamburg 50 / Tel. (49) (40) 850 0051 FAX (49) (40) 857892

India Millipore Pvt. Ltd. / 50A 2nd Phase Rind Road Pennya Bagalore 560 058 / Tel. (91 12) 394657 FAX (08 12) 396345 Telex 0845-5078 MIPL IN

Italy Millipore S.p.A. / Waters Chromatography Division / Via A. Grandi, 21/23 20090 Vimodrone Milan / Tel. (39) 2-250781 FAX (39) 2-2650324 / Telex (843) 312284 MILSPAI

Japan Nihon Millipore Ltd. / Waters Chromatography Division / No. 5 Koike Bldg. / 3-12, Kita-Shinagawa 1-chome / Shinagawa-Ku, Tokyo 140 Tel. (81) (3) (3) 471-7191 / FAX (81) (3) (3) 471-7116 / Telex 781-2324161 NHNWTRJ

Mexico Millipore S.A. de C.V. / Waters Chromatography Division / Avenida Ingenieros Militares 85 / Mexico 11230 D.F. Tel. (525) 576-9688 / FAX (525) 576-8706 Telex 383-1777 442 MISAME

Middle East, Eastern Europe and Africa Millipore Ges.m.b.h. / Hietzinger Haupstrasse 145 / A-1130 Vienna / Tel. (43) 222-8778926 FAX (43) 222-8771654

The Netherlands Millipore B.V. / Waters Chromatography Division / Penningweg 33 Postbus 166 / 4870 AD Etten-Leur (N.B.) Tel. (31) 1608-22000 / FAX (31) 1608-22436

Norway Millipore AB / Waters Chromatography Division / Enebakkveien 119 / 0680 Oslo 6 Tel. (47) 2-678253 / FAX (47) 2-685315

Peoples Republic of China (Hong Kong) Millipore China Ltd. / Waters Chromatography Division Room 1503, 15/F / Tower 3 / 33 Canton Road Tsim Sha Tsui / Kowloon / Hong Kong Tel. 852-7351616 / Telex 33140 MWBHKHX FAX 852-7354005

Puerto Rico Waters Chromatography Division P.O. Box 11977 / Cidra, Puerto Rico 00639-1977 Tel. (809) 747-6553 FAX (809) 747-8449

South East Asia (Singapore) Millipore Pty. Ltd. #26-03 United Square / 101 Thomson Road Singapore 1130 / Singapore / Tel. 65-2532733 Telex 786-56556 MILLIP / FAX 65-2544056

Spain Millipore Ibérica S.A. / Waters Chromatography Division / Entenza 24 / 08015 Barcelona Tel. (34) 3-3259616 / FAX (34) 3-3259896

Sweden Millipore AB / Waters Chromatography Division / Box 233 / Långebergsgatan 30 421 23 Västra Frölunda / Tel. (46) 31-289860 FAX (46) 31-681126 / Telex 854-21064

Switzerland Millipore AG / Chriesbaumstrasse 6 8604 Volketswill / Tel. (41) (1) 945-3242 / FAX (41) (1) 945-3766

Taiwan Millipore Asia Ltd. / Room 804 / 8th Floor No. 136 / Sec. 3 / Jen-Ai Road / Taipei / Taiwan 10628 / Tel. (886) 2-7001742 FAX (886) 2-7553267

The United Kingdom and Ireland Millipore (U.K.) Limited / Waters Chromatography Division / The Boulevard / Blackmoor Lane / Watford Hertfordshire WD1 8YW / Tel. 44-923 816375 FAX 44-923 818297

USSR Millipore-Intertech / Franco-Soviet Chamber of Commerce / Pokrovsky BD. 4/17 101000-Moscow-USSR / Tel. 207.70.39 Telex 413326 CCFS SU / FAX 230.22.77

For all other countries: Waters Chromatography Division / Millipore Corporation / 34 Maple Street Milford, MA 01757 / USA / Tel. 508-478-2000 Telex 174166 / FAX 508-872-1990

Waters
Division of MILLIPORE

Waters Chromatography Division Millipore Corporation 34 Maple Street Milford, MA 01757 508-478-2000